URBAN PLANNING PROBLEMS

Edited by

GORDON E. CHERRY

Contributors

J. G. Birch
G. E. Cherry
Cynthia Cockburn
M. J. Croft
P. J. Hills
E. A. Rose
Barbara M. D. Smith
C. J. Watson
Margaret Willis

LEONARD HILL – LONDON

Published by
Leonard Hill Books
a division of
International Textbook Company Limited
Kingswood House, Heath & Reach, nr. Leighton Buzzard,
Beds LU7 OAZ and 450 Edgware Rd., London W2 1EG

© Gordon E. Cherry 1974

First published 1974

ISBN 0 249 44138 1

Printed in Great Britain by Pitman Press, Bath

Smoke from the train-gulf hid by hoardings blunders upward,
    the brakes of cars
Pipe as the policeman pivoting round raises his flat hand, bars
With his figure of monolith Pharaoh the queue of fidgety
    machines
(Chromium dogs on the bonnet, faces behind the triplex
    screens)
Behind him the streets run away between the proud glass of
    shops
Cubical scent-bottles artificial legs arctic foxes and electric
    mops
But beyond this centre the slumward vista thins like a diagram:
There, unvisited, are Vulcan's forges who doesn't care a
    tinker's damn.

Splayed outwards through the suburbs houses, houses for
    rest
Seducingly rigged by the builder, half-timbered houses with
    lips pressed
So tightly and eyes staring at the traffic through bleary haws
And only a six-inch grip of the racing earth in their
    concrete claws;
In these houses men as in a dream pursue the Platonic Forms
With wireless and cairn terriers and gadgets approximating
    to the fickle norms
And endeavour to find God and score one over the neighbour
By climbing tentatively upward on jerry-built beauty and
    sweated labour.

On shining lines the trams like vast sarcophagi move
Into the sky, plum after sunset, merging to duck's egg,
    barred with mauve
Zeppelin clouds, and pentecost-like the cars' headlights bud
Out from sideroads and the traffic signals, Creme-de-menthe
    or bull's blood,
Tell one to stop, the engine gently breathing, or to go on
To where like black pipes of organs in the frayed and fading
    zone
Of the West the factory chimneys on sullen sentry will all
    night wait
To call, in the harsh morning, sleep-stupid faces through the
    daily gate.
                Louis MacNeice, *Birmingham*, 1934

Contents

Biographical Notes

JOHN G. BIRCH trained at Loughborough College as a teacher of Physical Education. After 12 years in Secondary Schools, in 1965 he joined the staff of the Central Council of Physical Recreation as Research Officer, later transferring to the Sports Council where he played a major part in the establishment of their research programme. He was author of the Report *Indoor Sports Centres* published by HMSO and was closely involved with the preparation of the Sports Council's publication *Provision for Sport*. From 1970-1974, he was Senior Regional Officer for the Greater London and South East Sports Council with responsibility for their work on facilities planning. He is now Chief Officer for Leisure and Cultural Activities for the Waverley District Council in Surrey.

· · · · · · · · ·

GORDON E. CHERRY is Deputy Director of the Centre for Urban and Regional Studies at the University of Birmingham. He is a London geographer, a professional planner and chartered surveyor. Before joining Birmingham in 1968 his career was with local planning authorities, and latterly he was Research Officer in the Newcastle City Planning Department. He has published widely, for example: *Town Planning in its Social Context*, Leonard Hill Books, 1970, *Social Research Techniques for Planners* (with T.L. Burton), Allen and Unwin, 1970, *Urban Change and Planning*, G.T. Foulis, 1972, and *The Evolution of British Town Planning*, Leonard Hill Books, 1974. He is interested in recreation planning and he is chairman of a research committee that advises the Sports Council. He is a member of the Council of the Royal Town Planning Institute.

· · · · · · · · ·

CYNTHIA COCKBURN is at present engaged in research at the Centre for Environmental Studies, London. She worked for a period as a journalist, qualified as a social worker and spent some years in research, at University College London and elsewhere, on aspects of the construction industry in Britain and in developing countries. Her research interest since 1968 has been mainly in local authority planning and policy-making. She is the author of a number of research papers and was the secretary of the Amos Working Group on Education for Planning which reported in 1973 (Pergamon). She is joint editor of a forthcoming book, *Community Action*.

. . . .

MICHAEL J. CROFT is a geographer from the University of Leeds and a professional town planner. A career with local planning authorities has included a period (1964-67) in the Research Section of Newcastle City Planning Department and subsequently in the West Riding, when between 1971 and 1974 he led the Doncaster Area Joint Structure Plan Team. He is a part-time teacher at the Department of Town Planning, Leeds Polytechnic, and currently Chief Planner (Structure Plan) with the South Yorkshire County Council. In 1969, he contributed the Location of Offices Bureau Research Paper No.3, *Offices in a Regional Centre*.

. . . .

PETER HILLS is a Civil Engineer and a specialist in highway and traffic engineering. While working at the Ministry of Transport in the Urban Road Planning Division, he spent a year in the early sixties as a member of the Working Group on the Buchanan Report, *Traffic in Towns*. Subsequently he was a lecturer in Transport at Imperial College, London. In 1973 he became Assistant Director of Research in the newly established Institute for Transport Studies at the University of Leeds. He has acted as a consultant in urban transport planning in Britain and Nigeria. His publications include co-authorship of *Motorways in London*, 1969.

. . . .

EDGAR A. ROSE is a practising Urban Design and Planning Consultant. He holds the Chair in Town and Country Planning at the University of Aston in Birmingham and was formerly Head of the School of Planning and Landscape in Birmingham Polytechnic. He formerly held posts in local government in London and Manchester where he was the first Deputy City Planning Officer. He was a member of the Panel of Inquiry into the Greater London Development Plan.

. . . .

BARBARA M.D. SMITH is a lecturer in the Centre for Urban and Regional Studies at the University of Birmingham. She has had a continuing interest in industrial history, development and planning in the West Midlands for a decade or more. This has been geared, in turn, to business histories, industrial location and movement studies and, more recently, to the examination of the employment problems of localities in the Region. Her publications include the chapter in 'Industry and Trade, 1880-1960' in the *Victoria County History of Warwick*, **VII**, 1964; *The Administration of Industrial Overspill*, Centre Occasional Paper No.22, 1972; and with Ruddy and Cherry, *Employment Problems in a Country Town – A Study of Bridgnorth*, Shropshire, Centre Occasional Paper No.16, 1971.

. . . .

CHRISTOPHER J. WATSON, a geographer from the University of Bristol, is a Senior Research Associate at the Centre for Urban and Regional Studies, University of Birmingham. He was formerly a member of the Scottish Development Department's Housing Research Unit. He is the author of several publications on housing, including *Housing in Clydeside* 1970 (with J.B. Cullingworth); *Estimating Local Housing Needs: A Case Study and Discussion of Methods* (with Pat Niner, Gillian R. Vale and Barbara M.D. Smith) and *Household Movement in West Central Scotland*.

. . . .

MARGARET WILLIS has a degree in Sociology from the University of London. She was the first sociologist to be employed by the London County Council's Architects' Department to carry out surveys with different aspects of housing. After a spell in market research and a break to work for UNDP she is now a Senior Research Officer in the Department of the Environment where she has worked on new towns, sports and recreation surveys, social aspects of development planning and currently Inner Area Studies. Her publications include articles on these subject.

Introduction

Recent town planning literature has concentrated on a number of very distinctive topics. Our energies and outlooks seem to have been captured by some particular fashionable discoveries. This is not an unusual episode in the evolution of any professional or academic activity and indeed is no bad thing. Speculation and innovation pursue an unpredictable and spasmodic course during which each new direction has its devotees and enthusiasts who make the running vigorously for some years. At the end of this time the subject matter and outlook of the discipline or core-interest will have been influenced and reoriented to some degree. The incremental process of accretion to a body of knowledge then restarts from another point in response to related intellectual stimuli, and a new cycle begins.

Perhaps four emphases can be recognised over the past decade, and inevitably they are related. The one of longest standing is that concerned with advances in method or techniques in plan making. Model based, analytical geography replaced the more descriptive, classificatory discipline, and its use of mathematical models gave it common ground with economics and regional planning. It is not surprising that many planners, with geography as their first degree, made contributions in this field. The spread of new mathematics through schools, availability of new and larger computers, the wider developments of quantitative methods and the intellectual fascination of model building prompted a sure revolution in planning practice. The important contribution was the recognition of interconnectivity amongst the issues with which planning was concerned: the systems approach stressed how events in the planning process had a chain reaction of consequences. A cyclical concept of planning as a process from objectives to results replaced the former idea of planning as a matter of preparing unitary plans for a set point of time in the future. With the advent of structure plans a new impetus was given to representing proposals in these terms, but in the meantime a number of sub-regional studies had given full rein to the possibilities inherent in the new model building approach.

The second new contribution has been one which brought together the fields of operational research and political science by describing how the decision making process in planning at different spatial scales actually operated. A relatively small band of investigators has produced new insight, the importance of which is out of all proportion to the numbers of workers engaged. The interrelationship of the town planning process with that of other public bodies and agencies has been shown locally at Coventry by Friend and Jessop and at Droitwich on a regional scale by Friend, Power and Yewlett.

Closely linked again is the emphasis on corporate planning in local government. Once again, the activity of town planning was seen as part of a wider canvas of management of local authority affairs as a whole. The idea of specialist management based on largely separate services has been recast in favour of an integrated system of relating all activities to corporate goals and objectives, regardless of particular departmental and committee responsibilities. In the new framework a system of ongoing planning as a continuous operation is emphasised, one in which learning and feedback become crucial to the cyclic process. Once again, reliance on the former weight of the one, authoritative master plan which lays down a schema for (say) twenty years, is eroded.

Linked yet again is the current concern with the planner's role both in urban and regional management and in society as a whole. New methods and techniques in planning have been both the cause and effect of new concepts of planning. The former design bias to which architect and engineer could contribute has almost been replaced by the contributions of cybernetics and operational research: planning, formerly seen as the preparation of an end-state master plan is now better described as the management of process. In these circumstances the planner has seen how he is simply a part of the network of public authorities and agencies responsible for planning: he has no prescriptive skills that outweigh any other and he is not in any way outside the political system of management, but indeed very much part of it.

Encouraged generally by developments in the social sciences, the planner has looked again at his social role. He has inherited a particular ideology shared by the social reformer and he thought himself capable of acting almost as sole spokesman for the responsibility of shaping the environment and engineering social change. In recent years, however, planners have redefined both the social objectives of planning and the ways in which these objectives might be achieved. A number have emphasised the need to politicise planning in order to make progress on reducing the inherent inequalities in our social system. Many would still rely on a policy of gradualist amelioration, or short-term incrementalism designed to achieve what improvements one can with the resources available and the institutional frameworks existing. But no one relies on a single, land-use master plan to integrate the targets of economic, social and environmental change.

These have been the recent fields of concern. It is clear that in the meantime a
number of aspects of planning have largely been ignored or at least played down.
Urban design for example has received relatively little attention, although a
hunch must be that in the next few years it will revive in importance with
renewed emphasis on the importance of local environments and that aspect of
quality of life. Further, the question of ecology and the environment has
spluttered inconclusively for the town planner, although it must receive more
prominence shortly. Equally, there have been no conceptual steps forward on
questions of road planning since *Traffic in Towns* (1963); although the promise
of public transport systems and the invective against urban motorways keeps the
issue prominent. On a wider scale, thinking about strategic national issues has
ossified: for example, regional policies for the distribution of people and jobs or
attitudes towards urban containment and countryside protection, have changed
little. Housing matters continue to be fragmented into separate responsibilities
and we seem unable to operationalise a local authority housing policy. Similarly
with recreation: fashions of the moment come and go, but attempts to integrate
the various elements in a comprehensive package that balances supply and
demand have largely failed.

In many instances therefore our contemporary enthusiasms in matters of
planning are imbalanced. There is too great an obsession in some quarters, not
enough concern in others. It is timely therefore to do at least two things. One is
to re-identify the nature of the problems and issues with which town planning as
a comprehensive activity is concerned. The second is to review the main ways we
are, and have been, tackling these problems. These are the main objectives of the
book, and we concentrate on a selection of urban questions. This is not to say
that rural matters are not important: they are, and it is certainly high time that
countryside planning received more attention. The Scott Report of 1942 is
virtually the last comprehensive review of the countryside to take place. But this
book has an urban focus.

Town planning is an activity centred on land, land use and activities and the
development process. It has a very distinct social context and takes place within
economic and political systems. For at least 150 years Britain as an industrial
society has been engaged in planning of one kind or another to meet the needs
of our rapidly growing towns and cities. From about 1830 those responsible for
urban government began to tackle the human and physical problems thrown up
by unprecedented urban and industrial growth; initially the emphasis was on
housing and health. Gradually, during the 19th century, state or municipal
intervention saw that British cities were lit, paved, watered and sewered; their
houses and roads regulated; their population aided and assisted through various
means of social policy; recreation needs were met; transport systems provided;
and that an effective governmental machine was created. This approach was

necessarily fragmented but an additional measure of coherence was given by the development of the town planning movement, with its early emphasis on housing, town design and land use control. In the 20th century, a centralist planning approach helped in tackling social and environmental problems in a more coordinated way. Town planning as a sphere of activity has widened, but the total field of what we now recognise as planning is wider still. It is usually unprofitable to draw disciplinary or any other boundaries round these areas of concern.

In many ways, the problems which are presented in urban Britain today have been broadly similar throughout the last hundred years. On the other hand, it is very often the case that our perceptions of problems have changed and the way we tackle them is very different. Problems are not valueless objects; the very way we recognise a particular matter as a problem, actually constitutes the problem. But broadly there was a 'state of our towns' problem in the 1890's, just as there is in the 1970's. There was urban poverty and a range of intractable social problems in Victorian cities as there is today; the Victorians relied on voluntary institutions and philanthropic endeavours, whereas, today, there is relatively greater reliance on public support via the state. The processes of urban change, whereby suburban expansion has leap-frogged outwards, characterise, not just post-war Britain, but a period of over a hundred years. The search for decent housing is not just a feature of the 20th century, neither is the solution of urban transport problems; and there are many other examples.

Once political and institutional forces in Britain allowed the development of broadly interventionist policies to deal with urban and community problems, a comprehensive town planning movement could emerge. It soon had its own insight to the nature of the problems which beset Victorian cities and it developed a range of skills (not so much unique to itself but overlapping with other disciplines) to tackle them. This is still the basis of a town planning approach — identification of issues and problems and harnessing of skills to deal with them. The problems change and our perception of them changes — what is important to one generation is not necessarily to another.

Planning, therefore, to a large measure emerged as, and remains, a problem-oriented activity. It has a basic core of knowledge and expertise relating to land, environment and development, but shares other skills with a number of different disciplines and interests. It is supported by a broad ideology which attempts to relate social needs to the provision of bases of satisfaction and fulfilment in everyday life. Planning is an aspect of public policy making and there are many areas of planning today where the gap between policy and the problem to which that policy package relates is a wide one. In these cases the process of feedback and monitoring has not been rigorous enough, and old policies have been overtaken by events.

The book unfolds from this point. Eight problem fields are reviewed: urban form and structure, urban society, the housing question, employment, the physical environment, transport and communications, recreation and urban government. Emphatically this is not a book which brings together essays on, for example, spatial strategic planning, economic planning, urban design, transport planning, recreation planning or community planning. Rather it selects a number of fields to which these aspects of planning clearly relate, and it examines them from the point of view of the problems they currently present and the way they are being tackled. The collection is admittedly selective. To be otherwise would be too massive an operation. The essays chosen are those which have the greatest bearing on the operation of town planning at the present time. There are certainly others, and we do not touch (except in passing) on the provision of essential services (water supply, use and reuse for example), refuse (its collection and disposal), education, police, maintenance of law and order, health facilities, provision and distribution of shops, public health and so on. Some of these have been *the* problems of the past, as we have seen. In addition to being selective, the essays have a topic focus (housing, jobs, transport, for example). They could have been written from a functional point of view: the role of city centres, inner areas, suburbs and so on. These aspects are drawn together in the concluding chapter.

In Chapter 1, Michael Croft considers the question of urban form and structure which has long been a matter of town planning concern. Indeed it might be said to have been amongst those which promoted the growth of a town planning movement in the first place. Fear of unmanageable growth of cities (particularly London) at the turn of the century gave a favourable setting for Ebenezer Howard's concept of the Social City based on satellite garden townships. Within the structure the attainment of spatial order based on a neighbourhood pattern became a general requirement. Over a period of 70 years, the forces of urban change have strongly encouraged dispersal and reduction of densities. Strategic concepts for urban growth since the 1940's have reinforced the former, although the effect of the Green Belt has been to keep residential densities higher than would otherwise have occurred. Since then, we have also toyed with alternatives such as linear towns and corridors of growth, and the traditional star shaped town with limbs of growth following radial routes has been replaced by figures of eight, rectangular grids and other designs. But the planner's sureness of touch has long since gone. The full realisation as to the scale of the metropolitanisation of England has only just dawned, and we need to get back to first principles: what are the problems and what policies do we need to tackle them? Michael Croft reminds us of the essentials: the technological, economic, social and physical forces underpinning urban change, and their effect on urban form from the point of view of size, density, shape, uses and condition.

Margaret Willis in Chapter 2 examines important aspects of our urban society. Post-industrial society throws up a range of problems in cities with which planning has to deal: the consequences of our structure and inequality in the distribution of rewards have consequences in poverty and deprivation, which territorially are brought together in an acute way in the difficulties of the inner city. These are not new recognitions. The social sumps of Victorian London sparked off protest literature and produced legislation just as the problems of Islington or Southwark do today. The early planners were as conscious of the need for social 'improvement' as we are; they simply went about it differently. Today we are groping towards a concept of social planning, a new form of urban management involving many professional and other skills with political objectives of reallocating benefits and rewards to groups in society previously denied them. Town planning as a professional activity is touched by this new development, and Margaret Willis reviews present day policies such as those relating to race relations, community development and urban aid programmes, with which the planner becomes involved.

Housing and town planning have long been linked and in Chapter 3 Chris Watson reminds us of this. Although housing in local authority affairs is a separate function, nonetheless many of the statutory functions of planning are related to housing: allocation of land, design criteria, phasing of development, associated community facilities, clearance and improvement of dwelling stock and so on. Above all one of the consequences of planning policy, particularly that to contain urban spread and to protect the countryside (with or without a Green Belt), has considerably influenced land and therefore house prices. Intervention in housing matters has often been a very blunt instrument. The complexity of the situation behoves careful analysis and sensitive treatment; Watson helps us in this respect by close examination of questions concerning housing conditions, housing needs, housing choice and the problem of land.

The importance of the economic base of cities became an issue during the inter-war period when certain regions of this country were long at risk due to down turns in commercial activity. Sustained unemployment and under capacity in certain areas, compared with relative prosperity in Greater London and parts of the Midlands prompted the Barlow Report in 1940 to echo advice from many quarters to advocate dispersal of population and jobs from the larger cities and various forms of help to underprivileged regions. It became a plank for post-war policy. But manufacturing jobs are not the sole criteria; the office boom and the development of tertiary and quarternary employment has seen to that. The problems associated with job location are changing, but the way we integrate our knowledge of the situation with the overall planning policies is feeble. In Chapter 4 Barbara Smith looks at some of the underlying questions to which town planning is directed: the broad location of industry, its siting within a particular urban area, obsolescence and renewal of plant and industrial districts, land needs and the selection of land, and finally with the factors concerned with the dynamics of industry – the birth and death of manufacturing enterprises.

With regard to the physical environment (Chapter 5), one of planning's earliest contributions was to civic design. Raymond Unwin's classic text of 1909 was an *Introduction to the Art of Designing Cities and Suburbs*; Patrick Geddes was a landscape designer and all the leading early figures engaged in a form of town planning which unmistakably had a design end product. The concern with visual amenity and townscape has been maintained; town planning as an art form is still recognised. But what is the place of civic design in town planning today? Why is it not the force it was? What do we mean by design? Design for whom and at whose cost? Why have we failed so badly to conserve our ancient urban heritage? Does pollution control of air, noise and water offer a new way of considering environmental management? Is it possible to approach civic design in the old sense any longer? These are some of the questions which Edgar Rose explores.

The transport question (Chapter 6) is another long standing element in town planning, although as a concern of Government the Ministry of Transport was divorced from town planning for 50 crucial years between 1919 and 1969. The arterial road, a question in Greater London as long ago as 1913, represented an occasion for local authorities to come together in joint action. Today an urban fabric has to accommodate parked and moving vehicles to a degree that has necessitated environmental destruction on a scale quite beyond that of an earlier transport system, the railway. A variety of road solutions has come in quick succession: ring roads and roundabouts to urban motorways and grade separated junctions. Peter Hills shows how the problems are more than physical: they are social and cultural. Car possession has become one of the great status symbols of an acquisitive society; its demotion as an object of value in the face of wider, environmental values seems to hold out greatest possibilities of ever containing this remarkable trojan horse. But that particular thought has to be seen in the context of all the problems reviewed in this chapter.

Planning for the mass use of leisure time is a relatively new activity, particularly in towns, although the provision of parks, swimming baths, libraries and community buildings has long been a responsibility of local authorities. Today the problems are compounded by a blend of factors and John Birch in Chapter 7 reminds us of these: availability of free time, higher disposable income, mobility through car ownership and exposure to new experiences through education. The present situation is that the supply of public and private facilities fails in many cases to meet demand, and forecasting is made particularly difficult by the fact that the creation of demand is supply-led. The difficulties are compounded by the fact that so far we have failed to create a satisfactory institutional framework for recreation planning, and an *ad hoc* fragmentation dominates in place of a comprehensive service. Birch highlights these matters in a review of the main areas of recreation service – sport, the arts and community activities.

Urban government is perhaps at the heart of the matter and in Chapter 8 Cynthia Cockburn emphasises three aspects which are of vital importance in the planning of complex systems; coordination, intelligence and democracy. Planning is a form of urban management, a problem-oriented activity. The questions asked today in our social and political climate are particularly searching: whose problems? Whose solutions? Who plans, and on whose behalf? The war time years saw a high water mark for the British centralist system with a well established bureaucracy. But paternalist planning has broken down and we are now witnessing explorations into new systems of government both within and without the established framework. There is a general wish to create an open government with full participation from the community at large. Professionals and elected members hold no monopoly of wisdom, and the alternative of micro-politics at the neighbourhood or community council level is a distinct possibility. In the meantime, the art of management has had its own revolution in administrative circles. This has opened up local authority affairs to corporate thinking, stressing the cyclical, ongoing nature of planning from objectives to action with feedback and monitoring important stages between.

In the final chapter (9) I draw together the main themes from these essays. I stress the historical dimension which we should bear in mind when considering urban problems, and offer a 'processual' view as to how problems have changed over the years. In relating the keypoints of the individual chapters to each other I stress the interconnectivity of the problems with which urban planners are dealing; perhaps this is well seen in the question of poverty, where the influences of education, housing, employment, income, and family size are singularly reinforcing. But in their interrelatedness, problems compound in severity and I emphasise the importance of multi-problem areas of territorial significance in the inner city. The way we tackle problems also forms an important section of this chapter, because the lessons for planning are profound. I conclude with a look at the future: have we an incipient urban crisis on our hands, or is this gloomy introspection bolstered by a passing phase of lack of societal confidence?

Cities are exciting phenomena. They embrace all that we hope for and despair about. Their problems present a continuing agenda for analysis, speculation and prescription. Undergraduate and post-graduate students, for whom this book is particularly intended, often require a synoptic presentation of the urban scene, one against which their own individual specialism might be set, or, if they are town planning students already with a generalist awareness, one against which to compare their own understanding. *Urban Planning Problems* has this intention.

1 Urban Form and Structure

The town planner has always claimed the physical appearance of towns and cities, and the way they are organised physically, as very much his own concern. Embracing the civic design movement, and stimulated by the pressing need to tackle a whole range of housing problems at the turn of the century, he was keen to develop his analytical and prescriptive skills and to press for legislation to give greater control over the urban environment. When Abercrombie wrote of town planning being a matter of "beauty, health and convenience" (1.1) he had in mind the planner's self-imposed obligation to create cities worthy of a technologically advanced society.

This provides the basis of town planning's concern for the internal form, structure, function and appearance of urban areas. Much of this concern falls under the general headings of *urban form* and *urban structure*; these interchangeable headings provide the focus of a wide range of planning problems affecting the physical base of our urban areas. These problems are constantly developing concerns for the planner in an increasingly complex age, and they continue to provide a major challenge for his skills today no less significant than the challenge faced by his predecessors when the town planning profession crystallised in the early years of this century.

These problems, the way they have come about and changed, and the developing attempts of planners to deal with them, provide the focus for this chapter. We start with a definition of urban form, and this is followed by a simple classification of the various forces which affect urban form. A broad overview of the complex relationships between urban form and the forces at work follows. The particular contribution of planning to this relationship is then examined, and the chapter concludes with a look at some of the many remaining problems.

The meaning of urban form

Three major definitions of *urban* are available to us. These are the 'formal' definition of the area covered by urban uses, the 'functional' definition of the often extensive area for which an urban centre provides services, and the administrative definition of the area controlled by a local authority. This chapter is concerned essentially with the formal urban area, although changes in the relationships between a town and its surrounding area are bound to affect its internal functioning and form, and much of the statistical data on urban form, and its changes, must relate to administrative units.

The emphasis in this chapter is a physical one, as it is buildings, roads, land uses and the like which make up urban form. But the realistic planner has never looked at these physical aspects in isolation from the social, economic, and technological forces which have produced the environment we have around us. The physical equipment of our urban areas exists only to perform functions which are thought necessary, desirable or profitable in a particular social, economic and technological environment and this broad context cannot be ignored in this examination.

Urban form may be conveniently considered as consisting of five facets or variables. These are the size of an urban area, its density, its shape, the uses to which it is put, and its condition. None of these variables operates independently as the discussion which follows later in this chapter will show.

The first two variables, *size* and *density*, are particularly interlinked. There is ample documentation of the spatial spread of built-up areas, and evidence of continued growth has led to popular forecasts of what Peter Hall calls a "horrendous sort of super-city hundreds of miles long" (1.2) stretching from London to Manchester. At the same time the administrative areas of the larger towns (with their often tight boundaries) are tending to suffer (or perhaps enjoy) population decreases as decentralisation occurs. As Table 1.1 shows, the nine largest British towns in 1961 *all* had population decreases in the ten years to 1971.

Falling densities, the link factor between urban spread and the decreasing populations of the largest urban centres, are long-established phenomena. The 19th century, with its poor facilities for mass urban transport, was a period of very high densities as people sought to live near their work: for instance, Manchester's innermost 2½ square miles contained 187 000 residents in 1851 at an *average* density of 126 people per acre (1.3). In 1971 however, the 270 acres of the *most* densely populated of Manchester's wards (Moss Side West) failed to reach an average density of even 60 people per acre (1.4).

The *shape* of an urban area, the third variable that will be considered in more detail later in this chapter, has long been the subject of attention from urban designers. This stems from the planner's traditional concern for providing optimum living conditions in a way that harmonises technology and social preferences. The planner's investigations into urban shape have involved both the theoretical advantages and disadvantages of linear development, radial cities, satellite finger growth, grid patterns, and so on, and the practical application of theory to real-world situations.

Table 1.1 Population changes in the largest British towns, 1961-71.

| | Population in thousands | | Decrease 1961-71 | |
	1961	1971	Number (thousands)	% p.a.
Greater London	7992	7379	613	0.8
Birmingham C.B.	1111	1013	97	0.9
Glasgow City	1058	898	160	1.5
Liverpool C.B.	746	607	139	2.0
Manchester C.B.	662	541	120	2.0
Sheffield C.B.	540	520	21	0.4
Leeds C.B.	511	495	16	0.3
Edinburgh City	468	449	19	0.4
Bristol C.B.	438	425	13	0.3

(a) Based on Office of Population Censuses and Surveys: *Census 1971, and Wales, Preliminary Report* (HMSO, 1971), Tables 4 and 6, and General Register Office, Edinburgh: *Census 1971, Scotland, Preliminary Report* (HMSO, 1971), Table 3.

(b) Populations relate generally to areas as constituted at the date of the 1971 Census.

(c) Apparent errors are due to rounding.

A fundamental concern of urban form is that of urban land *use*. All urban areas have a variety of different uses (housing areas, work places, and shopping streets for example) and we need to consider what uses there are and how their distribution is changing. Here the planner has had a major impact in rationalising the chaotic Victorian land use plan and separating out the assortment of conflicting uses – a process which, as we shall see, is not without its critics.

The final variable of urban form might be termed its *conditions*. This relates to the ability of an urban area to carry out its functions efficiently for the benefit of its inhabitants, and includes the variation in condition from one part of an urban area to another. Planners have always been concerned with the improvement of conditions and standards. They have played a significant part in the improvements which have taken place in residential and other areas in the last century and in the continuing battle to improve and renew our outworn urban fabric.

The forces of urban change

The forces of urban change may be conveniently classified into technological, economic, social and physical. Once again, the distinction is not a hard-and-fast one: transport changes, for instance, first become technologically possible and then economically feasible and socially acceptable, provided, of course, that the physical terrain of an urban area makes changes possible in a particular urban situation (1.5).

Technological forces provided the basis for the very origin of urban areas. This occurred when foodstuffs surplus to the needs of rural areas could be produced in sufficient quantity to support a class of specialists: these specialists were able to congregate together to provide goods and services for the food-producers. In succeeding periods improving technology has revolutionised urban life. Transport improvements (i.e. improvements in both vehicles and tracks or roads) have allowed workers to live at increasing distances from their work-places. Multi-storey buildings have been a practical proposition for a century now, allowing great concentrations of workers or residents in small areas. Improvements in *communications*, particularly in terms of the transmission of information, show some signs of making the need for *transport* much less significant in the future. Above all, technology provides greater choice: in short the ability to solve urban problems in a greater number of alternative ways.

Economic forces are also strong. Towns themselves are economic entities: in economic terms they exist to exploit localised resources (often originally a natural resource like iron ore or a natural harbour, but increasingly to use concentrations of labour to the full), to make the most of technological linkages (for example the working-up of semi-finished goods), and to save transport costs. Looked at internally, urban areas are economic entities in that they need to make the best use of the limited resources available for efficient functioning. Put another way, at any given location and at any given point in time, certain urban forms, uses and processes will be more economic than others: it is for good economic reasons that specialist shops and large department stores, for instance, have traditionally been located in town centres.

Social forces can perhaps be divided into two kinds. Firstly, there is the changing social composition of the population: this includes not only demographic changes (for instance the one/two generation family having replaced the two/three generation Victorian family) but also the changing way in which the population is divided into income groups, socio-economic and occupational groups and the like. Planners are increasingly having to take account of the ways in which their plans impinge differently on different groups. Secondly, there are the long-term changes in social values which need to be considered. The last few decades have seen the growth of an acquisitive society in which (at its simplest) 'keeping up with the Jones's' has been the norm; however, with the growth of the conservation movement and the increasing awareness of the finite limits of the planet on which we live, perhaps there will be a major change in attitudes which would be bound to have a significant planning impact. Social forces of this kind are reflected both in the private interests which express their points of view, often vociferously, and which the planner ignores at his peril, and in the public sector in the form which planning legislation and statutory planning activity take. Indeed, the very origins of planning legislation owe much to social attitudes represented in the reaction against the obvious ills of 19th century urban Britain.

Physical forces explain much of the form of our towns and cities. 'Grand Plans' from the theorist can be of little use in practical situations, and many towns show the influence of topography, drainage factors, the varying fertility of agricultural land, and other physical factors, either in their overall shape or in their internal arrangement. Many towns still have their major industrial belts along river valleys, for instance. Tyneside, Sheffield and Leeds are all cases in point. This stems from the facilities which river valleys offered for power (in pre-Industrial Revolution days) or for transport, or because flat plains adjacent to rivers provide good sites for extensive industrial land demands. Agricultural implications, as another example, often play a major part in influencing directions of urban growth, as, for instance, recently at Ipswich (1.6).

Urban form and changing forces

Having listed the element of urban form and classified the forces which affect these elements, we can now investigate how the forces affect each element in turn. This is important for those seeking to influence urban environments as in the last resort urban planning must at least come to terms with (and sometimes can do very little about) the fundamental forces involved. Space only permits a brief examination of the interplay between forces and elements in the recent past, at the present time and in the foreseeable future. For convenience of description most of the influences which affect urban form are allocated to one or other of the four headings already given. But just as the various aspects of urban form are themselves often closely interrelated so are the forces which affect them. For example the outward expansion of a town away from first-class agricultural land may reflect physical factors (inherent fertility of the soil), economic factors (the possibility of cheap development elsewhere), social factors (social attitudes on the community value of such agricultural land), and technological factors (the improbability of achieving large-scale production of 'synthesised food' at an early date).

Size and *density* are facets of urban form which must be considered together in this context. The influences which have long been affecting size and density have, in the main, been bringing about larger towns and lower densities. The major influences have been those concerned with transport changes: as already intimated, such changes are considered here as a combined set of 'technological-economic-social-physical' forces. Historically there is a close interrelationship between the nature of urban transport provision and the form of urban growth. Each affects the other: without available public transport, most people lived near their work in or near town centres and this was only made possible by having very high densities in residential areas; when public transport developed, notably along routes radiating from town centres, towns were extended along such routes and overall densities fell. The growth of private transport in recent years has likewise done much to encourage urban growth, and in fact has created additional environmental problems related to urban conditions. As for the future, many kinds of improvements in communications are possible, but the planner's current emphasis is towards the increased use of public transport (1.7), whether this be encouraged by more bus-only lanes, swingeing parking charges, or automated control of rapid transit systems. The development of new capital-intensive forms of public transport is clearly helped by high densities of population, allowing larger numbers of people to live closer to terminal points. Town size has its effect *on* transport also as the centres of large towns cannot cope with the proportions of private car travel for journey-to-work purposes accommodated by smaller towns: in the 1960's public transport in British towns with between 10 000 and 50 000 commuters to their centres (about up to the size of Cardiff) accounted for from 40 per cent or less to 80 per cent or more of journeys to work, but for towns with more commuters (more than Cardiff that is), the corresponding figure was never less than 80 per cent (1.8). Urban size and density clearly, then, cannot be considered in isolation from the complex question of public versus private transport.

Technological forces, outside the field of transport, are generally bringing about lower densities. It is true that technological innovations have made higher densities *possible*: the development of the elevator, or lift, around 1870 made multi-storey buildings practicable (1.9) and contributed greatly to the concentration of commercial activity in modern city centres. A major influence, however, is on industrial densities (in terms of, say, the number of workers per acre), and here the movement towards automation and mass production, frequently in single-storey buildings, is clearly leading to lower densities and urban spread — often reinforced by the physical outward movement of industries as cramped central sites become unsuitable for modern methods.

Economic forces again operate in complex ways on town size and density.

Urban areas come into being and are maintained so that people can associate together for various purposes, and this provides the economic basis for activities to be located close together. But construction costs rise with increasing density. Evidence for this comes from many sources, and the Department of the Environment's housing cost yardstick is as good as any: this gives guidance, based on actual experience, to local authorities on how to assess what would be reasonable expenditure to incur (excluding land) on new housing schemes. For instance costs per dwelling for three-person dwellings are nearly a quarter more at 120 persons per acre than at 60 persons per acre (1.10). At a broader scale, examinations of the relationships between town size and costs suggest that there are both economies and diseconomies of scale: congestion costs per head, for instance, tend to rise with increasing size beyond a fairly low level; the cost per head of providing public utilities, such as sewage works, however, tends to fall with increasing size. But this is a complex field indeed for the analyst, one of the very few clear features being the awkward fact that diseconomies start to occur at different sizes for different services (1.11).

The technological forces acting on industrial densities have their counterpart in social forces which influence residential densities and therefore town sizes. Although there have been short-term fluctuations, the long-term trend towards small families is clear: this is due more to the falling average age of people when they marry, and the associated decline in the tendency of three-generation families to live together as a single unit, than to any reductions in the number of children born to average parents. The long-term effect of this is equally clear: for any given number of people an increasing number of dwellings is needed and more space is needed to accommodate them. This has facilitated and, indeed, reinforced an emphasis on high-quality living conditions, reflected, for instance, in families' increased needs for separating different activities and for more space for storing labour-saving and recreation equipment. More houses are being occupied by fewer people (1.12). The contrast between most housing dating from the late 19th century and the private housing of the 1930's and since can be seen in virtually every town in Britain. More land is required to house even population levels which remain largely unchanged: in Doncaster, for instance, the average residential density (persons per acre) was falling at an average rate of 1 per cent p.a. during the late 1950's and the 1960's (1.13). This reflects a long-established national trend, for in the 40 years following 1920-21 the average number of urban residents per urban acre in England and Wales fell (at first rapidly, and then more steadily) from 17.2 to reach 11.5 in 1960-61 (1.14). Nor has this trend ceased: average residential densities are expected to fall in Leeds, and Leeds is only one of the many examples, by 11 per cent between 1961 and 1981 (1.15). The pressure for the achievement of higher space standards is reflected not only in housing but also in the many uses associated with housing, particularly schools and open spaces. The contrast between old and new is very evident when street after street of 19th century housing is cleared to make way for much smaller amounts of housing with far greater areas than before being devoted to schools, open spaces, and so on.

This kind of trend has been so long established that one would be rash to prophesy its end. Nevertheless the possibilities are with us. Most of the highest-density 19th century housing has already gone, and the process of urban renewal is unlikely to result in such a major 'loosening up' of existing uses as in the past. A major social imperative could reinforce this heavily: the proliferation of second homes (generally in *non*-urban situations) points to the *possibility* of urban areas becoming increasingly high-density areas used for week-day living close to work, with the pressures for affluent living in relaxing surroundings being syphoned off to low-density second homes in the country (1.16).

The effect of physical forces on town size and densities is a marginal one in most towns. Very few towns are completely surrounded by physical constraints (such as land which is undrainable or very difficult to drain) which *prevent* their expansion. The usual effect of constraints such as this is to channel the expansion of a town in particular directions, and even if expansion is totally prevented the frustrated developer generally has the option of finding his way to another town, where such constraints are less in evidence, rather than developing at higher densities.

The effects of the various forces on town size and density, therefore, are fairly common to a wide variety of towns: urban expansion and lower densities are the common theme. Similarly, although town *shape* inevitably varies from place to place in accordance with local geography, the kinds of influence are fairly common. Physical factors act as a powerful influence on the shape of towns. Some of these are entirely 'natural', such as the tendency for urban expansion to avoid areas of low load-bearing rocks or areas of steep slopes: Halifax is a good example of the latter. Other constraints, such as the need in many situations to avoid urban expansion in areas of high-quality agricultural land, reflect social attitudes to the importance of unalterable physical resources. Still other forces, while not natural constraints in these senses, have the support of the 'planning system' in strongly influencing urban shape, and will be considered later. The close relationship between land use and transport, already referred to, is also evident in terms of town shape. Transport provision gives to particular points (or lines or areas) changing levels of accessibility to a range of facilities and services: particular locations therefore become more, or less, attractive to potential residents and employers. Thus, by the end of the 19th century the typical British city had an 'octopus shape' as a result of the development of the steam train and electric tram along radial routes; but from the 1914-18 War onwards the development of the bus, with its more frequent stops and greater route penetration, freed urban development from a few radial routes, and cities became more typically circular in shape.

The relationships between the *uses* to which land is put in urban areas, the distribution of those uses within towns, and the forces creating the pressures for change are again complex. Dealing first with the relative importance of the various uses, we may take Doncaster once more as a reasonably typical example. The breakdown of the urban (developed) area here was as follows in 1968: residential 40 per cent; education 5 per cent; open space (playing fields, parks, allotments, cemeteries, golf courses, etc.) 19 per cent; town centre 2 per cent; district shopping centres 3 per cent; civic, cultural and other special uses 4 per cent; industry 9 per cent; railway and waterway 7 per cent (rather higher than usual in this particular example); other uses 11 per cent (1.17). With regard to the distribution of these uses several theories of urban growth have attempted, during the last half century, to explain the internal functioning of towns. It is sufficient for our purposes, however, to note that all British towns of any size have a recognisable centre, usually but not necessarily close to the geographical centre of the town. The centre provides services, such as certain types of shops and offices, used by the population of the town and that of its surrounding area, many of these services not being found elsewhere within the town. Towns generally have an identifiable industrial area or areas, often located in close proximity to a major communications route, either road, railway or canal (note again the relationship between transport and land use). Interspersed with housing areas are local service facilities, such as schools, shopping areas less significant than those of the town centre, and, particularly in the outer part of towns, areas of open space. In the next few paragraphs we consider what forces are working to reinforce or modify this kind of situation.

Transport changes are the most important influence. Any urban land use is related to other urban land uses: residential areas, for instance, are linked to employment areas by the fact that residents need work and employers need labour. These links are achieved by a communications system, in the form of some combination of roads, cars, buses, railways and trains, telephones, and so on. Since the availability of communications is frequently changing it follows that uses requiring particular kinds of links will tend to gravitate towards new locations in accordance with such changes. At the town scale, developments in communications considered from the point of view of the employer could well bring about major changes in the future. We can already see the development of distribution depots on the edges of towns in association with the use of heavier lorries on improved inter-urban roads and motorways, rather than in association with central railway stations, a common former location. The automated handling of data in offices allows routine functions to be decentralised from town centres, and this process may well be more in evidence in the future. If electronic communications can be developed to the point where they can substitute effectively for most face-to-face meetings in a working office situation, the physical tie between residential locations and office locations could be completely shattered, making it possible for certain workers to live scores or even hundreds of miles from their 'work'. The increasing spread of residential locations, closely related again to transport changes but in evidence longer than the spread of employment, has already been traced. It has gone on long enough, in fact, to create its own pressures: it contributes in part, for instance, to the pressures making for the decline in the importance of some traditional town centres and to the development of large supermarkets or even larger hypermarkets near the edges of towns; these are good locations to meet the requirements of at least the car-users of the suburbs. Perhaps the most significant, however, of the changes brought about by transport improvements is that people have more contact with an increasing range of locations (both in their work and leisure pursuits). This means that the importance of a specific physical 'place' is in some ways reduced. The links between physical 'places' and the social and economic realities which give rise to the 'places', important though they are, become increasingly difficult to trace (1.18). At the more local level the same kind of phenomena are at work, but since at this level current pressures are seriously modifying a major tenet of much 20th century local planning (the neighbourhood concept) we shall examine this later in relation to the impact of planning.

Economic forces play a major part in the location of land uses within a town: shops tend to occur in town centres primarily because the superior accessibility of such locations makes it more worthwhile for a shop-keeper to set up shop there than for a resident to set up house: in short, it is a more economic proposition. However, the factors which 'push' a particular use to a particular location are not constant, and hence land uses are constantly changing. In other words, in a free market there is an economic reaction to changing technology, social attitudes and physical constraints. At the same time, though, a change in technological, social or physical circumstances (even if reflected economically, as in the changing rental level for a shop) will not automatically cause a change in the land use pattern. This is because, in spite of the pressure for demolition of old buildings and the construction of new ones to cater for different uses, such changes are very costly and therefore change in land uses is a slow process and the economic reaction is a muffled one. This is particularly the case when a *group* of uses, for instance a collection of solicitors' offices, insurance companies and brokers, other professional offices, and banks, have developed important linkages which no single office among the collection can afford to rupture by physical movement (1.19). Nevertheless, changes which are largely the result of economic pressures do occur. For instance, arguments for economies or diseconomies of scale, already mentioned at the town scale, can also be put forward for individual land use activities. Current views tend to favour larger units: school campuses are becoming larger to allow greater specialisation and therefore wider choice for individual students; distribution depots are becoming larger to reap the advantages of bulk containerisation.

Another factor affecting urban form, basically economic in character as it represents an attempt to make the maximum use of limited resources, is the pressure for dual use of certain facilities: the increasing use of school facilities (both classrooms and recreational facilities) is an example. Perhaps even the growing adoption of staggered working hours (flex-time) may be included under the economic heading, as it represents an attempt to make the best use of the limited amount of road space available for journeys to work.

Turning to social forces, perhaps two points need to be made. The first is that, although leisure time has not been growing as significantly as is commonly supposed (the average length of the working week, including overtime, has remained steady in recent years, for instance (1.20)), it might be anticipated that there will be real increases in leisure time in the future. Taking perhaps extreme possibilities, if the average amount of working time required per annum falls by half, we might see either a four-hour working day or six months' annual holiday. The scale of local leisure provision required will clearly be very different between these two extremes. The second point concerns the increasing emphasis being placed on environmental quality in social attitudes. This means that rather higher quality sites tend to be sought for housing areas (where most people spend the majority of their lives) while other areas (which, in earlier periods, might have been devoted to housing) are developed for other uses. It is in these subtle ways that changes in social attitudes bring about changes in the distribution of land uses.

Turning to what we have described as urban *condition*, certain features are again obvious in a visual sense. Many town centres have for some time been sprouting *new* shopping and office developments, normally surrounded by areas of decay, often with mixed housing, commercial and industrial uses. The surrounding housing areas tend to improve in quality as one moves outwards, although marked differences between private and local authority housing can sometimes be observed. Any town will reveal varying qualities and conditions, both between different uses and, perhaps more significantly, for the same use. This reflects the fact that individuals and organisations, acting privately or commercially, can afford to pay for the occupation of land and buildings to varying degrees; the existence of variations in condition within a town is an economic reaction, the supply of particular facilities tending to meet the demand. The disadvantage, particularly in the housing field, is that wide variation in condition may be increasingly inappropriate as egalitarian attitudes become more prevalent.

So far as particular influences on condition are concerned, transport and technological factors can again be discerned. The problems associated with traffic congestion are a major feature, but these are examined elsewhere in this volume. A number of 'transportation effects' relevant to urban form may be mentioned here. The spread of car-ownership means that people are less concerned with local accessibility than before: this puts a premium on living in areas with advantages other than those of local accessibility, notably high environmental standards, often in association with people of similar social backgrounds. Technology is also being brought to bear in providing the kinds of standards of comfort, convenience and safety in 'public' areas (such as in pedestrianised covered shopping centres) which are already expected inside buildings.

Even if technology provides the possibilities for improving urban conditions, there are always economic limitations, not only for individuals (here the limitations vary, as already suggested) but also for the country as a whole. For instance, we have the technical ability to overcome congestion, pollution, poor housing and all kinds of urban afflictions by the end of this century, but the capital resources necessary are unlikely to be made available to deal with all of them: the problem here becomes a social and political one of allocating scarce resources between competing sectors of activity (1.21).

The limits of economic resources, however, also have their effects on particular parts of towns, and these are most evident in what has become known, at least in large towns, as the 'zone of transition' around town centres. Buildings in the past have normally been built to last 60, 80, 100 years or more; they may still be structurally sound at a time when they are no longer in a suitable location or of an appropriate character to meet their original purpose, or the precise original purpose may even have disappeared. At the same time, many buildings built for one purpose can be converted to other purposes: churches converted to warehouses are now becoming fairly abundant, and one warehouse, at least, has been converted into a Department of Town Planning at a Polytechnic (Leeds)! Such conversions are cheaper than new buildings and this type of supply helps to satisfy particular sectors of demand. Not all demand, of course, can be met in this way; if it could, the scope for fundamental urban change would be drastically reduced; nevertheless, this process is a powerful agent for change. Zones of transition, where this kind of activity is concentrated, often were former mainly fashionable residential areas highly accessible to 19th century town centres, now overtaken by the outward spread of commercial uses as the service sector grows, and by an associated deterioration in environmental conditions, reinforced by the process of ageing. Once this kind of process sets in the area tends to succumb to a positive downward spiral momentum as different uses and groups move in by a process of 'invasion and succession'. Prospects and rumours of redevelopment may well even encourage decay. Such areas become the home of mixed uses, their housing dominated by the privately-rented sector occupied by lower income groups, and they contain most acute social problems, especially in large towns. Where the occupants of an area of this sort are an obviously distinct group, for instance an immigrant group, the area's problems may have an unfortunate focus in the public imagination. Many towns contain concentrations of coloured immigrants in areas such as this, and we do not have to look only to Bradford, Southall or Wolverhampton for examples. To take Doncaster, again, 10 per cent of the town's enumeration districts (the areas covered by enumerators on their house-to-house rounds) at the time of the 1971 Census, containing 12 per cent of the town's population, contained as many as 44 per cent of those of Doncaster's residents who were born in the 'new Commonwealth' (1.22). In some cases, the succession of different immigrant groups can be traced over time as in the case of parts of inner Leeds, where Irish immigrants were in turn succeeded by Jews and then by West Indians.

Not least among the problems of these areas is the fact that not only is it here that the need for improvement or renewal of the physical fabric is concentrated, but they are also areas where the occupants are in the least favourable positions to pay for better environments. Moreover, they are areas which particularly illustrate the fact that planning is concerned not merely with physical equipment, but also with the relationship between physical equipment and people and their needs and activities.

By now we have moved into the field of social forces in their influence on urban conditions. The way in which Britain's economic wealth is distributed through society is a social and political decision area, and the present position, rightly or wrongly, is that there are wide differentials between the various sectors. It is not surprising, therefore, that there should be wide differences in the standards, ages, and conditions of buildings which people use. The danger, of course, is that the existence of these different types of physical fabric, often in extensive uniform areas, tends to reinforce the lack of contact between social groups; the growth of racial ghettoes in London or the West Midlands or of religious ghettoes in Belfast are among the more spectacular examples of what can happen. Social attitudes also affect urban conditions in other ways. Changes in housing standards are due, in part, to changes in social attitudes, and the rate of change appears to be increasing; lighter, less permanent materials are likely to be used to an increasing degree to permit more flexible physical arrangements within dwellings and less costly construction and demolition (1.23). The idea of the plastic housing estate may not necessarily be a science fiction dream. To take another example, the growing pressures which may lead to the re-emergence of public transport are due in part to society's recognition of the fact that land-use and transport planning policies do not necessarily have to lead to congestion.

The influence of the planning system

Powerful forces have been shown to be at work in creating the problems associated with urban spread, decreasing densities, the zone of transition and a host of others. How, then, has the planning system in Britain attempted to deal with these problems in the context of economic and physical limitations (and how is the system changing its attempts) — and all this at a time of louder demands from the public for better standards?

Firstly, it is as well to remind ourselves that the planning system is only one (and a relatively late) set of community interferences in the exercise of individual rights over land. These interferences have generally formed the responses to the existence of very evident problems for society; the rise of planning is no exception to this. In fact the physical aspects of urban form have been a crucial stimulus to the rise of planning. The growth of towns in the 19th century was the significant factor: Glasgow's population grew from 77 000 in 1801 to 762 000 in 1901; Manchester grew from 89 000 in 1811 to 303 000 forty years later; Birmingham's population increased from 102 000 in 1821 to 401 000 in 1881; Leeds grew from 84 000 in 1821 to 429 000 in 1901; and the population of the area now defined as Greater London increased from 3.9 millions in 1871 to 6.6 millions only 30 years later (1.24). In the 19th century urban areas were overdeveloped with houses, and houses were overcrowded with people. Pressure for community action increased and this gradually formulated itself into the two main elements of modern planning, a *policy element* and a *control element*. The policy element has always been concerned with the prescription of improved urban forms. It had shown itself, for a very limited sector of the population, in the Georgian planning of Edinburgh, Bath and other cities; it was evident in the workers' settlements built at Saltaire, Bournville, Port Sunlight and elsewhere; and it flowered with Ebenezer Howard and the Garden City Movement at the turn of the 19th century and later. The control element represents a continual attempt to ensure that the prescription is properly administered — control of street widths and building heights in the second half of the 19th century foreshadowed the comprehensive planning control system of today.

These two elements were not adequately combined, comprehensively, until the coming into operation of the Town and Country Planning Act, 1947. Planning legislation dates from 1909, but it was cumbersome and fell far short of the present system. For instance, ten years after the passing of the Town and Country Planning Act 1932, only 5 per cent of England was subject to operative planning schemes (1.25). Other legislation was fairly narrow in concept, such as the Restriction of Ribbon Development Act, 1935, designed to control the then rapid spread of development along major roads. From 1947 onwards, however, planning legislation has had some direct effect on all the aspects of urban form which we have considered (and therefore an indirect effect on all the 'natural' forces operating on urban form). Under the 1947 Act each local planning authority was required to prepare and periodically review a development plan showing how all of its land was to be used in the future. These intended patterns of land use were to be achieved on the ground primarily through their control over development, widely defined to include the erection of buildings and changes of uses. The degree to which a proposal was in accordance with the development plan was a major influence on whether permission was granted. The local planning authority could also take direct action in implementing its development plan by means of compulsory purchase powers. The aim, quite simply, was to encourage a rational pattern of land use based on (usually implicit) *community* objectives rather than on *individual* profit-and satis-faction-maximising ones; and to this end the planning authorities have had con-siderable control over the quantity of facilities to be provided in any urban area, their distribution, and their quality.

The influence of the planning system, however, has been reduced by a number of factors: local planning authority areas have often been unrelated to the functional realities of urban situations; the links between land-use planning, transport planning and economic and social planning, so necessary in view of the nature of the forces affecting urban form, have often been tenuous; many of the factors which influence urban form are outside public control; and the increasing pace of changes in population levels, housing standards, car ownership, and so on, has tended to overtake an often slow-moving bureaucratic process. The reforms brought about by a new development plan system, initially under the Town and Country Planning Act, 1968, and a new local government structure, under the Local Government Act, 1972, will solve some of these problems but, as the earlier reorganisation of local government in London has shown, will inevitably bring others in its train. The split of planning functions between two tiers of local planning authority (county and district) is the most notable example of this.

A number of cogs in the planning machine, other than those operated directly by the local planning authorities, were also established in the early post-war years. To solve some of the problems caused by pressures for urban spread, the New Towns Act, 1946 allowed the setting up of New Towns with Treasury finance (although other pressures have also contributed to the setting up of New Towns). The Town Development Act, 1952 gave powers to local authorities for the major expansion of existing towns. The Distribution of Industry Act, 1945 and its successors controlled industrial location in a national context by means of negative control in 'over-heated' areas and the more positive provision of financial assistance in specified decaying areas. The National Parks and Access to the Countryside Act, 1949 allowed National Parks and Areas of Outstanding National Beauty to be designated and generally foreshadowed the current explosion of concern for the environment.

These are the bare bones of the statutory planning system as it affects urban form. We can now briefly examine what those effects have been in the context of the powerful 'natural' forces already at work. In some cases the planning system works with the natural forces, in others it seeks to modify them or their effects, while in yet others it may even attempt to work in converse directions.

Taking urban *size* first, we recall that the 'natural' trend has been for towns to grow. Is the growth of towns, then, to be without limit? Clearly not, for perhaps *the* major goal of land use planning since 1947 has been the containment of the physical spread of urban areas over the countryside (1.26). Early 20th century thoughts on desirable town sizes were a reaction against the atrocious living conditions to be found in the larger 19th century cities and reflected the clear feeling that cities were less good places in which to live than rural areas: Ebenezer Howard's proposals in 1898 were for towns in the 32-58 000 population range (1.27). Large cities were regarded as being far from ideal in the first half of this century (1.28), and this had its practical effects, for of the first twelve New Towns designated in England and Wales (1946-50) none was to be built for a population over 80 000, the median size being only 45 000. The tide then began to turn, however, partly as a result of good sites for 'semi-independent' towns becoming increasingly scarce. The five New Towns designated between 1961 and 1964 were all designed for the 80-100 000 range. The wheel had almost turned full circle by 1967-70, when all but one of the six New Towns designated were for populations of between 190 000 and 430 000. With Britain's population increasing, and most of this population being urban, the planner's basic choice is between many small towns and fewer larger ones. He is increasingly opting for the latter, taking the view that unstoppable forces have to be accommodated and that the physical environment can be best protected by means of concentrating urban growth in a smaller number of more suitable locations.

Just as towns have been accommodating more people, the average person in towns tends to need or want more space. Planners have argued long and furiously about the advantages and disadvantages to the individual and the community of living at high and low *densities* (1.29). The 'urban design' element in the profession since the war has supported higher densities, and this culminated in the development of Cumbernauld, a New Town north-east of Glasgow. Indeed, it is probably fair to say that the operation of the planning machine has generally kept densities higher than they would otherwise have been. Sprawl, particularly ribbon development, generates substantial social costs, such as costs of piped services, and loss of environmental quality, and the worst aspects of this have been firmly controlled under the 1947 Act following the more tentative efforts of the 1930's. Pressure for higher densities tends to grow when there is an emphasis on the value of natural resources such as agricultural land (1.30), although the main effect here is to channel urban growth to other locations. In the future, if the problems of traffic congestion continue to grow in association with the clamour for better public transport, the planning machine may find itself in the forefront once more of a battle to push up densities, a process which would considerably assist public transport operation. Nevertheless the forces producing lower densities are strong and, with the expectation of real income and standards rising considerably in the future, much may have to be done in convincing the public, particularly the more affluent sectors, that the trends towards lower densities must have their limits. On the one hand this may contribute towards a greater degreee of standardisation in densities, while on the other the need for public plans to give scope for individual choice suggests a requirement for substantial variations in density. In the end, density provisions (at least for housing) will consist of the planning system's reflections of social attitudes to egalitarianism, life-styles, environmental protection, and all the other factors which need to be balanced in decision-making.

Planning has had a powerful influence on the *shape* of our towns. At a time of both population growth and urban growth, one of planning's main tasks has been to ensure that the physical distribution of that growth is appropriate in terms of the community's objectives. Some examples of the kind of land which tends to be avoided because of the planning system and not because of free-market forces are worth listing:

(a)   where the costs of public utilities (e.g. drainage, water supply) would be high;
(b)   where public water supplies might be polluted;
(c)   where long-term surface mineral resources are located;
(d)   where there is high quality agricultural land;
(e)   where there are areas of high natural landscape quality and nature conservation interest;
(f)   where a Green Belt has been established under the planning system to control urban growth in 'sensitive' locations.

These have a real effect on the shape of our towns: for instance, between 1948 and 1958, nearly 7000 acres (sufficient for 46 000 houses) were kept free of development, simply as a result of the operation of the Planning Acts, in the Solihull-Coventry Green Belt (1.31). In many other cases, such as the attempts to minimise urban development in areas subject to noise pollution, or to locate development (other things being equal) to minimise journey-to-work costs, the planner tends to work with natural forces. Whether the planner works with or against pre-existing forces, this kind of concern will tend to produce different urban shapes in different situations, each with its own specific collection of influences. But recent years have seen a renewed *positive* interest in urban shape, an interest which involves the question of whether certain urban shapes, *per se*, are better than others. One example is linear urban growth in which development is encouraged to take place in specific corridors related to transport facilities, either highways or public transport, or both. For successful implementation, however, this kind of proposal must be accompanied by a strong control mechanism to prevent 'normal' outward urban growth in all or many directions. Others would argue that order and convenience are not to be found in simple mappable patterns of this kind, as planning must cater for complex social and economic organisations which require complicated patterns of interaction.

As the planning machinery has been geared to provide direct control over changes in land *use* it would be surprising if planning had not had a major effect here. But let it be remembered that powerful forces affecting land uses are at work anyway: planning cannot run entirely counter to these in what is partly a free-market economy. Many industrial areas, for instance, have grown up where they have, without comprehensive planning control, for good reasons, and these reasons do not disappear simply with the advent of a comprehensive planning system. If one wanted to criticise the operation of planning in this respect, one might perhaps argue that planning's approach has often tended to deal with yesterday's problems, in that it has tended to accept the forces of the past when those of the present need to be considered in greater depth and those of the future anticipated. For instance, the spread of population, increased mobility, and the problems of congestion in town centres have tended to undermine, at least, the economic basis of shopping facilities in town centres; but planners have generally resisted proposals for out-of-town shopping centres in accordance with the natural forces of the past (1.32).

Although the 19th century town generally contained an identifiable town centre and an area or areas devoted almost entirely to upper and middle-class housing, because of accessibility requirements in pre-public transport days there was usually a fine inter-mixture of industry, often heavy polluting industry, and working-class housing. The reaction to this was evident by the turn of the century when the Garden City Movement powerfully stated the case for order, whereby each use was to have its own specific zone in a location which would not 'damage' other uses (1.33). The idea of fairly extensive use-zones of this sort has lain at the heart of much 20th century planning. Through the operation of the development plan and development control mechanisms this has done much to improve many aspects of the quality of urban life. Clearly here we have learnt from the mistakes of the 19th century. The improvements have been brought about mainly in areas of new development, where past mistakes could be avoided from the outset. Less success has been achieved where already existing 'non-conforming uses' have long economic lives before becoming due for redevelopment: these can only be eliminated on payment of substantial financial compensation. Even in areas where it can be easily applied, however, the concept of coarse zoning is under attack from some quarters. Most industrial establishments are not the polluters that they were and housing areas in close association with them have the potential advantage of keeping down journey-to-work lengths and traffic congestion. Since different uses depend upon one another for their economic survival, the argument runs that a much finer zoning system (if indeed a 'zoning' system at all) provides a more highly developed form of order than a coarser pattern (1.34).

Another conscious attempt to influence the distribution of land uses in residential areas has been focussed on the neighbourhood concept. This has involved the division of the urban area into physically recognisable units, devoid of through traffic, each with its own neighbourhood centre to provide local services and having sufficient, but not too many, people for face-to-face relationships and community life to develop. The application of this concept reached its peak in the early post-war New Towns like Stevenage and Harlow. As people at that time looked more to their own locality for the provision of many of their needs, such as local shopping, doctor and school, than they do now this approach clearly made sense in influencing the physical design of urban areas. Again, however, the concept has recently had to face severe criticism. We saw earlier how residential populations are becoming more geographically mobile, and urban areas are becoming more complex than the simplistic neighbourhood concept would have us believe: people are able to seek services over greater distances, and they increasingly seek contact with selected interest-groups rather than with the more random collection of people living within, say, half-a-mile of their homes. A much more realistic area of social connectivity, in any case, is probably a street or a group of a few houses, rather than several thousand houses. A more flexible system, which makes physical provision for easy cross-connections between neighbourhoods and avoids physical demarcation of individual neighbourhoods, is now a more frequent aim, as shown, for example, by the proposals for the new city of Milton Keynes (1.35) and the Sheffield overspill town at Mosborough (1.36). At the same time, the neighbourhood concept is far from dead: New Ash Green, a comprehensively planned 'new village' of 7000 people in Kent has been recently designed and brought into being very much on neighbourhood lines. Indeed the neighbourhood concept can still be regarded as valid (at least for the physical planning of service provision) as a basis for the planning of small towns, where there are fewer neighbourhoods and where consequently cross-connections between them are less prolific. In addition, neighbourhood planning is still very relevant for the large sectors of society who are less mobile than others: children, young mothers, old people, and the poor are bound to rely very heavily on what services are provided close at hand. A matching of physical structures and social needs is required without artificial physical separation.

This leaves us to consider the effect of the planning system on urban *conditions*. The extent to which the planning system can improve conditions, such as in the quality of housing provision or the extent of traffic congestion, depends as much on the availability of resources as on appropriate administrative systems and the availability of professional skills. Perhaps some of the major contributions that physical planning can achieve are social ones. The planning system, for instance, has its effect in attempting to secure better layouts in both local authority and private housing areas, and tends to keep densities in private housing areas to levels higher than free market forces would probably have them. By means such as these a small part is perhaps being played in reducing social differences. The planner's aim to constantly seek improvements in conditions, while obviously in line with the commonly held wider objectives of society, has its dangers, however, for areas of poor quality cheap buildings, suitable for use in embryonic business ventures or as housing for people hoping to move on to better things later, are always in danger of being planned out of existence prematurely. Jane Jacobs has suggested that the concept of zoning policies should be directed towards producing a variety of different ages and conditions in a given (small) area in order to cater for inevitably different needs (1.37). The planning system is perhaps becoming more sensitive to influences of this sort. It is important that this is the case for, as with other facets of urban form, the focus of the delicate balance of economic, social and other factors affecting urban conditions must lie substantially within the planning system.

Planning and urban form: some remaining problems

As a 'man-made' force rather than a natural one, the purpose, validity and benefits of planning can always be called into question. Firstly, though, is the effect of planning significant? Some would argue that much of the development of post-war urban Britain would have happened anyway, planning or no planning: the success, for instance, of an elaborate control system in diverting employment from the faster-growing to the more stagnant or declining regions of the country has only been partial (1.38). At more local levels, however, the effects are clearer, and a number of examples have been given of how the planning system contributes to the 'common good'. Most people would probably accept that, for all its faults, Britain is a better place for its planning system than it would be without it, and some would maintain this point strongly (1.39). At the same time, the search for improvements is a constant one, and the current changes in both the development plan system and the local government structure continue to be a source of much comment in this context. The focus for much of this concern may well lie, so far as urban form is concerned, around some of the aspects raised in the remaining part of this chapter.

A growing concern is not only what is planning for, but also *who* it is for. All activities controlled by the planning system transfer costs and benefits (whether in the form of money or more intangible costs and benefits) from one section of the community to another: the urban motorway, for instance, many provide benefits, such as easier and quicker journeys for middle-class surburban commuters, but it imposes costs, such as noise, on people living in areas through which it passes (costs now partially 'absorbed', so far as the individual is concerned, by the provision of compensation under the Land Compensation Act 1973). At one extreme one could argue that the planning system should be working towards particular patterns of wealth-distribution by providing for, and permitting, proposals which benefit particular sectors of society. If so, who states what these patterns should be? Alternatively, one might support the more traditional view that if there are to be changes in wealth-distribution these should be allowed to emerge as an implicit by-product of a planning system which works towards predominantly physical objectives and expresses itself in physical terms. That wealth-distribution is expressed spatially is obvious in Britain: variations in housing tenure and condition appear to be critical factors related to different incomes, life styles and occupational characteristics (1.40). As an example, one may examine, again, the situation in Doncaster (which has no particular reputation for being the home of extreme conditions) in order to see what kinds of space and mobility contrasts exist between different housing areas, space and mobility being two of the most persistent demands relevant to urban planning today. When the 1971 Census was carried out in Doncaster, there were 16 enumeration districts where housing was predominantly (90 per cent or more) in owner-occupation and 44 which were predominantly local authority housing. In the owner-occupation areas, the proportion of households living at densities of one or more persons per room ranged from nil to 4.5 per cent, with a median of 1.2 per cent; in the council housing areas, the range was from 1.0 per cent to 15.8 per cent, with a median of 6.6 per cent. Perhaps even more noticeable is the car ownership differential: the proportion of owner-occupant households without cars ranged from 7.7 per cent to 61.4 per cent, with a median of 24.5 per cent; the corresponding range for council tenant households was 42.1 per cent to 85.9 per cent, with a median of 68.6 per cent (1.41). Since these highly distinct kinds of areas tend to exist in our towns in fairly large blocks (partly as a result of the operation of the planning system) discriminatory planning in the future could perhaps play a considerable role in influencing conditions in *some*, and deliberately some rather than all, of these areas.

Planning in this kind of system must have strongly political aims. Even if politicians are not prepared to see the planning machine directed to these purposes, recognition of the importance of political decision areas is fundamental to progress in planning. The way in which Britain's anticipated long-term growth in prosperity is 'spent' (the proportion spent, for instance, on major improvements in urban form, especially its *condition*) is a continuous political decision area which affects planning. On a more local level there are signs that politicians are taking the initiative to an increasing degree; the 1972 change in Nottingham's transport policy, from an urban motorway emphasis to a public transport emphasis, was essentially a function of strong political will (1.42). As the technological possibilities of different kinds of urban form increase, this kind of strength may well be decisive.

Planning, of course, is by no means the only area in which the political will plays its part. Indeed, there is perhaps increasing recognition by planners of the importance of other fields of concern. The relationships between the distribution of buildings, land-uses, and roads and people's social and psychological reaction to them is now regarded as being far more complex than half a century or more ago when particular physical distributions were expected to produce clearly defined effects (1.43). As a result of this, associated perhaps with past over-concern for physical structures, the attention of even the planner interested mainly in physical urban form should be increasingly directed to consideration of human activities and human communication to ensure that he is planning with relevant ends in view. There must also be increasing links between spatial physical planning objectives (for example to provide so many units of housing at a particular standard in certain types of locations) and non-spatial objectives and policies (such as those related to the availability of housing finance).

In our brief look at some of the future possibilities for the development of urban form, we frequently noted the theme of the wide divergence between possibilities. This theme of uncertainty accounts, in part, for the development of new techniques in planning at sub-regional, metropolitan and urban levels. New techniques, centred on the building of models which allow us to simulate the major relevant elements of real world systems in a computer, facilitate the explicit exploration of alternative policies for urban structure. These techniques are of great value and planning is increasingly relying on them in reaching decisions on future urban form. But the dangers are there: the items that are left out of models may be significant, and the fact that models which predict the future normally rely on the present relationships between variables remaining the same over long periods (say between condition of housing on the one hand and age of housing and income of householder on the other) may lead to an artificial fossilisation of existing relationships and trends. In other words, the range of future uncertainty may not be undergoing such deep examination as is required. The role of new techniques of this kind, like urban form itself, needs to be carefully monitored (1.44).

In view of the great importance, if not the dominance, of transport changes among the forces which influence urban form, our final conclusion can perhaps be a simple one. This is that planning for land use and planning for transport must be approached as an integrated whole. This will influence both the structure of planning organisations concerned with urban form and the techniques which will influence future forms. Land use no more develops outside a transportation system than transport changes occur outside land use patterns, and one of the major challenges of planning future urban form lies in finding techniques appropriate to producing optimal land-use-transport patterns, whether these techniques be based on mechanistic predictive models, on vivid imagination about future possibilities, or perhaps on some happy combination of the two.

References

1.1   Patrick Abercrombie, *Town and Country Planning*, Oxford University Press, 3rd edition, 1959, p.104.

1.2   Peter Hall *et al*, *The Containment of Urban England*, George Allen and Unwin, 1973, Vol.1, p.40.

1.3   *Ibid.*, Vol.1, p.76.

1.4   Office of Population Censuses and Surveys, *Census 1971, England and Wales, Lancashire County Report*, HMSO, 1973, Table 3.

1.5   Transport facilities occupy a good deal of urban land and could have been included as a facet of urban form. However, as land use and transport interact in significant ways, it is convenient to consider communications, and changes in them, as forces which bring about urban change (which, themselves, encourage further changes in transport and, indeed, in communications generally).

1.6   Shankland, Cox and Associates, *Expansion of Ipswich, Supplementary Report on Comparative Costs*, HMSO, 1968.

1.7   See, for example, the proposals for Nottingham – David Lock, 'Bringing Back the Bus', *Town and Country Planning*, **41**, 1973, pp.329-331.

1.8   Peter Hall, 'Transportation', in Peter Cowan (ed.), *Developing Patterns of Urbanisation*, Oliver and Boyd, 1970, p.133.

1.9   Carl W. Condit, *The Chicago School of Architecture*, University of Chicago Press, 1964, p.21.

1.10   Department of the Environment, *The Housing Cost Yardstick*, Circular 88/71, HMSO.

1.11   European Free Trade Association, *Regional Policy in E.F.T.A.*, 1968. P. Stone, 'Town Form and Value for Money', in *Official Architecture and Planning*, **34**, 1971, pp.522-525.

1.12   Generally speaking, houses are not getting larger nor are they occupying larger plots – Peter Hall *et al, op.cit.*, Vol.2 pp.278-280.

1.13   Doncaster Corporation, *Development Plan, Second Review, Report and Analysis of Survey*, 1968.

1.14   Robin H. Best, 'The Future Urban Acreage', in *Town and Country Planning*, **32**, 1964, Table 1, p.352.

1.15   City and County Borough of Leeds, *First Review of Development Plan, Written Statement with Modifications*, undated.

1.16   The background to this can be found, for instance, in Peter Willmott, 'Some Social Trends', in Peter Cowan (ed.), *op. cit.*, pp.20-25, and in Ortrude White, *Societal Determinants of Urban Form – Some Thoughts on the City in the Year 2000*, Centre for Environmental Studies, Working Paper 45, 1969.

1.17   Doncaster Corporation, *op. cit.*, Table 5.

1.18   Melvin M. Webber, 'The Urban Place and the Nonplace Urban Realm', in Melvin M. Webber *et al, Explorations into Urban Structure*, University of Pennsylvania Press, 1964, pp.79-147.

1.19   See, for instance, M.J. Croft, *Offices in a Regional Centre – Follow-up Studies on Infrastructure and Linkages*, Research Paper No. 3, Location of Offices Bureau, 1969.

1.20   The average number of hours worked per week in Britain by male manual workers aged 21 and over in 1964 was 47.7, exactly the same as in 1938 – Department of Employment, *British Labour Statistics, Historical Abstract*, 1886-1968, HMSO, 1971, Tables 43-45. It has since fallen to 45.0 hours (1972), Central Statistical Office, *Monthly Digest of Statistics*, HMSO, October 1973.

1.21   Ortrude White, *op. cit.*, p.14.

1.22   Office of Population Censuses and Surveys, 1971 *Census*, Ward Library, Doncaster County Borough.

1.23   South Hampshire Plan Advisory Committee, *Technological Change*, Study Report G1, 1970, pp.6-8.

1.24   B.R. Mitchell, *Abstract of British Historical Statistics*, Cambridge University Press, 1962, Tables I6, I7.

1.25   J.B. Cullingworth, *Town and Country Planning in Britain*, George Allen and Unwin, 4th edition, 1972, pp.21-32.

1.26   This is the basic theme of Peter Hall *et al, op. cit.*

1.27   Ebenezer Howard, *Garden Cities of Tomorrow*, reissue edited by F.J. Osborn, Faber and Faber, 1946.

1.28   See, for example, Royal Commission on the Distribution of the Industrial Population, *Report*, Cmnd. 6153, HMSO, 1940, and New Towns Committee, *Final Report*, Cmnd. 6876, HMSO, 1946.

1.29   See, for example, W.G. Bor, J.B. Cullingworth, L.B. Keeble, J.P. Macey, and Muriel Smith, 'Residential Development Densities', in *Journal of the Town Planning Institute*, 47, 1961, pp.4-10.

1.30   Pressure for higher densities in order to protect agricultural land has been a major planning principle since 1947 (see, for instance, Ministry of Housing and Local Government, *Residential Areas – Higher Densities*, Planning Bulletin No.2, HMSO, 1962, p.4) buttressed by the subsidies granted to local housing authorities for high-density residential building.

1.31   This excludes areas for which applications were not made because of the improbability of gaining planning permission for development anyway. Quoted in Peter Hall *et al, op. cit.*, Vol.1, p.525.

1.32   To be fair, many planners would argue that this is a sacrifice of economic efficiency to provide the social benefits of better accessibility to town centres for particular sections of the community: in other words, economic and social forces have to be balanced by means of the planning system.

1.33   Ebenezer Howard, *op. cit.*

1.34   The most powerful statement of this view is to be found in Jane Jacobs, *The Death and Life of Great American Cities*, Random House, 1961.

1.35   Llewelyn-Davies, Weeks, Forestier-Walker and Bor, *Milton Keynes Plan, Interim Report*, Milton Keynes Development Corporation, 1968, pp.22-24.

1.36   Clifford Culpin and Partners, *Mosborough Master Plan*, Sheffield Corporation, 1969, pp.52-55.

1.37   Jane Jacobs, *op. cit.*

1.38   Peter Hall *et al, op. cit.*, Vol. 2, p.393.

1.39   See, for instance, Colin Buchanan, *The State of Britain*, Faber and Faber, 1972.

1.40   David Herbert, *Urban Geography – A Social Perspective,* David and Charles, 1972, p.183.

1.41   Office of Population Censuses and Surveys, 1971 *Census*, Ward Library, Doncaster County Borough.

1.42   David Lock, *op. cit.*

1.43   Ebenezer Howard, *op. cit.*

1.44   Recent warnings on these lines are to be found in John N. Jackson, *The Urban Future*, George Allen and Unwin, 1972.

Further reading

Patrick Abercrombie, *Town and Country Planning*, Oxford University Press, 3rd edition, 1959.

Colin Buchanan, *The State of Britain*, Faber and Faber, 1972.

Colin Buchanan, *Traffic in Towns*, HMSO, 1963.

Gordon E. Cherry, *Town Planning in Its Social Context*, Leonard Hill, 1970.

Gordon E. Cherry, *Urban Change and Planning*, G.T. Foulis, 1972.

Peter Cowan (ed.), *Developing Patterns of Urbanisation*, Oliver and Boyd, 1970.

J.B. Cullingworth, *Town and Country Planning in Britain*, George Allen and Unwin, 4th edition, 1972.

Brian Goodall, *The Economics of Urban Areas*, Pergammon Press, 1972.

Peter Hall *et al*, *The Containment of Urban England*, George Allen and Unwin, 2 vols., 1973.

Ebenezer Howard, *Garden Cities of Tomorrow*, re-issue edited by F.J. Osborn, Faber and Faber, 1946.

John N. Jackson, *The Urban Future*, George Allen and Unwin, 1972.

Jane Jacobs, *The Death and Life of Great American Cities*, Random House, 1961.

J. Madge, M. Smee and R. Bloomfield, *People in Towns*, BBC Publications, 1968.

J. Brian McLoughlin, *Urban and Regional Planning – A Systems Approach*, Faber and Faber, 1969.

Benjamin Reif, *Models in Urban and Regional Planning*, Leonard Hill, 1973.

Murray Stewart (ed.), *The City – Problems of Planning*, Penguin Books Ltd., 1972.

Melvin M. Webber *et al*, *Explorations into Urban Structure*, University of Pennsylvania Press, 1964.

Ortrude White, *Societal Determinants of Urban Form – Some Thoughts on the City in the Year 2000*, Centre for Environmental Studies, Working Paper 45, 1969.

2   Urban Society

In the town planner's approach to urban design, environmental quality and land use control, the influence of the social reformer has been marked and of long standing. From the earliest days of the Garden City Movement the planner saw his objectives in a distinctly social context. The pervading concept of 'physical determinism', whereby the nature of physical conditions was held to have a causal relationship with an individual or community response, threw great emphasis on the importance of satisfactory living conditions in meeting many of the community problems of the day. The early forties saw a renewal of the marriage of social idealism and physical, environment-oriented endeavour, but it was not long before disillusionment set in. Social engineering through a combination of either the New Towns Act, 1946, or the Town Development Act, 1952, and the Town and Country Planning Act, 1947, failed to make much ground. Many of the social problems which urban renewal and residential relocation posed were ignored or misunderstood, and in the sixties planners were challenged to reassess their objectives and methods in the light of searching questions and new assumptions.

This chapter picks up the contemporary position, reviewing the major issues which the present day urban planner has to consider in his plan making and other statutory functions. First, by way of introduction, we look at the broad social problems that are national in scale which impinge on planning: the nature of modern society, particularly its internal divisions and class structure, and the major problems thereby presented. Second, we review a number of specific issues with which the planner by implication is concerned, both in the inner city and suburban areas. Thirdly we look at contemporary policies in which the planner is inescapably involved such as race relations, the Urban Programme, and spatial concentrations of deprivation in city areas.

Planning and social problems

Planning is moving away from a development or master plan approach and is becoming more involved with the mechanisms and institutions which bring about change. Urban sociology, in its turn, is becoming interested in the interaction between planners and their client groups and, consequently, the management of urban resources. Pahl, (2.1) for example, has put forward the 'concept of constraints', that is because resources are scarce, various factors operate to constrain people's access to them. These constraints can be spatial or social, the latter including bureaucratic rules and procedures. Sociology, therefore, is looking more critically at the nature and consequences of planning action in urban areas, while the planner is attempting to understand the social context in which the plan is to be set and to look at plan-making more as a process than a specific end product.

Planning is no longer concerned primarily with land use control but in the comprehensiveness of the context for problem solving. As few urban problems and issues can be isolated and considered as purely physical it is necessary to look at the inter-connectedness of the physical, social and economic aspects. Plan-making, therefore has to become involved with policies and activities of other departments, agencies and bodies, i.e. with the process of government.

The problem approach is more likely to bring the planner into contact with the community and their immediate problems as the people see them. Because the community is not homogeneous there will inevitably be different issues resulting in conflict. To the planner no one group's interests can be followed without considering the effects on other groups and those of a wider or longer term nature. The decision-making process is, therefore, the political content of planning described by Cullingworth "as a process of balancing conflicting claims on scarce resources . . . . . . and of achieving compromise between conflicting interests" (2.2). The role of the planner could be regarded as providing information to the decision-maker which identifies the choices and conflicts and the distribution of advantages and disadvantages from the different choices.

But this emphasis given to conflict is fairly recent in the thinking of planners and has probably developed from an understanding, and greater recognition, of the pluralistic nature of modern society. The dichotomy between consensus and conflict in social policies is one that is currently being discussed. The consensus model for social policy can be illustrated by the Welfare State which is seen as a result of 'general will' and for the 'public good'. The concept of consensus implies that values are unnoticed or taken as universal. But the dominant values of society make for a generally held ambivalent attitude to those who claim support, particularly financial, so that many claimants feel a loss of respect. The current policy to provide selective help to those in greatest need requires people to undergo a means test. Although the theory is that benefits should be accepted as of right with no stigma of poverty attached, the prevailing social values have meant that many who need benefits do not claim them, and those who do frequently feel a loss of dignity.

In contrast to the consensus view of social policy with its underlying value assumptions working against certain sections of the population, there is the view that it is the power relationships in society which are important. If society is seen as composed of conflicting interests then, it is argued, the poor themselves must try and get a redistribution of power and resources in their favour. Whether this is achieved through 'the system' or whether the existing governmental institutions are regarded as reinforcing deprivation, the issues are ultimately about the way resources and power are distributed and therefore about politics.

Basic to the issues of conflict and distribution of power in society is the operation of the class structure and the inequalities which limit opportunity and choice. In looking at the class structure today there would seem to be two different aspects. On the one hand it is probably true to say that living standards have risen, and together with the implementation of social policies, there has been brought about a 'convergence' of tastes, consumption and behaviour with less status differences between the classes. Many features of middle-class life, particularly the ownership of material possessions, have become diffused, certainly amongst the more affluent manual workers, and encouraged by the TV and other media.

On the other hand evidence for a real change in the social class structure is difficult to find. Studies into the extent of social mobility, that is movement from one class to another, the distribution of wealth and the proportionate share of the working class in the available educational opportunities, have changed remarkably little. Two contradictory elements therefore exist: a more homogeneous society with an appearance of greater social equality but with the basic opportunity ladder still restricted and relatively unchanged over many years.

In a hierarchical society like Britain, but one which is consumption orientated and home centred, the home becomes not only a physical amenity but can indicate to the occupant himself and his neighbours that he has moved upward in the social scale. A better home is therefore sought by those with aspirations, and those who become owner-occupiers or move out to the newer municipal estates tend to have adopted middle-class values, as well as having the economic means to register this choice. Such a selective outward movement could well result in some parts of the city, for example, the older privately rented property and the older council estates, becoming enclaves of particular groups of people, often the poorest. This is an example of where increasing opportunity and choice can result in social polarisation and segregation. Planners have adopted ambivalent attitudes to social polarisation. They see imposed social hetereogeneity as restricting people's choice but the existence of large scale homogeneity – at the lower end of the scale – is also seen as harmful.

The limitations of opportunity and choice under which the poor live is regarded as the essence of the concept of deprivation. The limitations of choice operate, for example, in the workings of the housing market, including access to local authority housing. The latter is often restricted because of the rules and allocation policies which tend to exclude particular categories of families and individuals. Where points allocated are related to length of residence, immigrants are unable to qualify; where slum clearance schemes have concentrated on areas of two storey family housing, those living in crowded, multi-occupied dwellings have no opportunity for rehousing; and where there is a rigid definition of the categories of persons considered eligible for rehousing, the single, transients and others are usually excluded.

Definitions of deprivation are often linked to some measure of failure like scholastic achievement, (literacy, IQ tests, and others,) and socio-psychological surveys have concentrated on the popular reason for retardation — the lower class home. The notion of a 'culture or sub-culture of poverty' stems from the adaptation that is believed to be made by those who, in a hierarchial and meritocratic society, know that they are at the bottom and lose out on all the recognised and valued goods such as personal esteem, authority, congeniality and influence at work and in particular wealth with all its status and security. In addition there are degrees of racial, sexual and class prejudice presenting different problems to different groups. The different cultural responses demanded are then reflected in variations from the 'norm' of accepted and measured standards. It is suggested that anti-social behaviour could also be understood as a means whereby these people adapt to, and try to cope with, the relative deprivation of being so far removed from the standards enjoyed by the rest of society. Poverty also separates them from the stable working-class and they are therefore excluded from much of what ordinary society has to offer.

In recent years there has been an increasing concern with urban social problems. Some of these problems have arisen because of special circumstances, for example racial problems developed in the sixties when immigration increased; others have grown in importance because of changes in the structure of society, like those related to employment and mobility; while problems such as poverty, homelessness and destitution are being brought into prominence because of rising standards and increasing intolerance of such conditions.

This does not necessarily mean that there are more social problems but that more situations are being *defined* as problems. Becker (2.3) sees the process of problem definition as basically a political one — a way in which views are put forward by those with certain interests and others persuaded that public action is necessary. Institutions or agencies are set up to deal with it and the problem is redefined by the personnel engaged. The form the problem takes, therefore, is related to the way the problem is defined, and this, together with the type of organisations most concerned, influence the way the problem is tackled. Deprivation is an example. It is becoming defined in a certain way which is not always recognised as such by another observer, or even by the supposedly deprived person himself; and insofar as it is becoming a public problem taken on board by Government the possible solutions are likely to lie in institutional changes which they can control.

Attitudes exist in society which make it more likely that certain problems are selected for attention rather than others, and the same problem at different times can be treated more or less sympathetically. The elderly are a case in point. The elderly become divorced from the main stream of economic life, both as producers and consumers, and become separated, physically if not emotionally, from the nuclear family. The result has been segregation into institutions or retirement areas and a concentration of the elderly among those on Supplementary Benefit, in other words the poor. Recently, concern has been growing among those professionally involved, that institutional care actually increases helplessness and that more selective aid and community services would enable an elderly person to remain in his own home. Problems then become ones of material deprivation, loneliness and the 'delivery of services' to meet their needs.

By placing more emphasis on the home and the community the planners are becoming more aware of the harm that can be done by large-scale comprehensive redevelopment. The consultants (2.4) looking at Nelson and Rawtenstall actually suggested retaining the older houses near the town centre because they were so convenient and suitable for older people, apart from their wish not to disturb those who had lived there many years and had their roots in the local community. Organisations like Age Concern are trying to draw attention to the disadvantages that old people suffer in modern society, not least in the environment where traffic affects their safety, the major shopping developments undermine the existence of the local shops, congestion and declining public transport services make it difficult for them to get about and so on.

At the same time as the elderly have lost their role in society, and modern urban conditions have brought increasing problems for them, the young have become important as an identifiable group. In part this is due to their influence in the economic market as consumers, in the fashion and leisure industries in particular, and in part because it is through the education of the young that society sees itself progressing with the new technological skills. These trends have probably increased the generation gap, and the 'problem of youth' appears disturbing insofar as the younger people are seen to reject the values and institutions of society, with alternative life-styles and with deviant and 'anti-social' behaviour. Although such problems are often seen in the context of social, economic and political frustrations of youth, there are occasional references to the interaction of the urban environment, as for example the physical characteristics which encourage vandalism, the limitations of young peoples' mobility because of the dangers of cycling in heavily trafficked cities, the restricted opportunities for recreation in older residential areas, and the separation of educational establishments from the life of the community.

Demographic changes have led to differences in life-styles which affect the structure of towns and cities. More people are marrying and living longer so that the number of independent households has been increasing much faster than the population as a whole. The falling birthrate has meant that the typical family of parents and young children is one that exists for a shorter period of time and such households, therefore, are a minority. The consequences of these trends have resulted in a continuous demand for separate dwellings and a wider variety of housing types. With the shrinking of the private housing market the local authority's housing departments are being encouraged to take a wider responsibility for the housing needs of the citizens as a whole. Rising standards of living and the spending of leisure time as a family unit has increased the desire for greater space and privacy in the home. The move to surburbia and beyond has decreased the population in the cities and intensified demand for land and communications over a much wider area on the periphery. Increasing car ownership, longer holidays and the 5-day week have also altered recreational habits. Those with cars not only go further afield for their recreation but go more often. Pressures are therefore building up in the countryside — for more roads, second homes and caravan sites, golf courses, areas for water sports, car parks, picnics and so on.

The pressure for increasing material standards of living and the small size of modern families has led to a higher proportion than ever before of married women in paid employment. For the most part the double burden of home and job has not had much influence on the way towns and services are organised and planned, although within the home the manufacturers have provided more labour-saving devices. Only recently has flexi-time been introduced but work is still fairly rigidly and hierarchially organised with work-satisfaction as an objective only beginning to be discussed.

In defining urban problems the planner will collect data in order to measure deficiencies against some sort of standard, but the question arises — standards for whom? Faced with a multiplicity of communities and groups each with their own goal systems, the idea of there being generally accepted standards is unrealistic. To avoid this, planners now speak of 'needs'. But 'needs' imply absolute necessities and do not indicate priorities nor conditioned preferences. As in many other fields 'needs' have become determined by the professional on the presumption that he knows best. Webber (2.5) goes so far as to suggest that the 'social professions have been in the business of serving themselves rather than their clients' leading to an 'orientation to efficiency on the supply side' and to 'the neglect of equity on the demand side of the system'.

Certainly there is increasing criticism of the gap between the planner and the public. In defining problems people themselves often see them differently from the planner's assessment. For example, an area may be regarded by the planner as visually unattractive, as having high rates of noise and high pollution levels, an inadequate drainage system and a lack of open space; but the residents often perceive the area more in terms of social relationships – the presence of nice neighbours, relatives, the local shopkeepers, of ease and convenience of access to facilities, and of the opportunities it offers for jobs.

Problems can often arise from side-effects of carrying out existing policies and programmes. For example, a policy of redevelopment can produce many problems arising from planning blight and the need to move people to other areas. Often there is very little monitoring of public policies to see what is happening and the only recording done is in terms of input such as pounds spent, manpower employed, services rendered, slums cleared, and not output measures of consumer satisfaction.

The response by planners to problems has been criticised in the past because of their tendency to look for a 'key' solution. By concentrating on one aspect of the breakdown in city life – hygiene, slums, pollution, sprawl – the unbalanced consequences for the rest of the life and fabric of the city are ignored. Society is too complex and changes occur too rapidly to have a simple one-off solution. The character of social, economic and environmental problems have to be constantly redefined. As Cullingworth (2.6) concludes "problems are not 'solved': they are merely changed".

Specific issues

Much of the current discussion about social problems concerns various aspects of poverty and deprivation, and the increasingly political input into the planning process has probably developed from the way these are viewed in terms of social dynamics and change. Townsend (2.7), for example, considers the structure of society works to distribute resources so unevenly that some sections are forced into poverty. This is why economic growth can widen the gap between rich and poor. Cullingworth stresses the relativity of poverty pointing out "the 'problem' of the affluent is as relevant as the problem of the poor; . . . the crucial issue is the total social structure, not that part of it which is seen as 'poor'. Thus the problem of poverty is essentially the problem of inequality"(2.8).

The concept of deprivation is wider and more complex than that of poverty as it refers to a whole range of social and economic conditions experienced by those whose standard of living is markedly below the national average. Thus it includes poverty in the sense of low income, but its scope implies a more perceptive and more comprehensive approach to the problem of the poor than that inherent in the earliest work on poverty, which focussed exclusively on low income defined as less than the income required to buy basic necessities such as food, clothing, fuel and shelter. This approach ignored how far people were below the poverty line, the hard-pressed just above it and the complexity of the problems caused by or associated with low income. Nor could it reflect the changing needs and standards of society and how far its members were able to participate fully in the life of the community.

To be deprived is to have considerably less of the very many different kinds of goods and services which together make up much of what is included in the term 'the standard of living' and 'the quality of life'. The interaction and reinforcement of income inequalities with inequalities in education and employment opportunities, health and environment tend to make for physical concentrations of people who are deprived and for some of those people to suffer from multi-deprivation. The interlocking effects are well described in the American 1971 Manpower Report of the President:

"Disadvantaged city residents, particularly members of minority groups, have fared badly in competing for jobs because of a combination of obstacles that affects all aspects of their lives. Inadequate education, segregated housing, employment discrimination and other barriers — both real and artificial — have isolated these workers from the mainspring of economic activity and have resulted ultimately in relegating them to a secondary labour market, where jobs are poorly paid and likely to offer only irregular employment" (2.9). This broad concept of deprivation relates the problems specifically to the society in which they exist.

Part of this concept of deprivation is that it is possible to be trapped in poverty. It is therefore the effects on the children which is of particular concern. The continuation of deprivation from one generation to the next is related to a whole host of interlocking deprivations; inadequacies in their education, for example, make it difficult for them to obtain better jobs with better pay, so that they are forced, in turn, to bring up their families in the same conditions. The Department of Health and Social Security has recently commissioned research to be done to test the validity of this concept of a cycle of deprivation and ways in which the operation of the cycle might be prevented.

Similar to this concept is that of cultural deprivation related to deficient child socialisation experiences. Recent evidence from the Child Development Study has demonstrated that 7-year olds in overcrowded homes are retarded, on average, by about nine months in reading age. Children from families not having sole use of any of three basic amenities were also a further nine months behind in reading attainment. This remains true when allowance is made for social class, type of accommodation and tenure. The impact of this accumulation of disadvantages is described in *Born to Fail* (2.10). The nursery school and playgroup programmes are aimed at compensating for deficiences in the early experiences in the home.

Coloured people seem to suffer from additional restrictions in choice and opportunity over and above those of the 'deprived' because of the prejudice against their colour. Daniel (2.11) for example, indicated that discrimination on grounds of colour was taking place on a wide range of factors investigated, particularly housing and employment. This line of argument sees the coloured immigrants having particular problems. They are forced to take the lower status occupations vacated by the indigenous population, more particularly in the economically thriving conurbations. They form concentrated settlements in inner urban areas because of restrictions on housing choice. These areas suffer from physical and social deterioration, with disadvantages from inferior schooling and declining employment prospects. The situation is exacerbated by a stereotyped role for, and discrimination against, coloured people. As a result (the argument concludes) subsequent generations of coloured British citizens will become trapped in a vicious circle of deprivation.

Concern is already growing that the children of immigrants, particularly West Indian, of whom an increasing number have been born here, are finding it difficult to get jobs, and a growing number of school leavers are to be found 'on the streets', and at the same time, their crime rate is rising. To some extent their parents, as new immigrants, accepted the limited opportunities open to them, but their children, educated at British schools, have much higher aspirations and when these are not fulfilled there is considerable disillusionment and resentment; the difference in their skin colour exacerbating this feeling of rejection.

In schools it has been recognised that coloured children may fall behind in education because of cultural reasons. The higher than average incidence of West Indian children in educationally sub normal schools suggests that problems of language (the West Indian patois is very different from English) and culture shock (including the different standards held in the school and the immigrants' home) may be, at least in part, the operating factors. The problems of schools in deprived inner areas combined with lack of understanding and inadequate teaching give the coloured child additional handicaps which restrict his opportunities to benefit from the educational system.

The other side of the argument is that coloured immigrants form part of the wider problem of deprivation. In London, figures from the 1966 Census show that in no wards do they form more than a quarter of the population so that there are numerically more whites than coloureds in 'deprived areas'. The policies required therefore should be aimed at helping deprived people as a whole. Burney (2.12) takes the view that immigrants as a group have many characteristics of other deprived people such as "young families, large families; low paid workers, mobile workers, shift workers; unmarried mothers; and almost any non-English looking, non-English-speaking, non-conforming people ... Racial discrimination is perhaps the biggest single minus; but even this can generally be overcome unless combined – as it nearly always is – with at least one, if not several, of the other factors listed".

The problems of poverty and race have become associated with the inner areas of cities but on the periphery of towns and in developing areas new housing estates have been built which also present social problems. In the immediate post-war period the planning issues were seen in terms of avoiding the deficiencies of the inter-war estates — their vast size, monotony, the concentration of people from one class and lack of social meeting places. By planning in neighbourhood units, it was argued, community identity and neighbourliness would be fostered, while social class mix and 'social balance' should be the goals.

Criticisms of the post-war housing estates continued, however, as studies described the loneliness of wives separated from their kinfolk (Young and Willmott (2.13)) and the phenomena of the new town blues. Friendship patterns showed how neighbour contacts were selective and based, for the most part, on similarity of background. Neighbouring and community planning by way of physical development lost credence as criticisms built up against 'architectural determinism' and 'social engineering'. But as comprehensive redevelopment, with its mass movement of people, slowed down — because there were fewer large areas of slums — so the advantages of rehabilitation and modernising of existing houses were promoted. By this latter policy it was possible to maintain the community which, it was alleged, was difficult to build up anew by physical development.

But there was no agreement about this view of community. Some like Willmott (2.14) from his work in Dagenham found that a community can be re-established, while others like Parker (2.15) considered it had become of less importance than formerly. Parker concludes that:

"The evidence reviewed throws up contradictory findings, but on the whole it is suggested that the break up of working class communities by slum clearance has no more than a minor and short-term effect on most people. It is important to place slum clearance within the context of other social changes which are more important, for example, the economic progress of recent years has helped to reduce the interdependence of kin and neighbours, and the extended family group is fast disappearing."(2.16)

The aspirations for better housing and environment are ones which are held not only by middle class people but by many working class and slum dwellers too. In a sense, therefore, the local authorities are reacting to, rather than precipitating, social change. But the protests to the Docklands plan in London by the residents shows that there are communities which still have strong ties and who wish to remain together.

These are a few of the problems facing the planner but how far has he knowledge of them and a sound data base for understanding them? On the whole, social information in town planning has not played much part in what has been primarily regarded as a physical activity. Measurements of achievement for example, are principally in terms of houses built, roads constructed and so on. Social statistics and trends, analyses of urban structure and small areas have, however, begun to contribute to physical planning and to policy making.

In 1970 the Government published *Social Trends* (2.17), the aim of which was to try and bring out the relationship between different statistics and identify the gaps in the statistical framework. The General Household Survey (2.18) was begun to provide a regular picture of changing social conditions to help in the formation and discussion of social policies. Moser (2.19) believes that this system of social statistics could, if successful, throw light on the relationships between social investments and changes in social conditions and welfare, and on links between economic changes and social changes. The development of social indicators is one in which there is a considerable amount of interest at the present time. Moser (2.20) suggests there are three kinds: informative indicators (describing particular conditions), evaluative indicators (relating to particular policy programmes) and predictive indicators. Any tendency to look for a single index of 'well being' is criticised by Moser "as there is no objectively agreed weighting system"; although all policy statements and development plans make value judgements, weighting benefits in one sphere against benefits in another.

This difficulty is apparent in the work done by Craig and Driver (2.21). Their aim was to develop social indicators, from data in the 1966 Census, to identify and quantify adverse social need in small areas. The weighting of variables to use as indicators of social need was called by them the rules of an 'arithmetic of woe'. Only if area A, they alleged, had every indicator of a greater value than the corresponding indicator for area B might it be confidently claimed that A was an area of greater need than B. An alternative to the construction of an arithmetical index is to map the incidence of each indicator, and then identify areas of substantial overlap. This is a variation of an unweighted index and one which is popular with planners. However, the advantage is the spatial picture it gives and not as a method of aggregation.

Data from social service departments and other agencies, aggregated into wards or similar areas for reasons of confidentiality, have been used in addition to that from the Census to identify social problem areas. An example of this is the work done by the City Planning Office at Liverpool into social malaise. In this Report (2.22) the high incidence spatially of social malaise statistics was used to identify areas of special need "where present difficulties might be remedied by an influx of extra physical and social resources". The identification of such areas was therefore linked with a policy of 'positive discrimination', and the use of selected criteria, as applied to areas, has been the basis of Government programmes such as Educational Priority Areas, Community Development Projects, and the Urban Programme.

Once areas have been identified in terms of different social problems and therefore having different social *needs*, the question arises as to how far the delivery of public services and the distribution of resources meet these needs. Area management is a method of administration now currently being discussed which is closely linked with identifying area needs and area problems, information on which is essential to policy formation. The recently published urban guide lines for Sunderland (2.23) suggests the carrying out of a community review.

However, although the use of criteria identifies different areas, many programmes relate to the individual and his household. Special surveys need to identify particular groups such as the elderly and disabled, or, in the planning field, the non car owners, to assess their needs and see how far these are met by the existing provision. The proposed Housing Action Areas for example will be identified by some criteria of 'stress' but for the implementation of any programmes individual households will need to be interviewed as the composition, age, work place and aspirations of the residents can be radically different from house to house.

Contemporary policies

Social policies in this century developed in an *ad hoc* way, meeting different areas of social life and needs, for example in relation to housing, mental health, old age, the blind and so on. In the 1940's there was an extension of social legislation and an approach to social policy as a whole in the Beveridge Report of 1942 (2.25). The universal character of social policy 'conditioning the lives of all citizens' has gradually given way to the view that in a varied and pluralistic society the uniform and concentrated ordering of policy may not be desirable. With greater understanding of the complex process of formulating and implementing of social policies it is realised that not all policies are the outcome of conscious thought and deliberation but many evolve gradually, particular cases setting a precedent.

It is not surprising therefore that ideas about social policies are not static; they change with changing ideas, events and circumstances. There are also genuine and sincere disagreements about the nature and the urgency of a social problem or need, and the consequences about the appropriateness of an intended social policy. This can be illustrated by the policies directed to the coloured immigrants which are both ambiguous and faltering. The argument that the problem of coloured immigrants is merely one of general deprivation is often supported in the belief that any policies or resources specifically aimed at assisting the coloured minority could be regarded as socially unjust. There has always been the feeling that resentment and even a white backlash could follow, aggravating rather than reducing the problem of race relations. Policies, therefore, on this view should be generally directed at helping the deprived, although indirectly the coloured community may benefit more proportionately, as for example policies related to improving security of tenure or rent control in furnished accommodation would particularly help coloured people, proportionately more of whom are furnished tenants. On the other hand some policies have been directly related to reducing discrimination and disadvantage for coloured people. The Race Relations Act of 1968 for example has helped reduce discrimination, particularly in employment.

Other policies have been ambivalent like those towards dispersal of coloured immigrants. Dispersal was seen as providing access to better material conditions such as housing and improved educational facilities and environment, and reducing social conflict by assisting in integration. The Cullingworth Committee, however, warned that "any policy of dispersal in the field of housing must be implemented with great sensitivity, with no element of compulsion or direction, and can proceed only at the pace of the needs and wishes of the people involved. It must not be assumed that coloured people wish to disperse themselves rapidly among the whole community, but at the same time the opposite must not be assumed" (2.26). In education the bussing of coloured children has been criticised as separating them from their playmates and depriving them of specialist provision for language teaching. There was also such a density of immigrant children in some areas that dispersal altered the balance very little. Ideas recently put forward seem to be more towards the development of teacher training courses in language teaching for immigrants and the provision of pre-school groups and nursery schools in areas of significant immigration. Some are against dispersal because, they argue, such a policy could deflect from improving the conditions for those who cannot or do not wish to move. A report by the Housing Panel of the Birmingham Community Relations Committee says: "The difficulties of these areas will not be solved by moving sections of the population but only by concentrated action within the areas themselves ... What is needed is the injection of more interest, more effort and more money into the areas of decay and neglect" (2.27).

Social policies are also seen by some as primarily a means of eliminating obstacles to choice. Deakin and Ungerson describe these as, "making widely available information on which to base a choice, providing easier access to the particular institutions that can best provide it, and cutting down on the exercise of arbitrary powers by those who now take the crucial decisions about people's housing chances" (2.28). The setting up of housing advice and information centres, a number of which have been financed under the Urban Programme, is an example of making information on housing opportunities more widely available. Voluntary bodies, as well as statutory authorities, are also setting up advice centres — on legal matters, welfare rights and benefits and other types of information.

Social policies directed towards the areas of new development have been primarily concerned, not with choice so much, as with the adequate provision of social amenities. Problems of new communities were seen in terms of lack of meeting places, little provision for leisure or for young people, inadequate services and so on. The importance of such provision stressed for a number of reasons. Firstly, there was the view that old established communities have strengths which a new community lacks so that it was necessary to give them more support in the way of social provision. Secondly, the move itself was regarded as traumatic for many people and the breakdown of established relationships and patterns of activity meant that special attention should be paid to facilities, like community centres, to help build up community ties again. Thirdly, there was the underlying view that, by rehousing, the authority could free families and especially the children, from the destructive social influences of living in a slum. By providing community centres rather than pubs and working mens' clubs, middle class values were offered to the residents revealing a paternalism in planners often criticised by those now engaged in community development work.

Publications like *The Needs of New Communities* emphasised the deficiencies in current plans for new communities:
"By their very nature they are predominantly concerned with land use: It (a Town Map) will not show the position of, or even record the number of, doctors' surgeries, tenants' meeting places, children's play spaces and the like . . . the danger is that since such provision is not planned at this stage, it may be given insufficient attention at the detailed planning stage" (2.29).

The recommendation, therefore, was that in addition to a physical plan, each new community should have a social development plan and programme.
"It would show how the social services and community facilities were to be provided, by whom, and where. Its preparation would involve a great deal of consultation with existing statutory and voluntary bodies. Since it would be dealing with changing social needs it would require constant reappraisal in the light of changing conditions" (2.30).

Because much of the provision referred to was the responsibility of other agencies the stress was on co-ordination and the desirability of appointing a Social Relations Officer. But a number of new and expanding towns have been slow to appoint such an officer and none at all exist in the established towns. The administrative problems of co-ordination and securing the necessary financial resources have often frustrated the plans for social provision, while the political problems of determining priorities have led, on a number of occasions, to a rejection of 'non essential' community facilities.

Meanwhile it is being realised that some kinds of social policies are needed in relation to older council estates. The original preoccupation with physical and management problems of rehousing, redevelopment and overspill, and the tendency to think that a new home in a new environment was sufficient has resulted in some post-war housing estates now becoming 'problem areas'. Many families who were moved from slum areas still show the same symptoms of social malaise. In the Liverpool Social Malaise report it is held "that the rehousing of these people to corporation estates on the outskirts of the city has done little to alleviate the handicaps and difficulties that they face . . . The slum clearance and rehousing programme is not shown to have much statistical relevance to the problems examined in this Study, suggesting that a concerted attack on social problems will not be helped greatly by the mere renewal of the city's physical structure" (2.31).

The approach adopted at present has been primarily in terms of modernising the homes on old estates with the improvement grants made available by central Government. But Wigan, for example, in Operation Phoenix (2.32), appointed a family case worker and gave the Medical Officer of Health executive powers 'across the board' to cope not only with the problems of physical degeneration, but the community and personal problems associated with poverty, large families and personal inadequacies. In the Community Development Project in Vauxhall, Liverpool (see page 51), where there are many 1950's Corporation walk-up flats, the tenants themselves have been brought into the planning and execution of planning programmes and provision of amenity areas and playgrounds.

The emphasis in recent housing policies has been on rehabilitation which helps to maintain the existing community. But not all older privately owned housing areas are traditional, close-knit communities. There are also, particularly in large cities, the areas of 'transition' where population turnover is considerable and furnished renting and multi-occupation increasing, so that the different groups living there are determined primarily by economic circumstances rather than community of interest. These transitional areas could be especially vulnerable to the policies that local authorities have developed to deal with comprehensive redevelopment or renewal. Parker raises caution in dealing with transitional areas:

"Here there may be concentrations of ethnic minorities, newcomers to the city, the poor and deprived and deviants. In these situations the likely consequences of large-scale slum clearance are much less easy to judge. The social life of these 'communities' is likely to be much more complex than it is in the traditional working class slum areas and the inhabitants much more susceptible to disturbance" (2.33).

The recent White Paper *Better Homes: The Next Priorities*, 1973, proposed to introduce legislation to redirect priorities in dealing with older housing, and it is likely that more of these transitional areas will become Housing Action Areas. The aim in these HAAs will be "to give priority to the task of dealing comprehensively with the physical conditions ... and to help those people suffering hardship arising from these conditions" (2.34). The actual implementation of Housing Action Area schemes by the local authority could be critical, depending on how much knowledge of the varied needs of residents is obtained and how sensitively the officers react to meeting these needs. Rehabilitation, although less drastic to the residents than clearance, can change the type and price of property that is currently available and which is meeting a real need in these areas. A reduction of accommodation can force those who do not want Council or Housing Association accommodation to gravitate to other similar transient areas.

Increasingly it is being realised that to devise social policies for specific issues is not enough. Families with poor housing for example may have additional problems not connected with housing, while in certain areas it is the combination of deprivations which make the problems more acute for the residents. The belief that there are concentrations of people with 'multiple deprivations' has led to the idea of social policies directed to deprived areas. But opinion has changed only recently towards this approach. The Plowden Report (2.35) was published in 1967 but although committed to look at primary education it considered the home, environment and parental background and recommended a national policy of positive discrimination, the aim of which was to provide additional resources for schools in deprived areas. The educational priority area programme has been a consequence of this committee's report.

The Government-backed educational priority areas made the assumption that educational problems, i.e. low attainment at school, tend to be associated with a whole range of social problems: the children are likely to be in overcrowded housing, to be in families too large for the mother to cope with, to have fathers out of work, or to come from broken families. The findings of the EPA research programme, under the direction of Dr A.H. Halsey, were published in 1972 (2.36). The research recognised the limits of an educational approach to deprivation but concluded that more could be done for children in disadvantaged areas by the development of pre-schooling and the community school. His findings suggested that children are more influenced by the 'hidden' curriculum of friends' and neighbours' jobs and aspirations than by the school itself so that he concludes that there should be more links between school and family, school and teacher training, school and the economy, and school and school. This also includes extending the administrative principles of statutory/voluntary co-operation.

The EPA concept with its input of additional resources by Government has now been extended. The amount available in the primary school building programme is now £50 million a year allocated on the proportion of pre-1903 schools, many of which are in deprived areas. The criteria for areas of 'educational stress' include not only truancy, poor school attendance and a high turnover of teachers, but poor home conditions like a concentration of overcrowded, old and badly maintained houses and family characteristics such as large families and those with supplements of cash or kind. The nursery programme recently announced (1973), allocated two-thirds of the £34 million to deprived areas.

The Urban Programme also provides aid on a positive discrimination basis but covers a wider range of activities and is more experimental in nature than the

EPAs programme. It was authorised under the Local Government Grants (Social Need) Act, 1969, which provides money to local authorities in respect of aid to any urban area of special social need.

"Broadly it is intended to refer to multiple deprivation in urban (not rural) areas: localised districts (sometimes consisting of only a few neighbouring streets) with old, overcrowded, decrepit houses without proper plumbing and sanitation; old and inadequate school buildings; persistent unemployment; family sizes above the average; a high proportion of children in trouble or in need of care: or a combination of some or all of these. In addition, the presence of a large number of Commonwealth immigrants is only one factor, though a very important factor, in the assessment of social need" (2.37).

The total amount of local authority expenditure authorised under the Urban Programme was £20 to £25 million (1968-72) and up to £40 million for the next 4 years (1972/76). The total number of projects approved so far (1972) is about 2800 in some 162 local authorities in England and 5 in Wales. Voluntary projects are also eligible and made up 23 per cent of capital schemes and 49 per cent of non-capital schemes in 1972.

A wide variety of projects are now aided. In 1973 they included such educational projects as home-school links, youth and community provision, language teaching for immigrants; the personal social services' projects included play groups, luncheon clubs, care centres and other facilities for the elderly, good neighbour schemes, and projects to help the mentally and physically handicapped. There were other schemes supported such as short-term provision for the homeless, housing aid centres, legal advice and other services. The amount of money is modest and bids far exceed those that gain approval. One criticism is that there is very little information on how effective the grants are in meeting the most acute needs or whether they are going to the most socially deprived areas.

The assessment of deprivation and the means by which social improvement can be achieved is leading to the development of local community programmes of a character which is relatively new to Britain. The Community Development Projects are examples of this development. They were also set up by the Home Office in 1969 and consist of 12 neighbourhood-based action research experiments. They are aimed at the better understanding and the comprehensive tackling of social needs through closer co-ordination of central and local official and unofficial effort, informed and stimulated by citizen initiative and involvement. Supporting each project team is a research team employed by an appropriate university or polytechnic. The CDP began operating in 1970 in Coventry, Southwark, Liverpool and Glamorgan and further projects have since then been set up in the West Riding of Yorkshire, the London Borough of Newham, the Burgh of Paisley, the County of Cumberland and the City of Newcastle upon Tyne. The probable duration of any project is about 5 years.

Until very recently there has been very little documentation on the operation of these programmes. (2.38)

More recently, in 1972, the Department of the Environment set up three inner area studies in Liverpool, Birmingham and Lambeth, London, as part of the Six Towns Studies. The aim was to carry out research into the function and role of the inner areas in a city and, through action projects, to learn more about policies, techniques and resources to help meet the problems of deprived areas, with special emphasis on housing and the environment. The projects will run for three years. Interest in the 'delivery of services' has led the Liverpool project to experiment with area management and to carry out some research into area budgeting. Whereas the Inner Area Studies have put more emphasis on the 'provision' of services, the Community Development Projects recognise that areas of deprivation contain people who have no choice over the major aspects of their lives, and it is therefore the community as a whole which has to try and get more power on behalf of its members in the decision-making process.

Although a social policy based on positive discrimination has probably been accepted in principle, the extent to which a redistribution of resources from the better off to the poorer members will take place is far less clear. The various Government programmes directed at helping 'the deprived' are at present fragmented but the new Urban Deprivation Unit (2.39) at the Home Office has been set up to co-ordinate such programmes now operating from different Departments. Local government services are assisted financially by the Rate Support Grant allocated according to a 'needs' and a 'resources' element. Proposals regarding the basis of allocation of such grants are being reassessed with the aim of providing more support for poorer authorities. The history of social policies in aiding families and individuals financially has shown how *ad hoc* they have been, proving complicated, costly to run and confusing to the clients. One of the aims of the proposed tax credit system is to improve the take up of benefits. It is a simpler system enabling a "low income family to understand without difficulty what help they were entitled to" (2.40) and much of the provision will be available automatically and so reducing the need for a means test.

These examples show the variety of contemporary social policies. Some coordination is beginning to take place both in local and central government. For example, some local authorities have adopted a corporate planning approach, while central government have proposals to reduce the number of separate benefits and grants that have to be claimed by a family or individual in need. Nevertheless, there is still much further to go in tackling the urban social problems that exist today.

The town planner's contribution in the field of environmental quality is a real one, but of course it only goes so far. But the planner's activities have wider implications and repercussions: it is important to know that his actions have many social consequences. This chapter has shown the many interrelationships that exist between physical policies and community activity. Above all, however, the planner has to be sure of the nature of the urban problem with which he is dealing; the social aspects, as we have suggested here, are particularly complex.

References

2.1   R.E. Pahl, *Whose City*, Longman, 1970.

2.2   J.B. Cullingworth, *Problems of an Urban Society*, Volume 2:*The Social Content of Planning*, Allen and Unwin, 1972, p.156.

2.3   H.S. Becker (ed.), *Social Problems: A Modern Approach*, John Wiley, 1967.

2.4   Department of the Environment, *New Life in Old Towns*, HMSO, 1972.

2.5   M.M. Webber, *Planning in an Environment of Change*, in J.B. Cullingworth (ed.), *Problems of an Urban Society*, Volume 3: *Planning for Change*, Allen and Unwin, 1972, p.58.

2.6   Cullingworth, *op.cit.*, p.22.

2.7   P. Townsend (ed.), *The Concept of Poverty*, Heinemann, 1971.

2.8   Cullingworth, *op.cit.*, p.22.

2.9   United States Department of Labor, *Manpower Report of the President*, 1971, p.91.

2.10   National Children's Bureau, *Born to Fail*, 1973.

2.11   W.W. Daniel, *Racial Discrimination in England*, Penguin, 1968.

2.12   E. Burney, *Housing on Trial: A Study of Immigrants and Local Government*, Oxford University Press, 1967.

2.13   M. Young and P. Willmott, *Family and Kinship in East London*, Routledge and Kegan Paul, 1957.

2.14   P. Willmott, *The Evolution of a Community: A study of Dagenham after Forty Years*, Routledge and Kegan Paul, 1963.

2.15   B. John Parker, *Some Sociological Implications of Slum Clearance Programmes*, D. Donnison and D. Eversley (eds.), *Urban Patterns, Problems and Policies*, Heinemann, 1973.

2.16   *Ibid.*, p.248.

2.17   Central Statistical Office, *Social Trends*, HMSO.

2.18   Office of Population Censuses and Surveys, Social Survey Division, *The General Household Survey: Introductory Report*, 1973.

2.19   C.A. Moser, 'Some General Developments in Social Statistics', *Social Trends*, No.1, HMSO, 1970, para.4.

2.20   *Ibid.*, p.11.

2.21   J. Craig and A. Driver, 'Office of Population and Census Statistics: Identification and Comparison of Small Areas and Adverse Social Conditions', *Applied Statistics*, **21**, No.1, 1972.

2.22   F.J.C. Amos, *Social Malaise in Liverpool*,   Interim Report on Social Problems and their Distribution, p.1.

2.23   Department of the Environment, *Making Towns Better – The Sunderland Study*, HMSO, 1973.

2.24   Department of the Environment, *Better Homes: The Next Priorities*, Cmnd. 5339, 1973, pp.5-9.

2.25   W. Beveridge, *Social Insurance and Allied Services,* Cmnd.6404, HMSO, 1942.

2.26   Ministry of Housing and Local Government, Central Housing Advisory Committee, *Council Housing: Purposes, Procedures and Priorities,* HMSO, 1969.

2.27   'Birmingham Community Relations: Dispersal – An Irrelevancy', *Race Today,* 4,3, March, 1972, p.94.

2.28   Nicholas Deakin and Clare Ungerson, *Beyond the Ghetto,* D. Donnison and D. Eversley (eds.), *Urban Patterns, Problems and Policies,* Heinemann, 1973.

2.29   Ministry of Housing and Local Government, *The Needs of New Communities: A Report on Social Provision in New and Expanding Communities,* 1967, p.49.

2.30   *Ibid.,* p.50.

2.31   F.J.C. Amos, *op.cit.,* p.5.

2.32   J. Haworth Hilditch and W. Steels, *Operation Phoenix,* County Borough of Wigan, 1970.

2.33   B. John Parker, *op.cit.,* p.249.

2.34   Department of the Environment, *Better Homes, op.cit.,* para.19.

2.35   Department of Education and Science Central Advisory Council for Education (England), *Children and Their Primary Schools,* 1967.

2.36   Department of Education and Science, *Educational Priority,* A.H. Halsey, (ed.), 1972.

2.37   *Home Office:* Press Release.

2.38   *The National Community Development Project: Inter-Project Report,* CDP Information and Intelligence Unit, February, 1974.

2.39   *Hansard,* 1st November, 1973, Col.340.

2.40   Treasury, *Proposals for a Tax Credit System,* Cmnd.5116, 1972.

Further reading

J.B. Cullingworth, *Problems of an Urban Society*, Vols. 1-3, Allen and Unwin, 1973.
D.Donnison and D. Eversley (eds.), *London: Urban Patterns, Problems and Policies*, Heinemann, 1973.
R. Holman (ed.), *Socially Deprived Families in Britain*, Bedford Square Press for N.C.S.S., 1970.
R.E. Pahl, *Patterns of Urban Life*, Longmans, 1970.
R.E. Pahl, *Readings in Urban Sociology*, Pergamon Press, 1968.

3   The Housing Question

The housing situation in Britain has been a cause of concern for well over a hundred years. The search for solutions to the related problems of overcrowding, insanitary conditions and poverty gave impetus to the growth of the planning movement. There has always been a close relation between housing and planning, and it is significant that the first 'planning' Acts of 1909 and 1919 were, in fact, *Housing* and Town Planning Acts. The development of planning owes much to its initial concern with housing reform.

Many of our present housing problems have their origins in the nineteenth century. The history of housing and planning policy began with the emphasis on the 'health of towns' and was at first concerned only with public health and sanitation. These were the earliest housing responsibilities of local government and the public health tradition is still very strong today.

It was some time before a more positive attitude to the housing problem was reflected in public policy. The first step towards it was accidental. In 1915, rent control was introduced to prevent profiteering by landlords during wartime. Although it was promised that controls would be removed when conditions returned to 'normal', this could not be done immediately. In fact, it has never been done and in one form or another, rent control has continued to the present day. In 1918, there was a housing shortage, made worse by the virtual cessation of new building during the war; the problems of overcrowded and inadequate housing were still acute. Landlords and builders lacked confidence and there was little indication that the housing programme would be resumed on any scale. Another way of providing houses for the working classes had to be found and the task was entrusted to local authorities. The inevitable corollary was that the State should give the financial help that had previously been denied and subsidies were introduced to encourage new building. For the first time, the government acknowledged that to secure improved housing conditions and to increase the supply of housing, required political and financial commitments on a scale previously unknown. Though its consequences could never have been foreseen, the Housing and Town Planning Act, 1919, was a watershed in the development of British housing policy. Once the principal of direct intervention and subsidisation had been accepted, there was no going back, despite the hope that private enterprise would eventually resume its traditional function of providing housing for all. In the space of four years, the government intervened twice in the housing system, both times dramatically, and has gone on doing so ever since.

By 1920, the seal was set on many of the strands of present-day housing policy and practice. What began as a concern for public health and sanitation was gradually extended to include a whole range of interrelated issues and we now take for granted the government's ultimate responsibility for housing policy and for the success (or failure) of the housing programme. Together with health and education, housing is an area of social policy that directly affects everyone. Not surprisingly, it is one of the major topics of political and public interest.

For the town planner, therefore, the housing question enters deep into his area of concern. Its past significance has shaped a professional outlook, and its present importance in local authority planning is such that his work relates closely to both the formulation of housing policy and the implementation of housing schemes. In the earliest years of this century the practice of town planning was essentially that of shaping the residential environment, and Unwin and Parker in particular provided a distinct professional contribution in their expression of a new, suburban architectural form. Earswick was followed by Hampstead and Letchworth, and in the space of a decade the pattern for low density development was set. The reformer's idea of well-built dwellings in a setting of air, space and sunlight, seen at Bournville in the 1890's, was translated into various garden suburbs, and later into both private and local authority estates (3.1).

For many years, indeed well into the inter-war period, town planning schemes authorised under either the 1909 or the 1919 Acts were essentially housing schemes. For a long time, public control over housing layouts to the new dictates of low density and space around dwellings was the prime reason for planning as a statutory activity. The relative growth of other aspects of planning within the statutory process has not diminished the importance of housing in planning matters. In post war Britain a programme of clearance, improvement, redevelopment and new building has been a fundamental part of the process whereby British towns and cities have been transformed in appearance and structure. The planner has been part of that programme: he has helped to shape policy by making land available, coordinating linked projects, programming the phasing of development, relating concepts of house *and* environmental improvement, and fostering participation between planners and the planned.

Today the planner may have lost the simplicity of outlook of a 19th century housing reformer, but he still has a fundamental role to play in housing matters in local authority planning. Housing administration may now be a professionally distinct operation, but in practice the town planner's own prescriptive skills and coordinating function should result in a close working relationship. Sometimes he may assume that role without full understanding of the issues with which he is expected to deal. This chapter seeks to help him in this situation by reviewing a number of key problem areas: housing conditions and standards, housing needs, choice in housing and the land question.

Housing conditions and housing standards

On any objective criteria, housing conditions in Britain have been greatly improved in the last fifty years. Not only have nearly 13 million houses been built since 1919, but the worst excesses of overcrowding and unfit housing have now been dealt with. It is this very success in dealing with the general problem that makes the specific problems which remain all the more unacceptable. It is an unpleasant fact that despite the general improvement in standards and conditions, many thousands of households do not have the separate accommodation that they need. There are still more who, even today, live in conditions only marginally better than those regarded as intolerable at the turn of the century.

But the scale of the problem has changed. Whereas the Victorians and Edwardians were concerned with conditions that affected the majority of the population, we tend to regard these inherited problems as residual. This does not make them any less serious or intractable, particularly in the larger cities and conurbations where they are concentrated, but they have to be dealt with at the same time as new problems that have emerged in the intervening years. Housing policy today cannot be directed to the single objective of clearing or improving the remaining slums. There has to be a balance between all parts of the housing programme. Though our first concern may be with the total resources devoted to housing, our second is invariably with the way these resources are shared between often conflicting demands. Nowhere is this more clearly illustrated than in our attitude to slum clearance.

Many people would argue that the continuing existence of a slum problem in British cities is totally unacceptable. But what *is* a slum? Officially, it is a dwelling that is statutorily 'unfit for human habitation'. The present definition of unfitness has remained virtually unchanged since the 1957 Housing Act, though a small but important amendment was made in the Housing Act, 1969: "In determining . . . whether a house is unfit for human habitation, regard shall be had to its condition in respect of the following matters, that is to say −

(a) repair
(b) stability

(c) freedom from damp
(cc) internal arrangement
(d) natural lighting
(e) ventilation
(f) water supply
(g) drainage and sanitary convenience
(h) facilities for the preparation and cooking of food and for the disposal of waste water

and the house shall be deemed to be unfit for human habitation if and only if it is so far defective in one or more of the said matters that it is not reasonably suited for occupation in that condition." (3.2)

This standard is open to wide interpretation and although the Central Housing Advisory Committee sub-committee on Standard of Housing Fitness (3.3) recommended that it should be made more precise, the only one of their proposals to be adopted was that the standard should include 'internal arrangement' as one of the items to be considered in determining unfitness. The 1968 White Paper *Old Houses into New Homes* acknowledged that "an important contributing factor making for an unfit house may be that it has a very bad internal layout: for example, a w.c. opening directly from the living room or kitchen, and narrow, steep, or winding staircases" (3.4). Other recommendations, including, for example, that "to be habitable a dwelling should . . . have a suitably located and satisfactory sanitary convenience for the exclusive use of the occupants, with access under permanent cover" (3.5) were not accepted. Only in Scotland, where a similar sub-committee was appointed by the Secretary of State (3.6), was the unfitness standard substantially revised and replaced by a new 'tolerable standard' in the Housing (Scotland) Act, 1969.

Although public health inspectors may be scrupulous in their application of the unfitness standard, there can be little doubt that its interpretation changes almost imperceptibly from year to year, in response to changing attitudes about what is 'acceptable' or 'tolerable'. In some respects, this is a great strength, since flexibility in housing policy is very important. But it is now well-known that the number of unfit houses reflects only part of the problem of quality in the older housing stock. It is also known that the way in which the standard is interpreted has, at times, varied greatly in different parts of the country. From returns made by local authorities to the Ministry of Housing and Local Government in 1965, it was estimated that there might be about 771 000 unfit dwellings in England and Wales, representing 5.5 per cent of the total housing stock (3.7). In 1967, the Ministry carried out its own National House Condition Survey, which revealed that there were about 1.8 million unfit dwellings; this was 12 per cent of the total housing stock (3.8). Similar enquiries among local authorities in

Scotland gave an estimate of 99 000 unfit dwellings in 1965 (5.9 per cent of the total) (3.9). But the results of a Scottish housing survey suggested that the total might be as many as 273 000 or 16 per cent of the total housing stock (3.10). It was thought that some local authorities might, as a matter of policy, consider as 'unfit' only those dwellings which they hoped to be able to clear within a reasonably short period (3.11).

The Department of the Environment carried out a second National House Condition Survey in England and Wales in 1971. It was estimated that there were about 1.25 million unfit dwellings (7 per cent of the total housing stock) and that nearly 3 million (17 per cent of the total) lacked one or more of the basic amenities*(3.12). The latest estimate for Scotland suggests that about 190 000 dwellings or 10 per cent of the total housing stock, are below the statutory tolerable standard (3.13).

With figures like these, it is unlikely that statutory minimum standards could be raised, or made more precise, in the immediate future. For example, to regard all dwellings lacking basic amenities as statutorily 'unfit' would be politically unacceptable, even though it might be desirable for other reasons. But there is an important issue here: to what extent does the State have the right to dictate to its citizens the conditions under which it is 'fit' for them to live? The underlying purpose of statutory minimum standards has always been to safeguard public health. Whether they should be raised to meet 'social' objectives is a question that merits serious discussion, not least because of the economic costs that would be involved, both for government and individual households.

The House Condition Survey in England and Wales confirmed that the highest proportion of unfit housing was in the northern regions, where over 10 per cent of all dwellings are unfit, compared with only 4 per cent in the South-East. Eight per cent of dwellings in the English conurbations and nearly 7 per cent in other urban areas are unfit. Together, these represent 64 per cent of all unfit dwellings in England and Wales. In a recent Scottish survey, it was estimated that 9 per cent of all dwellings in the Clydeside Conurbation and 12 per cent in Glasgow were definitely below the tolerable standard. A further 21 per cent in the conurbation and 30 per cent in Glasgow were classified as likely to be below the tolerable standard. A significant proportion of the houses in this category were built between the wars (3.14). This demonstrates clearly that the slum problem is not "a nineteenth century legacy which will gradually wilt away as housing programmes move forward" (3.15). It is a continuing problem and the sooner this is realised, the better. Since at least the 1920's, politicians have been arguing that "the housing crisis would be over and done with quickly" (3.16). In 1954, Mr. Harold Macmillan said that "many local authorities should be able to solve

* The basic amenities are: w.c. inside dwelling; fixed bath in a bathroom; wash basin; sink; hot and cold water at three points.

their housing problems in five years or so . . ." (3.17), and as recently as 1972, Mr. Julian Amery, then Minister for Housing and Construction, said that he was launching a new drive on slum clearance and improvement. He expressed his conviction that if

". . .we. . . really set our hands to it we can beat the problem of slums and unsatisfactory houses within a measurable time . . . For the first time there is light at the end of the tunnel. We must strike out for it. There are times when the mere size of the problem seems so daunting that some may feel it is not in our power to solve it, at any rate in our time. Well, this is not true." (3.18)

Of course, every politician, whether local or national, would like to preside over the 'solution' of the housing problem. But the concept of solution is misleading. Even if all the houses presently regarded as unfit were cleared or improved by the 1980's, that would not be an end to the problem, because our definition (whether statutory or interpretative) of what constitutes a slum will go on changing, in response to rising standards and expectations, just as it has done ever since the nineteenth century. The need to replace or improve inadequate housing will be a continuing task and will always form a major part in any housing programme. The problems which will confront us when inter-war housing requires replacement will be even greater than those which now remain as a legacy from the 19th century.

In contrast to the rather flexible definition of unfitness, standards for new housing are much more precise. Their main purpose is to ensure that people are housed in safety and in conditions which are not a danger to health. They reflect prevailing attitudes of what is 'desirable' and also try to take account of what future expectations may be. A house is usually built to last for at least sixty years, and some attempt must be made to anticipate the standards of space and equipment that may be required in future. Even if these cannot be predicted with any accuracy, it is important that houses should be designed in ways that will enable them to be improved or adapted to meet changing requirements. This has been possible with many houses built in the past. It may be much more difficult with modern schemes, particularly those built to high densities and with a substantial proportion of multi-storey flats.

It might be asked why, when it is known that present-day standards are certain to result in the provision of housing that will be considered inadequate in future, we do not set even higher standards, to prevent these problems occurring. There are two simple answers. First, we can only guess at what will be 'acceptable' or 'desirable' in say twenty years' time. Second, we cannot afford the high costs that such a policy would require. The Tudor Walters Report in 1918 recommended standards that the committee considered would be "above the accepted, at least for the whole period of the loan with the aid of which (the houses) are to be provided, say 60 years" (3.19). Their idealism was laudable but misplaced. Although high standards were adopted by the government, the most telling comment on their long-term effectiveness is that in the first nine months of 1972 alone, nearly 104 000 improvement grants for dwellings owned by local authorities were approved in Britain (3.20). The majority will almost certainly have been used to improve houses built between the wars by the local authorities themselves. The upgrading of the existing stock to conditions approaching, if not equal to present day standards for new housing is now an established feature of the housing programme.

The Parker Morris Committee, which reported in 1961 (3.21), concluded that priority should be given to the consideration of standards of space and heating. It was recommended, for example, that a five-person house should have a minimum net floor area of 960 square feet; and that heating installations should be able to maintain living areas at 65°F (19°C) when the outside temperature is 30°F (-1°C). Like other recommendations of the Committee, there are precise standards; they were made mandatory for all houses built by local authorities from 1 January 1969, though they had already been widely adopted by that time. The Parker Morris Committee was as much concerned with the psychological well-being of families as with traditional considerations of health and safety, which are in any case safeguarded by the Building Regulations.

Parker Morris standards were recommended and adopted as *minimum* standards for local authority housing. But they have become *optimum* standards. This is not altogether surprising, as the cost of both building and renting houses continues to increase. One of the arguments about housing standards is the extent to which the present generation of occupiers should pay for space and equipment, the provision of which may be partly determined by an assessment of what future generations may expect or require. There is, thus, an uneasy compromise between building to the highest standards we can afford now, while recognising that money must be spent in future (as it is today) to maintain or improve houses to a standard acceptable to later generations. Alternative solutions, such as short-life or extendable houses, the size of which can be increased or reduced according to personal needs and preferences (3.22), have attracted interest but have been adopted only experimentally. There have sometimes been problems in securing planning permission and the role of the planning process in restricting, rather than promoting, the development of experimental schemes needs careful examination.

New housing is expensive. The government tries to control the costs by limiting the amount of money local authorities may borrow for new building purposes, in accordance with the 'housing cost yardstick'. This was introduced in 1967, following the Housing Subsidies Act of that year. The yardstick is based on Parker Morris standards and allowable costs are expressed in terms of building cost per person. They take account of a number of factors, including variations in density, sizes of dwellings and cost variations in different parts of the country. They have been widely criticised by architects and designers and there is now a serious problem because many builders cannot, or will not, tender within cost yardstick limits. It is claimed that this is seriously affecting the ability of local authorities to maintain their new building programmes. The problem of trying to improve housing standards in a period of rapid inflation is acute. The simple choice is between reducing standards or accepting higher costs. Since neither of these alternatives would be acceptable, housing policy must, once again, search for the inevitable compromise.

Parker Morris standards are not applied to the private sector though it was hoped by the Committee that they would be. It has been argued that standards based on the number of persons who would be occupying a house, while applicable to accommodation owned and managed by local authorities, could not be enforced for new owner-occupied housing. The consequence is that many of these houses are built to lower standards than those which are now mandatory for local authority housing (3.23). This is a matter of concern to many planning authorities, who endeavour to deal with this anomalous situation through their powers under the Planning Acts. The extent to which and the way in which these powers are used varies greatly in different parts of the country.

Housing needs and housing programmes

The need for new housing is partly determined by the prevailing standards against which the quality of existing housing is measured. Though in many urban areas there is still an absolute shortage of dwellings, it is made more acute by the concentration of bad housing conditions and the consequent need for replacement and improvement.

Housing need has many dimensions. It is a social concept and has been defined as "the extent to which the quality and quantity of existing accommodation falls short of that required to provide each household or person in the population, irrespective of ability to pay, or of particular personal preferences, with accommodation of a specified minimum standard and above" (3.24). Because the definition or interpretation of 'minimum standard' is constantly changing, estimates of need are constantly changing too. An increase in housing need is an inevitable consequence of population growth, whether caused by natural increase or migration. Even where the total population is relatively stable, additional needs can arise from an increase in the rate of household formation. The trend to earlier marriage, the tendency for many elderly people to continue living separately from their families, and the growing needs of many young single people for accommodation away from their parental home all have their effect on the number of separate dwellings required to house the population. For many years, the rate of household formation has exceeded the rate of population growth. In one County Borough alone, the net increase in the total housing stock between the 1966 and 1971 Census was about 5300 dwellings but the population increased by only 8700 (3.25). This was by no means untypical. Despite the widely held view that there is no longer an acute overall shortage of houses in most parts of the country, quantitative needs have not been fully met and there are still serious local shortages. Official estimates put the number of homeless families at about 20 000 but this figure merely reflects the number of places occupied in hostels for those registered as homeless (3.26, 3.27). It is not a measure of the needs of households in shared dwellings, nor of those young couples who are forced to begin their married life living in the home of their parents or in-laws. Still less is it a measure of the number of households in overcrowded or unfit dwellings, which organisations such as Shelter have claimed should be regarded as homeless, because they lack adequate accommodation (3.28).

There have been various estimates of total housing needs. In 1913, the shortage of houses was officially estimated at between 100 000 and 120 000 (3.29). By present day standards, this target was exceptionally modest. Even at today's relatively depressed rate of new building, it represents less than six months' output. In fact, over 4 million houses were built between the wars, and the net increase in the housing stock was probably about 3.7 million. It was not enough. At the end of the war, estimates of need ranged from 750 000 to over 6 million (3.30). Since 1945, nearly 8 million dwellings have been completed and about 1½ million demolished – a net increase of about 6½ million. And there is still a housing shortage.

In 1965, the government announced that its first objective was to reach half a million houses a year by 1970 (3.31). This target was never achieved, though there was a record 414 000 completions in 1968. The reasons for the failure of the programme will probably never be fully understood. It may have been too ambitious, and perhaps beyond the capacity of the building industry. It was certainly affected by economic difficulties which caused relatively rapid increases in the cost of materials and labour. The greater use of industrialised building techniques proved less economic than had been hoped and there was widespread concern about the wisdom of building at high densities. There was a reappraisal of many local housing programmes in areas where political control changed in 1967 and 1968. New estimates of housing needs were prepared; these suggested that far from a housing shortage, there might instead by an overall surplus of housing within the next few years. In 1969, Mr. Kenneth Robinson, then Minister of Planning and Land, announced that by 1973, there would be a margin of about one million more houses than households in the country as a whole. His statement went on to infer that this surplus would have beneficial effects on the housing market, for having achieved this margin, there would be an end to the national housing shortage "and with it an end to spiralling house prices in both new and second hand markets. Supply will at least balance demand and what the market will bear will no longer be inflated by scarcity" (3.32).

Unfortunately, this forecast was wrong, as so many previous forecasts have been. It is yet another example of the hope that 'solution' is just around the corner. It is significant that there is now *no* official estimate of quantitative housing needs (though they can be calculated from figures in government publications) (3.33, 3.34) and no target for the new building programme. Present day housing objectives are couched in much more cautious terms, such as "a decent home for every family at a price within their means" (3.35).

Although at the time of writing the full results of the 1971 Census were not available, it is likely that they *will* show a crude numerical surplus of housing in Britain as a whole. In itself, this is a remarkable achievement but it does not mark the end of the housing problem. Many houses are substandard and many are in the wrong places. A vacant house in Liverpool or Dundee is of no use to a family seeking accommodation in London or Glasgow. Cheap houses in North-East Lancashire cannot be bought by people who need to live and work in Birmingham. The geographical distribution of housing is an important factor affecting the level of housing need.

This is one of the reasons why it is becoming less and less meaningful to talk about housing needs and problems in national terms. The Central Housing Advisory Committee report on Council Housing said, in 1969, that "we no longer have a single 'national' housing problem: we have a large number of local problems of great variety. It is, therefore, essential that local policies be based on a well-informed understanding of the problems of individual areas and the context in which they arise . . . local authorities should take steps to ensure that they are better informed of the housing situation in their areas" (3.36). A Working Party of the Scottish Housing Advisory Committee concluded that "the responsibility of local authorities should extend far beyond providing for the needs of those who are actually to be housed by them: they should be looking at the totality of needs — hidden needs, needs which are not being met, and needs which may arise in the future. This includes the needs of those who do not wish to or cannot be housed in the public sector" (3.37).

The Working Party also emphasised the importance of a comprehensive approach to the housing programme. New building, slum clearance and improvement are complementary activities. Too often they have been carried out in isolation from each other and have not been planned as part of a coordinated strategy for housing, either locally or nationally. For many years, the housing programme has been dominated by a concern to provide the maximum number of dwellings in the shortest possible time. This was particularly true in the years immediately following the war, when the accumulated shortages caused by population increase, war damage and a housing programme of insignificant proportions produced a huge backlog of acute needs. Slum clearance was not resumed in any organised way until 1955 and the introduction of improvement grants in 1949 had little general impact. Inevitably the solution of the housing problem was seen mainly in terms of reaching and sustaining a large programme of new building.

The speed with which some developments were planned and built in the late 1940's and 1950's created problems of housing and environmental quality, and a lack of provision for social needs that it is easy to criticise today. As slum clearance got under way again in the late 1950's, many more large estates were being built on the outskirts of towns and cities. People were moved from areas in which many of them had spent their lives; they had to face problems of living in new and unfamiliar surroundings, often far from their work. Moving could be expensive too: not only were rents higher in the new houses but the costs of travelling to work, or to see relatives and friends left behind, were considerable. There were many adjustments to be made in life-style and standard of living. Though it is easy to risk overdramatising these human problems, they confronted hundreds of thousands of 'slum clearance' families and others (3.38, 3.39) moving to what were euphemistically described as 'new communities'. What is surprising is that so many of the people affected by these rapid social and physical changes accepted them with relative equanimity and even grew to like their new areas as much as they had always appreciated their new homes (3.40, 3.41). It is remarkable that people's capacity for resourceful readjustment was not more explicitly and frequently acknowledged as essential to the grand designs of government and local authorities. All too often, it was simply taken for granted.

In recent years, the doctrine of 'clear and replace' (which has its origins firmly in the 19th century) began to lose favour. Doubts were expressed about both the massive rehousing role adopted by many local authorities and the whole philosophy of regarding every 19th century house as a target for the ball-and-chain and bulldozer. It was argued that instead of trying to create new communities there might be advantages in attempting to revitalise old ones. The benefits of retaining population close to the centre of towns and cities were emphasised and it was thought that some areas of older housing could be improved, at a relatively modest cost, to provide a pleasant environment on a more human scale than that in many of the new peripheral estates. It was even suggested that it might be more 'economic' (at least in the short-term) to devote substantial resources to housing and environmental improvement, rather than to attempt to solve the housing problem by slum clearance and new building alone.

Until the 1969 Housing Act, the improvement of older houses had been left to individual initiative and was not coordinated in any organised way, except in Leeds, where ingenious use of 1957 Act powers had enabled the Corporation to embark on a policy of securing the comprehensive improvement of areas of older housing (3.42). The 1969 Act introduced the concept of General Improvement Areas, in which owners were to be persuaded and helped by local authorities to improve their houses by the availability of much more generous grants. A new grant was introduced to contribute to the cost of environmental improvement in General Improvement Areas. By the end of 1972, 296 local authorities in England and Wales had declared 546 G.I.A.'s, containing over 170 000 dwellings; grants had been approved for the improvement of 26 000 dwellings within these areas (3.43).

A different policy was adopted in Scotland, where local authorities were given powers to declare Housing Treatment Areas. Under the Housing (Scotland) Act, 1969, these areas (in which at least 50 per cent of the dwellings must be below the tolerable standard) could be for demolition, for improvement or a combination of both.

In 1969, 124 000 improvement grants were approved in Britain as a whole. The number rose to 232 000 in 1971 and to nearly 370 000 in 1972. In numerical terms the improvement policy has been a resounding success. It was undoubtedly helped by the introduction in 1971 of a 75 per cent Exchequer contribution for improvements carried out in Development and Intermediate Areas; in the rest of the country (the Midlands and South of England), where the need for improvement seemed to be less and the personal resources that could be devoted to it were thought to be greater, the Exchequer contribution remained at the original 50 per cent. The higher grant contributions were made available only until June 1974.

From 1969 to 1972, over 122 000 improvement grants were approved in Scotland and over 782 000 in England and Wales. The contrast between these figures and the modest 26 000 grants approved for work in G.I.A.'s in England and Wales is striking. "Up to the third quarter of 1972, about 12 per cent of dwellings in G.I.A.'s had had grants approved and about 5 per cent had had works completed. The Association of Municipal Corporations believed that the G.I.A. concept was not being realised and the Minister was equally disappointed by the results so far." (3.44).

The 1969 Housing Acts have been used to try to do three things: first, to encourage a unified approach to the treatment of *areas* of older housing; second, to encourage a general improvement in the quality of all but the most recent houses; and, third, to encourage, where possible, the improvement of houses below statutory minimum standards. To some extent, therefore, improvement has been seen as an alternative to demolition and replacement. Furthermore, "in retrospect, it is clear that objectives other than purely housing ones have subsequently been attributed to the 1969 Acts. It has come to be realised by local communities, and now by planners, that improvement is a housing technique which attempts to meet the needs of existing residents of an area, and prevents the blight of a neighbourhood while a redevelopment is being planned, as well as the social disruption of communities caused by the eventual clearance. Social objectives were not made clear during the passing of the Acts, but they have figured prominently in discussion of the effects of the legislation"(3.45). A report on the improvement potential of towns in North-East Lancashire went so far as to claim that "improvement is not only a physical process: an area improvement is a physical means of achieving social ends" (3.46). But these social benefits have yet to be demonstrated convincingly. There is no evidence that physical improvement *in itself* offers a solution to social problems. It has often been carried out as a substitute for comprehensive social policies, with the result that existing residents have been displaced in the process of 'gentrification'. This may not be a problem in North-East Lancashire, but has certainly been one in areas of high demand for housing, particularly the inner London boroughs. The numerical success of improvement policy since 1969 and its emergence as a new and important element in housing programmes has to be set against its relative failure to secure socially acceptable area improvement, and to improve large numbers of houses below statutory standards.

These problems are widely recognised and the White Papers published in June 1973 (3.47) proposed new improvement grant legislation and introduced the concept of Housing Action Areas, designed to deal comprehensively with areas of housing stress. New powers were promised to help local authorities carry through comprehensive action programmes; extra assistance was to be given towards house improvements "in ways which will protect and help existing residents"; and an important role was seen for housing associations, which it was hoped would help with "both housing and social problems by acquiring existing rented dwellings, providing new rented accommodation and undertaking major programmes of rehabilitation" (3.48).

Choice in housing

This emphasis on the role that might be played by housing associations highlights the polarisation that has occurred between the tenure sectors in Britain, particularly in urban areas. Before the First World War, most households were tenants of private landlords or companies; by 1947, the proportion had fallen to about 60 per cent. Today it is only 14 per cent. The place of the private landlord has gradually been taken by the local authorities and by the growth in owner-occupation. Over 49 per cent of the British housing stock is owner-occupied, and 31 per cent rented from local authorities and New Town Corporations. Five per cent of dwellings are rented with a job or business (e.g. 'tied' houses); less than 1 per cent are owned and let by voluntary housing associations (3.49).

These average figures conceal local and regional variations. In some of the larger English cities, the proportion of local authority housing is as high as 40 per cent; in Scotland, it is 52 per cent and in Glasgow nearly 60 per cent. The main supply of privately rented housing is also in the cities and conurbations and it is in this tenure sector that the worst housing problems are concentrated.

Successive attempts to decontrol rents in the private sector and the availability of more generous improvement grants since 1969 have been singularly unsuccessful in making private landlordism attractive and the continued decline of the privately rented sector is now regarded as inevitable. Many privately rented houses have been sold into owner-occupation; others are scheduled for clearance or closure. In some quarters, the disappearance of the private landlord is eagerly anticipated and it has been suggested that the process should be hastened by the 'municipalisation' of remaining private tenancies (3.50, 3.51). Others view the decline with concern and argue that the privately rented sector plays an important part in the housing market. The existence of privately rented houses of adequate standard reduces the need for housing in other sectors and can provide a 'stepping stone' to owner-occupation or a local authority tenancy. The privately rented sector is accessible to many people who cannot afford to buy a house, to others who may prefer to rent privately rather than from a local authority, and to those who may not have the necessary qualifications for admission to a local authority waiting list, or for the allocation of a council house. For every supporter of municipalisation who points to the evils of property speculation, harrassment, illegal eviction and extortionate rents, there are others who claim that such a policy would not allow a reasonable choice of tenure in the rented sector. To them, municipalisation simply means more bureaucracy, and the exchange of one set of access criteria for the more formal rules and regulations governing council house allocations. Is there (can there be) any guarantee that exclusive public sector ownership of rented accommodation would be any more successful in meeting needs in areas of housing stress than are the present procedures adopted by many local authorities when allocating the houses they already own? It is widely recognised that housing authorities have often failed to provide for many households who need their help (3.52). There is a continuing debate about this issue but government policy implies a hope that housing associations will eventually replace the private landlord and provide the alternative supply of rented accommodation that is considered desirable. The political philosophy behind this is the belief that there must be more 'choice' in housing.

At first, the objective was simply "a fairer choice between owning a house and renting one" (3.53). Now, however, it is proposed "to widen the range and choice of rented accommodation by the expansion of the voluntary housing movement" (3.54). Housing policy can never satisfy everyone and while many housing associations are delighted by the promised expansion, their ability to operate effectively has been doubted, particularly in some areas of local government. A recent NALGO Working Party report says,
"It should not be thought by the government that housing associations can possibly provide action on the scale required. In many cases, smaller voluntary groups, especially housing societies, compete unnecessarily with local authorities

and bid up the price of houses . . . It must be clearly acknowledged that housing associations do not have nor could they acquire from local authorities the necessary powers of compulsory purchase or the planning powers to designate improvement areas, and can, therefore, only play a supplementary and subordinate role to local authorities. Equally important is the fact that housing management skills are in short supply and local authorities are best equipped to provide them by expanding their existing services and training arrangements." (3.59)

The White Paper *Widening the Choice* extols the virtues of housing associations in a way that is bound to arouse antagonism from their critics.

"Housing associations already do valuable work, particularly in areas of housing stress. Because they do not operate for profit, they manage their properties in the interest of present and future tenants. Housing associations provide an opportunity for people – not least those with special housing needs – who have failed to find accommodation elsewhere. Housing associations can contribute to the mobility of labour because they are better placed than local authorities to offer accommodation to people who have recently moved into the area" (3.56).

All these points are, or *should* be, equally true of local authorities. The only exception might be on the encouragement of mobility, where many authorities are at a disadvantage because they impose residential qualifications on waiting list applicants. However, most have arrangements to house 'key workers' and the creation of new and expanded towns is a specific policy designed to promote mobility and relieve pressure in congested urban areas. Not surprisingly, the NALGO Working Party report emphasises, at some length, the housing achievements of the public sector " . . . the public sector has tended to cater for those on low and average incomes . . . many local authorities have, in practice, tended to treat housing as a social service. To some extent this may account for the apparent stigma of living in council housing, but it should be clearly stated that for over 50 years local authorities have met housing needs for which other sectors could not or would not cater, and their achievements ought to be recognised and applauded, not denigrated" (3.57).

The emphasis in present policy on the role of the private sector is seen most clearly in the attempts to encourage owner-occupation, "the most rewarding form of house tenure" (3.58). Half the households in Britain are owner-occupiers, about 55 per cent of whom are buying their houses with a mortgage or loan; for most people this is the conventional path to home ownership. That owner-occupation is 'rewarding' cannot be disputed. As Cullingworth has observed, "house purchasers buy at current market prices: with inflation, values increase while repayments remain at an 'historical' level. Indeed, continued inflation has greatly facilitated the 'filtering-up' process: house owners have been able to sell their existing houses at the inflated price level and purchase better houses by using the monetary 'profit' to provide the required deposit" (3.59).

While this is a recognised feature of the housing situation, many owner-occupiers would argue that they will never benefit financially from the continuing increase in the value of their houses, since, if they sell, their 'profit' must invariably be used to buy another house elsewhere. Nevertheless, the accumulated wealth (whether realisable or not) benefits only those who are, or can become owner-occupiers. One has only to look at the increasing assets of Building Societies to realise the extent to which this happening. House prices have risen dramatically in recent years. In 1968, the average purchase price of dwellings mortgaged by private owners in the United Kingdom was £4344, compared with £7374 in 1972, an increase of 70 per cent. During the same period, the average recorded income of borrowers increased by 53 per cent (3.60). The rise in land prices has been equally striking; the price per plot for private sector housing land in England and Wales rose by 85 per cent from 1966 to 1971 (3.61) and was reflected in the much higher prices of houses recorded in 1972 and 1973. The recent 'rationing' of mortgages by Building Societies and the increase in the mortgage interest rate to a record 11 per cent, have played a part in slowing down the rate of increase in house prices but the market has been depressed and the number of new houses for owner-occupation started, in England and Wales, in the second quarter of 1973 was down 14 per cent on the first quarter of 1973 (3.62). If this decline continues, and if the costs of land, labour and materials continue to rise, they are bound to be reflected in a further inflation of house prices, when mortgages again become more freely available. The proportion of people who can afford to become owner-occupiers may then be further reduced.

There is now the paradoxical situation that the government has tried, by both exhortation and legislation (in particular through the Housing Finance Act, 1972), to encourage more people to become owner-occupiers, yet some local authorities report an increasing demand for council housing, and lengthening waiting lists. This must, to some extent, be because many households feel they do not have an effective choice between renting and buying; but it also reflects the relatively poor house building performance of many local authorities in the last few years. In 1972, less than 123 000 public sector dwellings were completed in Great Britain, compared with 159 000 in 1971 and a record of nearly 204 000 in 1967. Some of the reasons for this decline have been suggested earlier in this chapter, but rising costs and land shortages affect the public and the private sectors alike. What cannot be determined is the extent to which the Housing Finance Act (promised in 1970 and brought into force in 1972) contributed to uncertainty about the prospects for new building by local authorities, thereby reducing the number of houses actually built.

The Housing Finance Act* brought about a major change in British housing policy. By extending the principle of 'fair rents' (introduced in the Rent Act,

---

* Since this chapter was written, the government has introduced a 'rent freeze' and has promised to repeal the 1972 Acts.

1965) from the private to the publicly rented sector, the traditional relationship was broken between the historic cost of providing council housing and the rents charged by local authorities. For the first time, the rent that is paid by council tenants is related not to the cost of building, managing and maintaining council houses, but to the open market, assuming a situation of no housing shortage. A national rent rebate scheme has been introduced for public sector tenants and rent allowances are available to tenants in the privately rented sector. The intention of the Act is to direct help to the tenants and the areas which need it most, and new subsidies have been introduced for this purpose. The Act has aroused a great deal of controversy (3.63) and is expected to have significant social and economic consequences, which must be carefully monitored. Except in Scotland, where the principle does not at present apply (under the Housing (Financial Provisions) (Scotland) Act, 1972), the progression to 'fair rents' is to be completed by 1975/6. What this will mean for the future of public housing is uncertain.

Although the 1972 legislation has been widely criticised, it has the great merit of attempting to treat the public and privately rented sectors on an equal footing. But it deals with only half the problem of housing finance, since the financing of owner-occupation was completely excluded from consideration. Many people think that a great opportunity was lost to tackle the inequality between the relatively favourable treatment of owner-occupiers (who, because of tax relief on mortgage interest repayments, receive indirect assistance with house purchase in inverse proportion to their needs) and the means-related benefits which are now available to tenants. The notions of 'fairness' and 'choice' are hard to square with this obvious anomaly.

Land for housing

The supply of land for housing is a perennial problem. There never seems to be enough, yet concern is frequently voiced at what appears to be the relentless spread of urban development. In 1900, less than 4 per cent of the total land area of Britain was in urban use; by 1950, the proportion had risen to 7.2 per cent (3.64). Today it may be as high as 8 per cent in Britain as a whole and 12 per cent in England and Wales (3.65). Thirty per cent of the population of England and Wales live in conurbations, which occupy no more than 3 per cent of the total land area (3.66). What is surprising is that the growth in urban land use has been so small, when compared with a population increase of over 45 per cent since the 1901 Census. The rate of loss of agricultural land to urban development in England and Wales increased markedly in the 1920's and reached its greatest proportions in the 1930's, when the net loss was over 60 000 acres a year. In the 1950's, the net loss was reduced to about 37 000 acres a year (3.67). These figures must be interpreted with caution but the decline may be partly accounted for by the introduction of relatively strict development controls in the 1947 Town and Country Planning Act, which marked an end to the unlimited spread of low density suburban development characteristic of the 1930's. These statutory controls were clearly necessary but they produced a conflict between the wider aims of planning policy and the then more limited aim of housing policy − which was to build as many houses as quickly as possible. This conflict has not been resolved, as Cullingworth has well illustrated: "Since urban growth is a matter for restraint, the pressure of demand (for housing) builds up inside the urban areas. Both political necessity and high land prices (one of the real costs of the restraint policy) force up densities. In the private sector this is limited by the willingness of people to accept high prices and high densities (and by the alternative which is open to the private sector of lower prices and lower densities beyond the green belts). In the public sector, shielded by overt and hidden subsidies, and catering for 'applicants' who have few alternatives, there has been little limit to the densities which can be achieved. As a result 'planned' environments have been created which, though far more sanitary, are in other respects reproducing the very congestion and inadequacies which it was their objective to abolish" (3.68).

As the 'urban' use of land within the administrative boundaries of urban areas increases, it is no wonder that the price of land (whether zoned for housing, or other purposes) has risen so much in recent years. This has had a marked influence on residential densities, particularly in local authority housing, where the building of high-rise flats increased significantly in the 1960's, both in inner city and peripheral developments. Although the number of flats built has decreased substantially in recent years, the continuing pressure for high density is reflected in the growing number of schemes which attempt, often successfully (3.69), to combine 'low rise/high density' solutions. The increasing cost of land is also reflected in higher densities for owner-occupied housing; in particular, new housing built for the 'lower' end of the private market now tends to be smaller and to provide the minimum size of garden permitted by local planning regulations. Almost any comparison of owner-occupied housing built in the 1950's and 1970's will illustrate this trend.

A factor contributing to the problem of land values is the restriction placed on urban growth, particularly by Green Belts. The policy of limiting such encroachment has had the inevitable consequence of maintaining, if not increasing, residential densities in urban areas. It has often seemed easier (and has at times been the explicit intention of national policy) to develop at higher densities within existing boundaries, than to attempt to 'breach' the Green Belt. Although successful in many respects, the growth of new and expanded towns has not solved the problem of pressure for land, particularly for housing, in areas immediately adjacent to our larger towns and cities. The unpopularity of local authority overspill schemes among 'receiving' authorities underlines this point.

But overspill in all its forms, and including the drift of owner-occupiers to commuter suburbs, is often unpopular with 'exporting' authorities, too. Many urban authorities have an understandable desire to retain population within their existing boundaries; this is essential if rateable values, rates income and the government's rate support grant (which is calculated with reference to population) are to be maintained or increased in real value. A city with a declining population and a possible loss of employment opportunities is in danger of losing income from these sources and having to charge its ratepayers more and more each year, to maintain essential services.

The land problem highlights a number of conflicts both within planning policy and between housing and planning policy. On the one hand, planning endeavours to achieve a reduction in residential densities; this is an inheritance from the 19th century concern for the 'health of towns'. At the same time, it is constrained by other policies designed to contain urban growth and to preserve Green Belts for agricultural, and (increasingly) recreational purposes. The conflict has not been, and shows no signs of being resolved. And apart from Scotland (where regional authorities are being created in 1975), the continued separation of conurbation areas from their rural hinterland in local government reorganisation is likely to strengthen the urban-rural conflict that has developed over more than fifty years.

It is ironic that within two years of abolishing the Land Commission, and in the face of a massive inflation in land prices, the government asked local authorities to give more planning permissions for housing and allowed authorities 'in the main pressure areas' additional borrowing facilities in order to assemble and service land for development by private housebuilders. In 1973, the government expressed its belief "that the release of land for housing needs to be further accelerated" (3.70). New planning guidelines were promised and later issued by the Department of the Environment in Circular 122/73. It was hoped that these measures would increase both the supply and use of land for housing purposes. Emphasis was placed on the need to restrict the bulk of future development "by rebuilding within existing towns and by expanding the towns within the limits of employment or local community capacity, e.g. infrastructure and social facilities". It was recognised that "problems may arise when development is proposed where the necessary infrastructure is not available and pending its availability the consequences of development would be unacceptable. The lack may be in the provision of physical infrastructure, such as roads, or in the social infrastructure, such as schools, welfare services amenities and recreational facilities. The issue on this type of problem is normally one of degree, related in part to the scale of possible harm and in part to its likely duration" (3.71).

There seems a danger that this advice may succeed only in repeating the mistakes of earlier years, when the provision of social infrastructure lagged so far behind the provision of housing – if it was ever provided at all. How long will it take to learn the lessons spelt out in *The Needs of New Communities* (3.72) and the even more devastating indictment contained in the Scottish report, *Council House Communities* (3.73)? The shortage of land for housing is not a new problem but the present proposals to deal with it carry great dangers, not least for the philosophy underlying the new Structure Planning process.

Underlying all these difficulties about the supply of land is the vexed question of land values. The evolution of planning this century has been closely concerned with this issue. Before the Second World War a continual complaint about the ineffectiveness of planning schemes was the impossible position local authorities were placed in respect of compensation and betterment. Legislation had not got to the nub of the problem: local authorities could not face the risk of paying large sums of compensation when planning permission for development was refused. Thus we had a situation featured by weak public control over use of land, residential use allocations in town planning schemes out of all proportion to actual requirements, and a reliance on voluntary agreements to reserve land from development in favour of recreation and amenity purposes.

The political climate concerning compensation and betterment changed rapidly during the early forties. The extent of war damage and the need for redevelopment by public authorities made a solution to the problem imperative. The Uthwatt Reports (Interim and Final in 1941 and 1942: Cmd 6291 and Cmd 6386) made radical recommendations, some of which were quickly acted upon. The Town and Country Planning Act, 1947, in its financial provisions completed the attack on the problem; the essential factor was that the development value in land was vested in the State. But this nationalisation of development rights proved unpopular, and the development charge was abolished in 1953.

The next attempt to tackle the land question was rather different: this time it was by way of a capital gains tax introduced by the Finance Act, 1967, and a betterment levy introduced by the Land Commission Act of the same year. But the new system worked far less than the previous one, for in 1971 the Land Commission was abolished. The problem however is even more acute than in the past and there is considerable public disquiet at the present situation of escalating land values. The Labour Party favours a solution which incorporates the idea of a land bank, and the Liberal Party supports the idea of site value rating. Either way, or indeed given the uncontrolled operation of the land market, there are very great implications for planning and housing.

Conclusions

This chapter has tried to show that there are very real conflicts both within housing policy and between housing, planning and other social and economic policies. There are no easy solutions to the housing problem; indeed, it is difficult to define what 'the problem' is. The preceding account has attempted to highlight some major long-term issues and to comment on a number of policies of topical interest. It does not pretend to be comprehensive; such treatment would require a book in itself.

The housing situation and the nature of housing policy in Britain today reflect the long-standing concern of central and local government with the collective and individual needs of households. Of all the 'services' provided or encouraged, housing is the most personal. But it is only one of a wide range of issues that confronts the policy-maker. Resources are scarce and must be shared according to some definition of 'need' − not just for housing but for industry, employment, social services, health, education, land, transport . . . the list is endless. The housing debate is essentially about the distribution of resources, for which there are many conflicting claims. And what applies to government and local authorities applies equally to individuals. How much can people pay for housing? How much should we be expected to pay? What priority does each of us attach to housing costs, tenure, dwelling type and size, location and so on? These are personal questions, the answers to which, though difficult to determine, are of central concern to policy-makers. It is one of the most important functions of housing research to try to provide the necessary information on these and other issues.

Central government has assumed increasing responsibility for housing in the last fifty years, but it does not have, nor does it seek, absolute control of the housing system. Through legislation, it can provide the powers, and often the financial means that are necessary if objectives are to be achieved. However, it is not government but local authorities, builders, building societies, landlords, housing associations and all the other agencies active in the housing field, which have the major responsibility for putting policy into practice. It is true that central government exercises control on local authority spending and it is probably for this reason that many authorities believe they do not have the freedom to determine their own local policies. This often leads to conflict, since there may be (and frequently are) disputes between central and local government about the objectives of housing policy and the way they can best be achieved. The introduction of a two-tier system of local government is likely to increase that conflict, at least in the fields of housing and planning.

It must not be forgotten, however, that local authorities often have wide discretion in many areas of housing policy, for example in housing management, the allocation of council houses, their sale to sitting tenants, the giving of discretionary improvement grants, the supply of local authority mortgage finance and the release of land for building purposes. There are different types of discretionary powers. Some give freedom on *how* a policy should be operated; others give freedom to decide *whether* and to what extent it should be operated. Council house allocations and eligibility rules are an example of the former;

council house sales an example of the latter. In both, a great deal is left to the judgement of individual local authorities. This can lead to wide variation in the way housing policy is implemented in different parts of the country. To the extent that this reflects the need for local solutions to local problems, it is more than welcome. Though there is always the danger that discretion can mean discretion to do nothing, it can be argued that these powers provide a means by which local and regional policies can be pursued within the framework of statutory obligations imposed through national legislation.

Great emphasis is now placed on the need to develop a comprehensive approach to housing problems (3.74, 3.75). This is seen as a particular responsibility for the new local authorities, and management structures have been suggested (3.76, 3.77) that may make this approach easier to achieve than under the traditional departmental system. These new developments may, however, be frustrated unless similar progress can also be made by central government. The tragedy of the last fifty years is that so many of our policies have been introduced in response to particular, and often unforeseen, crises. Sectors of the housing system have been treated separately, as if they were unrelated to each other. Legislation has been hurriedly introduced and frequently based on inadequate information about what is required and what is possible.

Though much has been achieved, it has not been enough. There must be a continuing search for ways in which housing policy can be made more responsive to needs and more effective in meeting them.

References

3.1   See Gordon E. Cherry, *The Evolution of British Town Planning*, Leonard Hill, 1974.

3.2   Housing Act, 1957, Section 4, as amended by Section 71 of the Housing Act, 1969.

3.3   *Our Older Homes: a call for action*, Report of the Central Housing Advisory Committee sub-committee on standards of housing fitness, HMSO, 1966.

3.4   *Old Houses into New Homes*, Cmnd. 3602, HMSO, 1968, para. 42.

3.5   *Our Older Homes, op.cit.*, para. 50.

3.6   *Scotland's Older Houses*, Report of the Scottish Housing Advisory Committee sub-committee on Unfit Housing, HMSO, 1967.

3.7   *Our Older Homes, op.cit.*, Table 1, p.56.

3.8   'House Condition Survey, England and Wales' in *Economic Trends*, No. 175, HMSO, 1968.

3.9   *Scotland's Older Houses, op.cit.*, Appendix II.

3.10   J.B. Cullingworth, *'Scottish Housing in 1965'*, Scottish Development Department, 1967, quoted in *Scotland's Older Houses, op.cit.*, para. 57.

3.11   *Scotland's Older Houses, op.cit.*, paras. 74-76.

3.12   *House Condition Survey, 1971, England and Wales*, Housing Survey Reports, No. 9, Department of the Environment, 1973.

3.13   *Towards Better Homes: proposals for dealing with Scotland's older housing*, Cmnd. 5338, HMSO, 1973, para. 6.

3.14   J.B. Cullingworth and C.J. Watson, *Housing in Clydeside, 1970*, HMSO, 1971.

3.15   *Scotland's Older Houses, op.cit.*, para. 80.

3.16   Marian Bowley, *Housing and the State, 1919-1944*, Allen & Unwin, 1945, p.37.

3.17   Quoted in Ralph Samuel, James Kincaid, Elizabeth Slater, 'But Nothing Happens', *New Left Review*, Nos.13-14, January-April 1962.

3.18   *Slums and Older Housing: An Overall Strategy*, Department of the Environment, Circular 50/72, 25 May 1972, Annex B.

3.19   Quoted in J.B. Cullingworth, *Housing and Local Government*, Allen & Unwin, 1966, p.137.

3.20   *Housing and Construction Statistics*, No.4, HMSO, 1973, Table 30.

3.21   *Homes for Today and Tomorrow*, HMSO, 1961.

3.22   For a useful review see, Andrew Rabeneck, David Sheppard and Peter Town, 'Flexible (?) Housing' in *Architectural Design*, XLIII, 11/1973, pp. 698-711.

3.23   Valerie A. Karn, *Housing Standards and Costs; a comparison of British Standards and Costs with those in the U.S.A., Canada and Europe*,

Occasional Paper No. 25, Centre for Urban and Regional Studies, University of Birmingham, 1973.

3.24   L. Needleman, *The Economics of Housing*, Staples, 1965, p.18.

3.25   C.J. Watson, Pat Niner and Gillian R. Vale, with Barbara M.D. Smith, *Estimating Local Housing Needs: a case study and discussion of Methods*, Occasional Paper No. 24, Centre for Urban and Regional Studies, University of Birmingham, 1973, para. 2.16.

3.26   J. Greve, D. Page and S. Greve, *Homelessness in London*, Scottish Academic Press, 1971.

3.27   B. Glastonbury, *Homeless Near a Thousand Homes: A Study of Homeless Families in South Wales and the West of England*, Allen & Unwin, 1971.

3.28   *Face the Facts*, Shelter, 1969.

3.29   G.E. Cherry, *Urban Change and Planning*, Foulis, 1972, p.112.

3.30   J.B. Cullingworth, *Housing and Local Government, op.cit.*, p.26 and p. 29.

3.31   *The Housing Programme 1965 to 1970*, Cmnd. 2838, HMSO, 1965, para.1.

3.32   Quoted in Gillian R. Vale, *Is the Housing Problem Solved? A Review of Recent Estimates*, Housing Centre Trust, 1971.

3.33   *Statistics for Town and Country Planning Series III Population and Households: No. 1, Projecting Growth Patterns in Regions*, Ministry of Housing and Local Government, 1970.

3.34   *Projections of Households for the Regions and Sub-Regions of Scotland*, Scottish Development Department, HMSO, 1972.

3.35   *Fair Deal for Housing*, Cmnd. 4728, HMSO, 1971, para.5.

3.36   *Council Housing Purposes, Procedures and Priorities*, Ninth Report of the Housing Management Sub-Committee of the Central Housing Advisory Committee, HMSO, 1969, para.448.

3.37   *Planning for Housing Needs: pointers towards a comprehensive approach*, Report by a Working Party of the Scottish Housing Advisory Committee, HMSO, 1972, paras. 22-23.

3.38   *The Needs of New Communities. A Report on Social Provision in New and Expanding Communities*, Report by a Sub-Committee of the Central Housing Advisory Committee, HMSO, 1967.

3.39   Barbara Weinberger, *Liverpool Estates Survey*, Research Memorandum No. 25, Centre for Urban and Regional Studies, University of Birmingham, 1973.

3.40   Pearl Jephcott, *Homes in High Flats*, Oliver and Boyd, 1971.

3.41   *Moving Out of a Slum*, Ministry of Housing and Local Government, Design Bulletin 20, HMSO, 1970.

3.42   *Our Older Homes, op.cit.*, Appendix 4.

3.43   *Housing and Construction Statistics,* No. 4, HMSO, 1973, Table 31.

3.44   *House Improvement Grants,* Tenth Report from the Expenditure Committee (Environment and Home Office Sub-Committee), HMSO, 1973, Vol. 1: Report, para. 59.

3.45   *Ibid,* para. 14.

3.46   *New Life in Old Towns,* Report by Robert Matthew, Johnson-Marshall and Partners on two pilot studies on urban renewal in Nelson and Rawtenstall Municipal Boroughs, HMSO, 1971, p.4

3.47   *Better Homes: The Next Priorities,* Cmnd. 5339, HMSO, 1973, and *Towards Better Homes: Proposals for Dealing with Scotland's Older Housing,* Cmnd. 5338, HMSO, 1973.

3.48   *Better Homes: The Next Priorities, op.cit.,* para.19.

3.49   *General Household Survey: Introductory Report,* HMSO, 1973, Table 5.14.

3.50   Malcolm Wicks, *Rented Housing and Social Ownership,* Fabian Tract 421, Fabian Society, 1973.

3.51   *The End of the Private Landlord,* a study paper prepared by the housing group of the Society of Labour Lawyers under the Chairmanship of Bruce Douglas-Mann, Fabian Research Series 312, Fabian Society, 1973.

3.52   *Council Housing: Purposes, Procedures and Priorities, op.cit.*

3.53   *Fair Deal for Housing, op.cit.,* para. 5.

3.54   *Widening the Choice: The Next Steps in Housing,* Cmnd. 5280, HMSO, 1973, para. 37.

3.55   *Housing: The Way Ahead,* Report of the NALGO Housing Working Party, National and Local Government Officers Association, 1973, Section III, paragraph 17.

3.56   *Widening the Choice, op.cit.,* para. 38.

3.57   *Housing: The Way Ahead, op.cit.,* Section VII, para. 4.

3.58   *Fair Deal for Housing, op.cit.,* para. 14.

3.59   J.B. Cullingworth, *Problems of an Urban Society,* Allen & Unwin, 1973, Vol. 2, The Social Content of Planning, p.56.

3.60   *Housing and Construction Statistics,* No. 4, *op.cit.,* Table 38.

3.61   *Housing and Construction Statistics* No. 2, HMSO, 1972, Supplementary Table 1.

3.62   Department of the Environment Press Notice, 30 July 1973.

3.63   For a useful review see, 'A guide to the Housing Act, 1972' in *New Society,* 28 December, 1972.

3.64   Robin H. Best and J.T. Coppock, *The Changing Use of Land in Britain,* Faber, 1962, p.229.

3.65   J.B. Cullingworth, *Problems of an Urban Society,* Allen & Unwin, Vol. 1, The Social Framework of Planning, p.87

3.66   *Ibid,* p. 86.

3.67   Robin H. Best, *The Major Land Uses of Great Britain,* Department of Agricultural Economics, Wye College, 1959, Chapter 7.

3.68   J.B. Cullingworth, *Problems of an Urban Society*, Vol. 1, *op.cit.*, p.79.

3.69   For example, articles in *Official Architecture and Planning* 34,4, April, 1971 (Theme feature: High Density Low Rise Housing).

3.70   *Widening the Choice, op.cit.*, paras. 11-12.

3.71   *Land Availability for Housing,* Department of the Environment, Circular 112/73, 1 October, 1973.

3.72   *The Needs of New Communities, op.cit.*

3.73   *Council House Communities: A Policy for Progress*, Report of the Scottish Housing Advisory Committee sub-committee on Amenity and Social Character of Local Authority Housing Schemes, HMSO, 1970.

3.74   *Planning for Housing Needs, op.cit.*

3.75   C.J. Watson, Pat Niner and Gillian R. Vale, with Barbara M.D. Smith, *Estimating Local Housing Needs, op.cit.*

3.76   *The New Local Authorities: Management and Structure*, HMSO, 1972.

3.77   *The New Scottish Local Authorities: Organisation and Management Structures*, HMSO, 1973.

Further reading

Marian Bowley, *Housing and the State 1919-1944*, Allen and Unwin, 1945.

J.B. Cullingworth, *Housing and Local Government*, Allen and Unwin, 1966.

J.B. Cullingworth, *Problems of An Urban Society*, in three volumes, George Allen & Unwin, 1973.

D.V. Donnison, *The Government of Housing*, Penguin, 1967.

Lionel Needleman, *The Economics of Housing*, Staples Press, 1965.

Adela Adam Nevitt, *Housing, Taxation and Subsidies*, Nelson, 1966.

4 Industry and Employment

This chapter, which deals with planners' involvement with industry as well as employment, considers both the existing concerns of physical planning in this field and the wider framework within which this takes place. Involvement came initially via the need to deal with immediate problems; it entered the statutory planning process with the development plan that embraced industry and employment. The structure plan too requires consideration of 'employment and income' and 'industry and commerce' (4.1), but much of this planning activity has been opportunist and fragmented, coping with obvious existing problems or filling a plan requirement, and hence may be criticised as inadequate. It may also be criticised because of the lack of synthesis into a framework of employment planning at the city level: every aspect of planning for industry involves intervention in the market and has an employment dimension which planners need to evaluate explicitly and to monitor subsequently.

Planning is concerned with industry and employment from the following points of view:

(a)   the location of industry as a broad concept
(b)   the siting of industry in a narrow, localised sense
(c)   journey to work, and the implications for transportation planning
(d)   unemployment and the implications for social planning
(e)   the structure of employment, and the economic base of cities.

This list, however, is too neat for when the headings are examined for motivation, they coalesce into two main themes. One theme concerns industry as a source of employment for local residents in volume, location and structure; the other concerns industry as a factor in the total environment, a possible source of nuisance. One theme, therefore, should lead to forward planning and the other simply to control, though the reverse may be the priority adopted.

Hence, on the one hand, there is an important link up with population planning, house provision, city size and transportation, and on the other with the age and condition of buildings and redevelopment or renewal policies. Always, the two themes react on each other and on others.

In the main, one suspects that narrow planning requirements like redevelopment schemes, elimination of nuisance in response to complaints, reduction in possible compensation claims, lack of supply of municipal industrial land or expansion of rateable income have often influenced what action has been taken. Perhaps mainly in more prosperous areas, the important employment issue has been left to look after itself and has not entered specifically into planning at the local level. Indeed, the development plan separation of industry from employment has been significant in planning implementation too.

There is, of course, a very real distinction between what may be considered desirable or necessary to plan (in other words, for what purpose to intervene in the market) and what is practically possible to achieve by intervention. The latter in the field of industry and employment for local authority planners at present is severely limited by the effectiveness of their direct and indirect powers (for most of the powers rest with central government) and by their knowledge of the parameters influencing events. This ignorance would restrict even an advisory plan but the former, in addition, greatly complicates an executive plan. Many of the key variables are exogenous to the plan, being political, economic and temporal factors outside the planner's influence, let alone control.

However, this powerlessness can be exaggerated. Many firms have a social conscience and will adapt their employment and other policies in response to a clear indication of community interest from an understanding planning authority − over, say, the employment of school-leavers and older workers or location on an employment-starved estate.

The powerlessness has, in my view, been exaggerated in the Layfield Report of the Greater London Development Plan (4.2). The quotation given below sets out usefully the forces involved in employment generation and the explicit limits of planners' powers to control or influence employment (these are usefully distinguished). However, it ignores the implicit effect of giving out information, having a plan, report of survey or mutual exchange of views, and underplays the possibility of planning employment, housing and transport in unison so that they complement each other. While Layfield puts what may be a necessary damper on the kind of planning that casually expects to move jobs about like pawns, it may also deter many planners from attempting to improve the economic life of their bailiwick and from attempting to learn how to do this. Yet the planner's powers to accomplish the alleviation of medium term problems seem to be exaggerated by Layfield in turn.

In discussing why a plan should include a statement of general policy on employment, the Report said:

"Employment, after all, is something over which planning authorities have very little control or influence. The number and location of jobs available and the number of persons available to fill them, result from innumerable decisions by employers and employees about where they shall build factories, where they shall establish offices, what sort of employment structure any given development shall contain, what sort of wages the employer can afford to pay, where the worker wants to live, and so forth. The local planning authority certainly has no control over these decisions, and it has precious little influence. A list of the major influences which might work on an employer who is considering expanding his work force in any given place, or on a worker, in adding himself to the labour supply, demonstrates in itself the unimportance of the planning authority . . . The local authority cannot greatly influence any of these considerations except, when it is wholly within its control, the transport network . . . and to some extent housing and educational opportunities.

"We are driven, therefore, to the view that the local planning authority can, can, within its area, over the long term, influence only marginally the tendency of employment to contract or alter, or retain its nature. It can somewhat more effectively exercise, or fail to exercise, its powers to inhibit expansion, but even here, the power of the market renders less than perfect the ability of an authority to check it consistently in the long term. But this is not to say that an authority is not left with important functions. These seem to be two:

(a) The precise physical location of individual developments. These can be influenced powerfully by normal planning control, particularly the grant, or withholding, of planning permission, by the provision of sites and services, by investment in infrastructure, etc. If the authority knows clearly where it wishes there to be a net expansion of employment, or where redevelopment without net expansion should take place, then, over the long term, particularly in co-operation with the Government, it can affect the physical structure of its area. But in a city the size and nature of London, the effect of even a determined and powerful authority will be limited.

(b) The alleviation of medium-term, i.e. three to ten years, problems of lack, or excess, of employment through financial assistance to firms, improved transport facilities, etc. It is impossible for them to move rapidly enough to affect really short-term problems, i.e. less than three years.

The local planning authority ought to have precise aims and policies for these two functions."

From these general points I can now turn to some of the major issues confronting the planner in connection with industry and employment. I have selected the following:

1. The location of industry, particularly from the point of view of inter- and intra-regional movement

2. The siting of industry, and local amenity problems
3. Industrial obsolescence and renewal
4. Employment and unemployment
5. Industrial land, needs and selection
6. The context of industrial change — the forces that influence firms to expand or decline.

There are, of course, other issues like the social problems concerning employment location in suburbs or the inner city, but these can be considered under the headings I have given. My examination has a West Midland bias because this is where my current research is being undertaken, but the problems identified and the principles discussed have a wide urban applicability, particularly at conurbation scale.

The location of industry

Concern with the location of industry, the term embracing all types of industry and all kinds of employment, though prone to limitation to manufacturing industry, has been an important feature of physical planning. The issue can be divided into two separate ones on spatial/distance grounds — location of industry within the nation, involving what we now call regional policy (inter-regional location); and location within the region and within sub-regions, which often involves the dispersal of firms from cities (intra-regional location). The location of plant within a particular urban area will be considered separately, as siting of industry.

The location of industry needs defining in another two respects. Location is a static concept; but planning problems arise mainly with *movement* of industry — either its voluntary movement or relocation in response to economic and social forces leaving populations without support, or its reluctance to move in response to local and central government's wishes to provide better for populations in their care. Movement involves the physical transfer of a plant from one location to another; it may also concern a firm spawning a branch. Another distinct kind of concept absorbed under the umbrella of location of industry arises from death and decline and, less problematical except in congested cities, birth and growth of firms. This is very much a dynamic matter. It may involve long drawn out changes, such as the decline in coal mining in some areas with one pit after another closing over fifty years, or sudden emergencies when a pit or plant or railway workshop shuts down leaving employees and communities high and dry with their previous livelihood gone. The seriousness of either kind of decline will depend largely on the health of employment in the area, which is often an independent matter.

The second definitional point involves the distinction between an industry and a firm, plant or industrial employer. Planners often talk about 'small industries' when they mean small firms in industries possibly employing many persons. There is danger in this slipshod thinking. While the location of an industry is affected by factors broadly shared by all firms in that industry, and these factors change over time, it is the firm, pit or plant that moves, declines, grows, or changes its product or technology and responds through the personnel at its head to pressures and incentives of public policy. While there has been a general trend against coal or rail usage, it is the circumstances of the individual pit or railway station that decides its future. There are, for instance, collieries in Staffordshire and Warwickshire expanding as rapidly as recruitment permits alongside others that are closing. Thus broad locating factors are only of limited influence on the location, movement and prospects of individual industrial firms. The key influences are the individual circumstances of the firm and its management, especially its supply of land (floorspace) and labour and its profitability and enterprise.

Reverting to the two types of location problem above, each has to fit in with the other and with other policies. Thus, while a city may be an exporter or importer of firms moving longer distances between regions, city planners will only be in touch with one end of this process and will have to work within the constraint of national and regional policies, which may not be consistent with their locally-based aims. The same is true in relation to sub-regional relocation, though the other end of the process here will be adjacent and more familiar (but possibly, therefore, less easy to work with). Hopefully, some form of coordination will usually exist amongst the planning authorities involved in the exporting and receiving areas when these are neighbours (4.3). (City planners have a larger measure of control, of course, over the *siting* of individual plants in their authority). Besides these relations with other planning bodies (and central government departments too), planners' powers to influence each type of location are severely constrained by the initiatives of the industrial plants and their managements (who, in turn, are constrained by internal and external factors).

Planners in a developing area where new industrial sites are constantly being taken up will have far more influence on location than in an area of stability or decline where location largely perpetuates past market decisions.

Although the two types of location process are basically similar, planners have engaged in each with a different objective and hence became involved at a different historical period. Interest in location at a regional and national level arose in the 1930's because of social rather than economic concern with unemployment and out-migration in areas where industry was declining, and this led to a call for industry to move to these areas from more prosperous regions on grounds of equity. More recently, in the 1960's, the benefits to growth from a more even use of resources was emphasised (4.4). 'A proper distribution of industry' (4.5) or a 'balanced industrial development' was demanded (4.6).

Concern with location at the regional and sub-regional level developed when cities seemed to be becoming too big and congested at the centre due to in-migration while people, pushing out to live on the periphery, were spreading commuting traffic and a range of urban problems over a wider and wider area. This generated feelings (and fears) about 'metropolis' and even 'megalopolis'. There were calls for restrictions on city size, which led to dispersal proposals. Although one can refer to Elizabethan and certainly Victorian concern about this, it is really in the 1930's and 1940's that concern turned into action. Interest in this type of location has also derived from the decentralisation tendency now spontaneously evident amongst industrial firms and population in many places (4.7).

The problems of urbanisation and unemployment were originally seen as separate but, since the 1945 Distribution of Industry Act (but not, rather interestingly, the 1944 Employment Policy White Paper, Cmd. 6527), the two have been seen as complementary — industry from congested areas providing the jobs needed in the development areas (4.8). The simplicity of this concept overlooked the economic, administrative and political difficulties entailed in its accomplishment (4.9). Whether for or against this dispersal process, planners soon became concerned about travel to work problems as the workplace and residence of the employed population diverged. Most recently, anxiety has tended to move from the problems of the overspill housing estates to the inner city areas and to the position of employees remaining in old housing and their employment opportunities. It is not yet clear whether decentralisation of employment has proceeded to a point where this anxiety is justified.

Industrial movement and change at the inter-regional level

As mentioned, planners in an individual city see only part of the process of inter-regional industrial movement, and in directly opposed ways according to the location of the city. Thus, amongst the major conurbations, London and the West Midlands are the only two located in exporting areas where the full force of industrial development certificate policy has been experienced for twenty-five years. The Manchester and Leeds conurbations have been betwixt and between but now lie in intermediate areas with some minor assistance to the inflow and growth of industry locally. Liverpool, Tyneside and Glasgow have been firmly in development areas since the last war (and Tyneside and Glasgow in the thirties too), their need for fresh employment bolstered by incentives to attract manufacturing firms and, more recently, service firms.

However, these incentives have been provided by central government. It is central government alone which has powers over the location of industry in this broad sense, both via the industrial development certificate and the later office development permit, required for all substantial new building, and via actual factory building and movement incentives (4.10). Local authority activity has been largely limited, first, to supporting these certificates and permits with planning permission for a particular site or building and, second, to developing the local infrastructure (4.11).

Inter-regional movement can be defined as virtually always going beyond travel to work distance and not usually involving the transfer of more than a handful of employees. It inevitably, therefore, affects infrastructure investment and rateable income. At the receiving end, it requires the planner to provide attractive and serviced sites, usually ahead of demand, and even to provide premises, perhaps through a developer or the government estates management organisations. It also requires attention, with central government support, for roads, housing, shopping and other general social facilities so that the incoming firms have a pleasant and properly provisioned environment. Publicity too is required to make this known to potential customers in competition with other areas seeking employment. Important also is the manner of dealing with industrial inquiries.

In the receiving conurbations and cities, regional in-movement of industry often creates some conflict with sub-regional and local types of movement, for incoming firms may choose to locate in areas from which the local authority is trying to disperse industry for local reasons. These conflicts have occurred particularly in Glasgow, Belfast and Liverpool.

At the exporting end, planners must also be conscious of the effect of the policy. When particular firms make a full move out, employees in the exporting area lose their jobs and, despite the assumed relatively full employment in the exporting areas, all may not find it easy to obtain equivalent ones. (Branch moves, which have been more common and larger in employment terms, only cause loss of potential job opportunities through diversion of growth rather than the specific job loss to individuals that occurs with a full transfer of a plant.)

The local authorities in exporting areas have been pressed to buy up the premises vacated by departing firms to prevent new firms arriving in their place to cancel out the departure. This has been proposed without much thought about the financial process or about an alternative use for the premises or sites concerned. The tendency to suggest commercial use merely suited the form of the industrial development certificate control and entailed no assessment of commercial suitability or demand. In any case, commercial development was likely to have already been boosted by developers and others kept out of factory building by the i.d.c. control. A city full of warehouses or empty factories was not the intention of the i.d.c. control. Nor was a city full of obsolete, decrepit factories but, until the recent concession in the West Midlands and perhaps more generally (for these concessions are veiled within the Department of Trade and

Industry's much vaunted 'flexibility'), modernisation schemes for factory premises have been difficult to implement even by the user because of the i.d.c. control on new building. Multi-storey, old factories have continued to be used because it was not economic to replace them. This leads on to the question of industrial renewal policies considered later.

Industrial movement and change at the sub-regional and local level

The distinction between sub-regional and local industrial movement depends very much on local circumstances, such as how tightly the civil boundaries have been drawn and whether there is spare land within those boundaries if expansion is needed, or a green belt prescribed outside them. As long ago as Chamberlain's Unhealthy Areas Committee of 1921, a measure of dispersal of manufacturing industry was advocated from London. The Barlow Commission on the Distribution of the Industrial Population (Cmd.6153, appointed 1937; reported 1940) in obedience to its terms of reference investigated the "social, economic and strategic disadvantages (that) arise from the concentration of industries or of the industrial population in large towns or in particular areas of the country". It was satisfied that the disadvantages were real in health, housing, recreation, nuisance, congestion, journey to work and strategic terms; indeed, it found little good to say for big cities except that they had some rationale in terms of industrial and public sector economies of scale.

The Commission's Report and the evidence it took are full of facts and thoughts on industrial location and concentrations, such that almost every apparently more recent innovation can find an echo there. In a very real sense the Barlow Report has been the base of post war industrial location policy, although the circumstances to which it reacted were very different in the late 1930's from those which obtain today. The concern expressed about the inadvisability of industrial concentration in view of the possibility of air attacks is just one example of that.

However, the Commission was rightly concerned about the problems of London. But it hardly noticed the problems of other conurbations such as the West Midlands, highlighted subsequently by the West Midland Group in *Conurbation* in 1948 (4.12). Since the war, the main force of central government policy has been behind moving industry out of London and the West Midlands Conurbation to overspill areas. This policy also operated to a lesser extent in other towns in the South and Midlands though most did not have official overspill schemes. It was assumed, on rather flimsy economic evidence, that much manufacturing industry was mobile and that its departure would relieve pressure on employment, traffic and land in the conurbations and city centres. The crucial factors that gave rise to the policy were, of course, first, unemployment in development areas and, second, shortage of housing land in the conurbations. The latter meant that much of the additional housing land had to be provided at some distance, making the transfer of employment for employed householders essential. Industrial movement just had to take place to provide for this. Whether there was enough potential industrial movement to meet both demands was not examined too closely since both policies were considered essential and urgent and, in consequence, there have been problems in new housing communities where decentralisation of population has not been matched by an equivalent flow of industry to provide employment.

Overspill (movement of population from one local authority area to places beyond its civil boundaries, ideally to self-standing and self-contained towns) has claimed most attention in the South East and West Midlands. There the scale was the largest, the overspill areas were more remote and the movement of employment to overspill areas come up sharply against regional policy. Because London's overspill process was underway before the regional problem became severe again after 1958, and because its housing problems and land values were sharp enough to generate out-migration, it was in the West Midlands, and in Birmingham most specifically, that the conflict between inter- and intra-regional industrial movement policies has been most evident. Planners in the New Towns and overspill areas in the West Midlands (Redditch, Telford, Tamworth, Daventry and Droitwich principally) and in the parties responsible for them (such as Staffordshire County Council and Birmingham, for Daventry), sought to attract employers from Birmingham; the Birmingham planners, less stringently perhaps, sought to induce movement out. Housebuilding in overspill areas largely depended on the contemporaneous provision of employment. Many factors were to blame for the failure to achieve this but the result was that the official overspill process slowed down, and some of the people, who had moved out to what were to have been relatively self-contained towns with their own employment, travelled back into the Conurbation to work. Problems occurred with this in farther off overspill schemes such as Daventry. The other consequence was that Birmingham felt forced to seek alternative sources of housing for its citizens, namely by building council housing itself on the periphery of Birmingham rather than depending on others building them in self-standing towns across the Green Belt. This alternative provided houses rapidly, at Castle Vale and Chelmsley Wood, for instance, in Warwickshire, but at the sacrifice of Green Belt land (and of green wedges within the city too) and without satisfactory solution to the employment problem either. These were dormitory estates and, where beyond Birmingham's boundary, outside the range of Birmingham City Transport with lengthy journeys to work to be paid for in addition to considerable rents. Their only advantage over the overspill alternative was the real one that they produced houses quicker (but nevertheless disappointingly slowly for those in need).

Neither the official overspill towns nor these peripheral dormitory estates can be described as well-planned solutions. This was largely because of constraints on the planning and provision required; because money, employment, land, and coordination between the officials involved were not made available in the quantities needed at the time they were required. Nor is the problem over. A housing land shortage persists in both London and Birmingham, the overspill areas remain as a commitment to be met, the development areas still need employment so that competition has not been removed and new constraints have appeared in house prices, rents and lack of economic growth.

The Birmingham situation described here is only an extreme example of a general 'overspill' problem experienced by many reception and exporting areas throughout the country.

One has some sympathy for the planner on two counts particularly. First, overspill was to provide public sector housing; in the private sector, individual families moved steadily out of cities to find houses without apparently considering employment a serious constraint on their movement. Second, in the United States, there was ample evidence of decentralisation of industry to areas equivalent to the overspill areas. But, in both instances, the parallel movement did not occur on the needed scale in Britain.

The factors involved in sub-regional industrial movement, movement to overspill areas or decentralisation of industry, whichever is preferred, are two-pronged — those affecting the movement of industrial plant and those affecting the movement of people. The former set affecting industrial movement includes the net growth of industry at the macro level in the local economy. This affects the demand on resources (both premises and labour) and their availability to growing firms in and around the firms' present location. It also includes the growth of firms at the micro level. For the individual firm, the need to grow produces a need for more space and, thus, in turn, for some, the need to move to find it. The choice of a new site by a firm on the move will be influenced by the macro situation already mentioned and by regional policy, including any Green Belt.

Most firms moving within the region expect to transfer some employees with them, and thus influences on the movement of people are crucial to the movement of firms. The main factors affecting the movement of people are housing considerations, and a range of personal factors including local ties; space in this chapter does not allow for their examination.

There is an important link between the provision of housing and the movement of industry. Although also involving decisions about densities, Green Belts, housing standards and the finance of council house building (which influences rents), the key requirement has been to provide dwellings that those in need of accommodation could and would afford. What they could afford was obviously affected by the kind of jobs they held and journey to work costs. So the type of industry that moved was important. Beyond the Green Belt, employment had to accompany population for the majority and, as the cost of housing rose, living in peripheral dormitory estates left some households with little money to spare for travel to work. Hence, here, too, there arose a demand for at least some local jobs for women, a provision deliberately excluded to avoid sapping job movement to remoter overspill areas. This, at least, shows up some of the complexity of industrial location policies.

The other key is regional policy, in the absence of which industry might readily have moved to overspill areas and, in the absence of a Green Belt, especially moved to the periphery. On the latter point, there is no doubt for statistics show considerable movement of this kind despite contrary planning policies and despite the lack of sustained national economic growth in manufacturing industry and employment.

Thus, given regional policy, given the Green Belt policy and given the lack of industrial growth, the preference of most firms for short moves (4.13) and the concentration of regional incentives until recently on manufacturing industry, the decentralisation of industry to overspill areas has been limited – and will continue to be limited. There seems no reason to consider these constraints as no longer operative. The i.d.c. concession (no i.d.c. is now needed for building up to 15 000 ft^2 outside the South East) is of minor importance for firms moving as opposed to expanding a little on site. 15 000 ft^2 accommodates about 50 employees at average space standards and most employment is provided in plants to which this amount of floor space does not represent much of an addition. Moreover, the concession also operates for firms in the old urban areas, thus providing less incentive for them to move out.

Attitudes and other policies also change. A crucial related policy is that towards road transport and especially public transport. Better roads, better public transport or wider car ownership could alter travel to work parameters. At present, there is a trend, probably strongest in the Midlands and South East, to build private houses on more remote pieces of land in an effort to price them at levels people can afford – even if that low price stretches the people's travel to work severely, especially where travel is dependent on inadequate public transport.

Ideally, from a travel to work by public transport point of view, houses should be concentrated in one area and employment, if not adjacent, concentrated in another so that adequate passenger demand justifies transport services between the two at a spread of times as hours of work range widely. This, although it illustrates the need to plan development as a whole, is not how we have been planning for the last twenty years.

City planners do not plan for local industry in isolation. Regional and sub-regional planning teams, financed if not directed by local authorities, central government departments and Regional Economic Planning Councils, separately or in combination, were commonplace in the 1960's. The strategies produced, even when approved by their sponsors, depended on the local planning authority for implementation, entailing interpretation in local dimensions. The experience of producing such a strategy has also been of value to the participant planners through the mutual discussion involved.

The siting of industry and the amenity problem

The question of where to locate industrial concerns within the urban area and how to control and lessen the environmental problems they create lies at the heart of town planning. Moreover, it is a concern likely to be approved by all, except by the offenders who may find excuses either in their technical inability to avoid the nuisance, financial justification (of shiftwork, for instance) or pre-emptive rights to an industrial site subsequently surrounded by houses – these excuses usually calling for subsidy or postponement of action. Unfortunately, the pressure tends to fall on particular industries (foundries, scrapyards, polishers and platers) and on small firms in older premises. Not all affected are mobile; cement works and open cast mines, for example, must stay with their raw materials.

There are two varieties of problem. First, where should industry be located in the urban area irrespective of any environmental problem? And, second, where should industrial firms that create environmental problems be located? In both instances, it is necessary to bear in mind the economic and employment constraints on firms. The two issues have tended to run together but it is not true that all industry is noisy or dirty. Some manufacturing firms, like people, object to unsatisfactory neighbours.

Planners on this issue are backed increasingly by the public, who, based on past experience which need not now be relevant, seem schizophrenic about factory development near their homes – though, at the same time, demanding the provision of adequate employment within a short distance of the same homes. There is a major dilemma here for planners to resolve. Some policy is necessary for, otherwise, the poorest, and most disadvantaged, areas will end up with the difficult plants, thereby adding to their environmental problems. ⌐

Planners have also been backed up by national legislation such as the Clean Air Acts of 1956 and 1968, though the primary problem dealt with there was smoke from the domestic chimney. On many counts, the verdict of the Barlow Commission on the unhealthiness and congestion of our cities has been outdated by improvements that have already taken place. However, standards of acceptability quite rightly have also advanced; so have our methods of detection and awareness of danger (on lead and asbestos poisoning, for instance) though not as far as one would wish.

The environmental evils produced by industry are noise, smoke and other pollution of the air, liquid effluents ideally to be rendered suitable for disposal through the public sewerage system, traffic and unsightly sites. Noise, which may become particularly objectionable outside normal working hours and thus is related to the economics of overtime and shiftworking, is one of the most difficult to cure. All, of course, are a problem for employees in the plant as well as neighbouring residents. The loading, turning and passage of heavy lorries is a general problem, especially in confined streets and sites, where, in fact, the street becomes the effective loading and even storage bay of the factory. The parking of employees' cars and the traffic congestion produced at opening and closing time is another aspect of the traffic problem, costly to resolve. Unsatisfactory factory buildings (overcrowded, decrepit, insanitary and even dangerous) may also be included, though the factory inspector may take responsibility for control (as the public health inspector will in other instances). The supposition that workers would leave the firms with bad working conditions has proved ineffective in many cases – though the reasons for this loyalty warrant investigation as it hints at unsuspected virtues in these kinds of firms perhaps worth preserving in some guise.

Clearly one answer is to require control of the problem at source if that is technically and financially possible within the existing buildings. If the nuisance is bad enough or the complaints strong enough, the offending firm can be served with a discontinuance order and even a compulsory purchase order and shut down. If it has an established use on the site, compensation may be considerable and, thus, implementation of closure is likely to be postponed.

A second answer has been to categorise industries according to their processes and nuisance potential. The categories were decided by the Ministry of Housing in the Town and Country Planning (Use Classes) Orders (4.14). Movement between classes requires planning permission and therefore it becomes possible to control the broad zoning of industrial uses. Firms in heavy and noxious industries are segregated in Class V-VIII while, at the other end of the spectrum, firms in Class III, light assembly industries, are such as can be permitted in residential areas.

A third answer relevant to both existing and new firms has been the allocation of zones of land for particular uses. This has served to concentrate industrial use on zoned industrial land to separate it from other uses with whom its purposes (other than employment provision) have been considered incompatible. Although existing non-conforming, non-industrial land users survive *in situ*, in time the separation will become clearer and cohabitation will only be required round the edge of the zones. Unneighbourly uses have thus been separated physically. This system dates back to before the war but was made general in the development plans of the 1950's, based largely on a principle of 'rounding off' existing land use.

Another form of this zoning is the trading estate, now sometimes called euphemistically an industrial park. Trafford Park in Manchester and Slough

Trading Estate were examples given to the Barlow Commission (4.15). In 1938, there were 200 firms and 50 000 jobs on Trafford Park plus 700 houses for keyworkers who needed to be within call; Slough, which opened in 1920, had 210 firms and 28 000 work-people before the war. Many so-called estates, for instance in the Black Country, are minute compared to these, occupying only one or two acres. Many new estates are now located beneath or along motorways as these are seen as the new key locating influence on manufacturing and warehousing concerns.

A trading estate is simply a group of factories (and warehouses even more often) on adjacent sites. The buildings can be freehold or rented. In some cases, the estate will have a formal organisation with one landlord and some communal policy and facilities, such as a canteen, security, power supply and maintenance of roads and grounds. (These communal facilities including children's nurseries and works buses, are something local authorities could provide to benefit the community and to attract incoming firms.) Trading estates in New Towns, for instance, can literally contain factories in a park but some elsewhere are frankly slums. Many estates are owned by local authorities who thereby retain control of their industrial land and can reserve places for firms moved by their own planning policies. In many places, the pace of redevelopment and the extinguishing of non-conforming uses depends on the supply of alternative sites in municipal control.

The tendency has been to separate industrial areas off from the rest of the urban area; in short, to segregate them, their traffic and their environmental problems. This is most evident in New Towns. It does mean that workplace and residence are separated and, even in a small town, this can create problems, especially for women workers. This is particularly so if the trading estate is large, for travel across can be lengthy. One communal facility, of course, could be the provision of a bus service; another could be a children's creche, referred to earlier.

One of the diseconomies of an estate for employers is the competition for employees and, often, the farthest off employer from residential areas or bus stops experiences added difficulties in recruiting and holding staff. This is evidence of fairly precise siting effects on an individual firm.

One implication of zoning and planning regulations generally is that non-conforming users are discouraged. This inevitably discourages the many forms of enterprise where a start is usually required in other premises; the home turned into a boarding house, the front parlour into an office, the garage or backyard into a workshop and the garden or field into a scrapyard. The cottage industry of the past that bred innovations and new firms, as well as squalor, is disallowed (if found out). It is difficult to see how this can be avoided. The problem is how to build flexibility and discretion into planning control without this inevitably permitting licence. But we need enterprise and employment opportunities. The jewellery quarter in Birmingham could never have developed under present planning regulations; this sounds like a criticism but, in fact, a desirable residential neighbourhood was gradually converted into a congested rabbitwarren of small premises and backyard shacks, the residents being driven elsewhere, leaving churches and schools redundant. What we need to do is to find some acceptable alternative for the new venture in terms of location, public health and amenity consideration.

Industrial obsolescence and renewal

The question of industrial obsolescence and renewal as discussed here relates almost entirely to manufacturing industry, though the problem is closely related to, first, the same problem in the housing sector and, second, to the siting and amenity problem just discussed. In both instances, planners are seeking to improve both the efficiency of industry and the environment. There is no reason to suppose that architectural determinism is limited to people and housing; it will also apply to firms and factories (4.16).

Much has been written about comprehensive redevelopment and its modified successors, renewal and improvement, (4.17) but nearly always these relate to domestic housing. However, the comprehensive redevelopment area (CDA) approach cleared factory premises together with houses and shops, and consequently required relocation policies for displaced firms. Outside these areas it seems to be assumed that industrial premises will renew themselves without local authority or central government intervention. In many cases this is only partially true and it may be very slow in operating. The scale of the problem and the process is likely to be very similar to that on the housing front (4.18). The better-off, who might have had the money to refurbish, move out of the older premises leaving them to other concerns in a kind of 'filtering' process. There will be instances where old premises are demolished and rebuilt for the same owner but this will usually only occur where adjacent land can be acquired and where the firm wishes to retain its existing position. Because of the inconvenience of operating in a factory during phased demolition and rebuilding, many firms will prefer to move to fresh premises.

Thus, inner areas, where factories are much of an age with the rest of the urban fabric, contain old, deteriorating factory premises (albeit with some brand new ones). Often these will be obsolete in design as well as merely old; thus refurbishing is not the complete answer. Obsolescence will embrace lack of parking, turning and loading space, lack of a canteen, multi-storey production space without adequate lift provision and the huddle of small workshops consistent with the production and social organisation of firms in the late 19th century. While parking and canteen facilities may be provided externally, it is difficult to introduce modern methods of production in multi-storey, multi-shop premises or to economise on material handling, though firms are resilient and ingenious on these issues, especially as the overheads and rents in older premises are far lower than in new.

On the first issue, account needs to be taken of the demand for factory premises in such areas, for the very lack of renewal of vacant property may reflect lack of demand. If this is so, alternative use for the land may be found. A positive policy is needed towards empty, unwanted or merely decaying industrial premises. However, in the Midlands and South East, such a policy is likely to come up against the i.d.c. control. This, in part, explains the continued existence of obsolete premises, because new building, especially of a speculative character, built ahead of specific demand, is severely controlled.

On the second issue, the problems are considerable and, in part, probably account for the present inertia. Old, obsolete premises tend to have low rents per square foot relative to new premises (but more square feet relatively to the landlord's benefit). This may be partly because some rents were fixed many years ago and partly because of the diseconomies of the building. (This is not inconsistent with demand maintaining rents relatively high in some areas because of the decline in the availability of such premises as redevelopment proceeds.) Low rents relative to those of new premises mean that relocation of present users to other premises is very difficult because many will not and, indeed, cannot afford the price of alternative premises. Moreover, if such firms have built up a place for themselves in the local community amongst linked firms and employees, relocation out of the area means hardship for others.

On the other hand, concerns that cannot afford current rents are being subsidised by the community if provided with premises at special rents, though this might be justified if employment provision was taken into the account.

Birmingham has provided alternative premises for small firms in inner city locations in its flatted factories, units in which can be rented from the Corporation. Two flatted factories containing in all about a hundred units of up to 3000 ft^2 each were provided in the 1950's and a third was recently opened by a developer in the jewellery quarter. However, economic rents were asked to finance the building. These rents might be twelve times the rent being paid by the firm for its (possibly near slum) existing premises. In any case, a hundred units could not have accommodated many of the 1500 concerns moved in the first five comprehensive redevelopment areas in Birmingham (4.19).

Another policy, which can be adopted by local authorities though more usually by property developers, is that of providing refurbished factory premises – taking over empty premises, splitting them up into smaller units if necessary and modernising them before renting them out or disposing of them. Quite a number of the industrial estates now in existence are based on such conversions, with sometimes additional new building on land around. The Kings Norton Trading Estate, opened by Slough Estates in Birmingham in 1931, is a pre-war example of this. Textile mills in Yorkshire and Lancashire have been dealt with similarly, providing low rental premises for immediate occupation. The cost of conversion must, however, not bring the price of the units up to the price of new ones unless there is a limited supply of the latter, which may be affected, in some parts of the country, by the i.d.c. control and land shortage.

This policy is related to employment location and generation as well as to urban renewal. It is also related to industrial land use policies discussed below.

Employment and unemployment

Much of the impetus to concern about industrial location derived from unemployment, and, as in that policy, the individual local authority was largely a participant rather than an initiator in subsequent employment planning. At the one end of the scale, there have been problems still epitomised by Londonderry, Jarrow and Glasgow (4.20). In September 1973, unemployment rates in these towns were two to four times the national average. At the other extreme, there have been towns and areas with, at times, problems of over-employment such as Dudley, Kidderminster, Redditch or London currently or Coventry in the past (4.21).

Persistent unemployment in an area has usually derived from a concentration of the local industrial structure on industries in decline nationally or increasing their productivity per head. Hence, concern about unemployment has led on to a watch on the industrial structure to see how it might respond to efforts to increase and diversify employment. Many methods geared to explaining decline and growth potential have been used – shift and share analysis and Colin Clark's economic potential may be mentioned (4.22). Linkages, multipliers, location quotients, growth centres, seedbeds, and basic industries are just some of the concepts brought into the discussion (4.23). Illustrative statistics were also used (4.24). This monitoring and analysis has not been confined to unemployment areas. The West Midlands, for example, has searched urgently for some explanation of its position (4.25). This is a growth area where manufacturing growth at least has been somewhat mysteriously lacking: existing growth industries like motor vehicles and non-ferrous metals not growing as fast as nationally or in Wales and Scotland and new ones like plastics, electronics and chemicals almost entirely absent. The success of the i.d.c. control and regional incentives in diverting growth elsewhere have not been thought to provide an adequate explanation.

This is perhaps better described as one common problem, a mis-match between workplaces and residences or between the supply of people and jobs. Jarrow and Glasgow have more people than jobs, while the South-East has more jobs than people. This mis-match can be measured (not entirely satisfactorily) by the statistics of registered unemployment and of unfilled notified vacancies in each area and is reflected in the availability and price of housing. Activity rates, migration, overtime working and travel to work distance are other indicators.

Why is there unemployment? First, there is unemployment that may be traced to trends in the national employment situation. These include the relative lack of demand for employees aged over 50 years and for the unskilled, and the changes in demand for labour in particular industries, these changes embracing perhaps not only numbers of employees but also their sex, skill and location. While, broadly, these changes involve declines in employment in agriculture, mining and manufacturing and the expansion of employment in services, this is too simple a division, for some manufacturing industries have been expanding and some services, notably rail transport, have been declining. Significant too at a narrower level are changes like that in the school-leaving age or in women's wage rates and hours due to the movement towards equal pay and opportunity, or towards shift working.

Unemployment may also be caused by a fall in general demand during a trade recession. Recently, such unemployment has often been induced by central government's (mis-) management of the economy in response to balance of payments or inflation problems, and it can be cured by a reversal of policy.

Other unemployment arises due to special local circumstances at the neighbourhood, city or regional level. These circumstances are special in the sense that the local employment experience differs from that generally occurring in the national economy. Nevertheless, this employment experience may be characteristic of particular types of area and thus may be present in comparable form in several similar areas. Examples include the employment problems of the central business district, of the inner city areas of older housing that usually surround the central district, of commuter areas where housing tends to be divorced from workplace, of development areas and of 'grey' areas in the interstices of present planning policies. Large conurbations may be experiencing common employment developments that need careful attention. Finally, there are the employment problems of areas where employment is seasonal or casual or exclusively for one sex or age group.

The mis-match between residents and workplaces may not lead to actual unemployment but to outcommuting, low activity rates and social discontent. More attention needs to be given to the composition of jobs in an area, provided through the aggregate employment requirements of principal employers to ensure that the needs of the local economically active are being met. The employment health of the local community will often depend on this. School-leavers, married women wanting part-time work, the older worker and the disabled may be at a disadvantage in the competition for local jobs; training opportunities may be inadequate with harmful effect on career prospects.

A recent study of an overspill reception area has indicated the effects of young in-migrant families on the age structure of the working population (4.26).

Entrants of school-leaving age have been exceeding in number retirements at 60 and 65 years each year at an accelerating pace; married women have been forming an increasing proportion of the labour force. The first has implications for the demand for jobs and training opportunities and for the staffing of the Youth Employment Service; the latter for the demand for part-time work and child care facilities. The apparent balance between employment and population growth was misleading: activity rates in the existing population were rising coincident with continued in-migration. In consequence, outcommuting was rising, which assumed a neighbouring labour market with persisting excess of jobs over residents.

The obverse of this is the inner city exporting area with an ageing and declining population, likely to include a disproportion of the older, unskilled and coloured workers who experience relatively more unemployment than other groups in our society. While this disproportion reflects age and immobility, it remains to be investigated whether local employment opportunities have in fact been changing to residents' disadvantage, perhaps towards lower-paid, menial service jobs, or jobs for women or for the more literate, as manufacturing jobs have moved farther away. An examination of both the workplaces of inner city residents and the residences of workers in inner and central employing concerns would indicate differences relative to others in the city region.

Description and diagnosis may not bring relief but it can indicate many points at which planning might adopt relatively minor remedial measures (child-care facilities, re-routed bus services, split shifts for part-timers) as well as longer term measures that alter the composition or expand the scale of employment. The local authority itself is a large employer and it can set an example.

Industrial land

Industrial location, obsolescence and employment present planners with a physical problem of land allocation; this is the one resource over which planners have some control, exercised through zoning and planning permission and direct acquisition. In relation to industrial planning, the planner's first concern is with industrial land. Indirectly, it is with housing land and the accommodation of employees within travel to work distance; also with transportation, and with the provision of the services necessary to both industrial concerns and the employed population.

In order to allocate land for industrial use, it is necessary to decide how much land is needed for industry, and where and when. Planners, therefore, have to know what land is in industrial use already (both in active use and in reserve, perhaps used as parking, storage or playing fields) and what the future demand will be. They will consider supply only at a later stage for they have some influence over supply through their zoning decisions.

The land demand and supply operation works at two levels – one in the planner's allocation assessment, and one in the market situation subsequent to the announcement of the allocation. The latter affects the supply and value of land, bringing some perhaps into the market not previously included.

In estimating future demand, planners can work from two directions. They can take the existing stock of firms and industrial land and see what changes will arise amongst these firms for land – for expansion or disposal. A survey will solicit this information, though it is of questionable reliability as firms do not plan ahead precisely or, rather, often do not implement their plans as their circumstances change. Such estimates, in any case, ignore new and incoming firms as these cannot be surveyed. However, analysis of past land use behaviour by firms can provide guidance on rates of expansion per acre and of net change.

The second approach starts from the points of view of population, housing and employment, and works back to land use. Estimates of housing sites and of the resident employed or working population of the future are made and converted into jobs per acre. This approach relies on full employment, largely demographic forecasts such as specific birth, activity and net migration rates, and levels of commuting.

In any conversion of employment opportunities into land use, there are certain technical factors to be taken into account. These relate to the use made of land by firms including the amount of building on each acre relative to parking and loading space and landscaping; to factory design including especially the number of floors and the height of the roof (which affects the volume of storage, for instance); to standards of accommodation, including especially the amount of non-productive floor space in canteens, training schools and circulation space; and to the amount of floor space occupied by machinery, conveyor belts and stocks. All these and others are influences on the density of employment per square foot of floor space and, gross, per acre of land. Employment density varies from factory to factory, process to process and from time to time in the same factory (according to how busy it is or how recently it added extensions). The best estimate available is probably an average figure for the present across all industry and some estimate of the likely change over the period under consideration. Basing the future on the present local situation (which will itself be difficult to discover) takes account of the existing industrial structure and balance of land use between industries. In estimating future change, account needs to be taken of expected changes in that industrial structure. With industrial floor space per worker ranging from as low as 30 ft^2 per worker in some labour intensive, crowded factories (like clothing), to 3000 ft^2 in iron and steel stockholding, there is plenty of room for error in any aggregation or averaging. The average is probably around 300 ft^2 and increasing because each worker and his activities and support facilites are occupying more space than in the past. Strangely on such a crucial matter, no definite figures are available but some reports of survey for structure plans do indicate data in a local area. But the floor space figures then have to be converted into acres of land, allowing for additional floors and land not built on. The usual allowance is 30-40 workers per gross acre on industrial land (4.27). (It is acknowledged that these figures should be in metric units, square metres and hectares but the statistics remain in the old units.)

The employment density figure should be applied to existing industrial land as well as additional land for, as employment densities fall (with more space per existing worker), so existing industrial land will provide less employment. If employment is to be maintained, therefore, more industrial land will be required to cope with present employment, quite apart from expansion.

Having decided how much industrial land is needed, it is then necessary to consider, first, the existing zoned land and, second, the opportunities for allocating additional land to the overall zoning in competition with other uses. The forecasting also presupposes that industrial land is in fact in industrial use and remains so. Non-conforming industrial users on other land may need to be accommodated on industrial land in the future, while industrial land may continue to be occupied by non-conforming, non-industrial users. Industrial land may also be semi-derelict, requiring positive reclamation or time to settle before development. Industrial land, actual and potential, may be in private ownership and, whilst compulsory purchase may be a legal possibility, it may be expensive to pursue. In particular, ownership and price influence the timing of land becoming available for development. Another feature that needs to be considered is the timing of the demand for land.

The allocation of enough industrial land to accommodate future employment demand does not, of course, ensure that those employment opportunities of themselves arrive. The local authority can influence that by advantageous location of the industrial land, by conversion of land into serviced sites and the provision of premises, and by promoting the area as an attractive industrial location to potential employers.

With regard to location, reference earlier was made to environmental influences on the siting of industry which principally decided where it should *not* be sited, for example, where it would cause a nuisance to neighbouring users, present and future. As to where new industrial sites should be located, the emphasis is on relatively flat land and links with the local road or motorway system or other good transport routes (invariably roads but lively places now mention air and port connections). New Towns emphasise the availability of housing for employees, the growth of local industry and their attraction to other firms; pleasant countryside and sports facilities like golf courses and salmon fishing are often featured. Existing industrial centres emphasise instead the pool of skilled and experienced employees and access to industrial services.

In most developed cities, the location of industrial land is largely decided by existing land use patterns while, in the outer areas where land may be undeveloped, a Green Belt will often restrict its use for industry. Opportunities for new industrial development on a large scale are thus severely limited. In a new or developing town, some of the less attractive land near transport routes is likely to be reserved for industrial land. There is no reason to suppose that precise siting is very crucial to commercial success; such factors as publicity and availability of bus routes to housing areas can make virtually any site successful. The key to its success in attracting outside firms will lie in the number of competitive sites, growth amongst potential customers and their knowledge that the site exists. Its price is, of course, crucial — but this encompasses all the previous aspects in so far as the seller is capable of evaluating them correctly. A local authority may want to maximise its capital gains and income from its industrial land holdings, or may be prepared to encourage rapid development through a favourable pricing system or mortgage facilities.

While accurate allocation of industrial land is a crucial function of planning, both in provision of employment and in siting of facilities, it is difficult to accomplish. The effective planning of employment through floor space controls (the industrial development certificate or the office development permit), relies on a regular relationship between jobs and floor space. The Greater London Council had to admit to the Layfield Inquiry that delineation of that relationship in aggregate had evaded them. However, trends in employment and floor space within the same plant over time could be helpful, at least in identifying the parameters of the relationship, and further planning studies would be helpful in this direction.

The forces acting on firms

To engage effectively in planning for industry and employment, planners need to understand the many forces acting on firms, both those that promote expansion and those that may lead to decline. It is the latter that are more crucial to policymaking and so are the ones considered here. Any of the following trends may be responsible for a local decline in aggregate industrial development.

(i) A slackening in the birth rate of new concerns. The Bolton Committee (4.28) and others have been examining this at national level. A high birth rate of small firms has been traditional (though largely undocumented since before the war) (4.29) in the West Midlands and South East and, even now, though the social and financial attractions of entrepreneurship may be flagging, and the industrial development certificate control and location costs may be diverting or frustrating entrepreneurs, the numbers of small plants in Birmingham is being maintained. This seems to be exceptional relative to other places outside the

South-East (4.30). However, although E.T. Penrose in *The Theory of the Growth of the Firm* (4.31) saw endless opportunities continuing for the small firm in the interstices of the larger ones (through the latter's incapacity to exploit all openings that existed), the ability of new firms to start up will depend on a continuing supply of premises, capital, opportunities and executives. On the first, redevelopment is rapidly eliminating sources of low-cost, small factories, while planning often prevents the use of unorthodox buildings for embryo firms.

(ii) A rise in the death rate of existing concerns. Death may come via bankruptcy, retirement, closure of premises (perhaps due to redevelopment), merger or rationalisation. The number of deaths may be increasing without a fall necessarily in output and employment. In some cases, death may be economically beneficial in releasing resources for better use elsewhere. However, if all those managements who report that they could make more money by investing in the Post Office transferred their capital there, the fall in employment might be disastrous.

(iii) The growth of existing firms being diverted to other areas. This might be due to influences such as industrial development certificate control, regional policy, changes in locating factors and availability of land and labour, and perhaps also dissatisfaction with an area from the environmental point of view. There are abundant instances of this relocation of growth, but whether it happens *more often* than in the past is uncertain.

It is important to realise that the scale of the operations of most major public companies now makes it impractical to judge the health of the local economy from the reports of even those traditionally associated with an area. Their growth may be located elsewhere or may result from relocation from the area. The hard work of local employees and managements may have provided the basis of growth but investment to develop this may go elsewhere to safeguard shareholders' interests with a spread of investment.

The disattraction of particular areas environmentally may present a very serious problem. Manufacturing is declining in the inner Black Country: one difficulty in generating new job opportunities there, especially in offices, may be the ugliness of the urban fabric.

(iv) The innovations of existing firms being diverted to other areas also for reasons similar to those mentioned in relation to growth. The industrial development certificate has had a significant effect on innovation and diversification in the south because an applicant has needed to justify a location there by evidence of ties and special locating factors. A new or innovating concern has difficulty in providing this, lacking even ties to an existing labour force. This has helped to maintain the predominantly metal character of the

West Midlands, for instance, though there is no evidence on whether, in the absence of the control, non-metal manufacturing would have developed. The control has not been, of course, complete and some existing firms, happily, have accommodated change within their existing plants or in premises taken over.

(v)   A lack of growth in the national economy, lack of investment in plant and new products and processes. This affects all areas.

(vi) The inertia created by the existing stock of buildings, which may be obsolete, and of industrial practices by management and workers, which may be equally obsolete. By analogy with old housing areas, a long established industrial area will tend to retain more older firms, more non-growing and non-innovating firms (as these do not need to change their premises), and to export the dynamic ones. A general demolition and modernisation programme is needed for factories as for houses with, similarly, enforcement by the local authority when the factory occupants fail to act (but retaining rents favourable to firms).

(vii) The net out-movement of firms. The flow from many cities is clearly outwards. This is especially true of Birmingham (from my own work) into which hardly a single manufacturing firm without some link to the town has moved in recent years. Most influences work against imports and favour exports. Several planning authorities have had restrictions on the disposal of industrial land to outsiders as it is needed for locals.

(viii) The decline in employment likely to result, and to have resulted already, from a reduction in jobs per acre coupled with limited additional industrial land in many cities. (Shiftworking is a counter-influence but is not changing very much in amount.) This means that employment drains away even in active, profitable firms. While existing firms may have expanded their turnover, output, profits and even floor space on their existing sites, the job opportunities involved have been declining as more land and real and potential floor space is given over to loading bays, single floor production, amenities, parking and more machinery. In a built-up area, additional industrial land is limited and, in the development plans of the 1950's, much land was necessarily zoned for other purposes than industry. Thus, in many older areas a combination of planning, price restrictions and existing usage limit the availability of additional land for employment maintenance, let alone its creation.

In many areas too, there has been a diversion of hitherto manufacturing land to warehousing due to the form of the i.d.c. control, (warehouses do not require i.d.c.'s) and due to planning relaxations in the 1950's and 1960's when labour was short. Attitudes have changed but the trend is difficult to reverse, especially as one assumes that the warehousing built by commercial firms is finding takers.

(ix) *The conflict with the environmentalists.* The problems of pollution, noise and nuisance have already been discussed. The danger is that, in process of taking care about siting and nuisance control, excessive safeguards will frustrate development entirely.

While changes in the individual firm, unless it is very large, may not be significant, they become important when the changes in a number of firms are all in the same direction so that their cumulative effect is considerable. Planners, therefore, need to monitor what is happening in their area. This is merely another application of the point about the composition of employment in aggregate already made; there the concern was with the situation at a point in time; here it is change that is important.

Conclusion

There are many aspects of the employment-income-industry-growth relationship that we do not yet fully understand. There are difficulties still in obtaining some quite elementary data that are needed, easily and accurately. Yet it is abundantly clear that it is better to be aware and watchful, even if policies and predictions prove mistaken, than to remain in dark ignorance. Research and experience will gradually reduce inaccuracy at the technical level, but that will not solve the problem of decision-making. We should always remember that there are plenty of people to consult, as in every branch of planning. Public participation is not excluded from industrial planning. Chambers of commerce or trade, the Confederation of British Industry branches, trades councils and trades unions can help in mutual understanding.

The success of planning for employment and industry is to have it in balance with other aspects of the local community. The industrial environment produced or amended by the planning system should add to the quality of life in the area economically and socially. It is therefore essential to provide an adequate employment and industrial base for cities. In attaining this long term objective planning has to be adaptive. Nowhere is this more true than with regard to the visual aspects of the industrial landscape. Sometimes ugly industrial structures cannot be avoided, but they can be made to fit in with other requirements in a way that develops their virtues and restrains their nuisances, and so that they continue to do this over time, adjusting to changes in standards and circumstances. There is a clear link between visual amenity, economic function and community creativity, and a heavy handed planning intervention can have unfortunate consequences. This confirms that the planner needs to be much more aware of the complex interrelationships with which he is dealing. In the past, the grounds and manner of his intervention in matters of industry and employment have been arbitrary to say the least. Let us hope that clearer diagnosis will lead to better prescription.

References

4.1   Ministry of Housing and Local Government, *Development Plans: A Manual on Form and Content,* HMSO, 1970, Appendix A.

4.2   Department of the Environment, *Greater London Development Plan: Report of the Panel Inquiry, Vol. 1: Report,* HMSO, 1973, Chapter V, pp.78-80.

4.3   Standing conferences of planning authorities and regional and sub-regional plans are two forms of coordination. Local government reform will have eliminated some inter-authority problems while introducing fresh ones.

4.4   *The National Plan,* Cmnd. 2764, 1965. On concern in the 1930's, see the Barlow Commission on the Distribution of the Industrial Population, Cmnd. 6153, 1940,*Report*, pp. 3-5.

4.5   Distribution of Industry Act, 1945.

4.6   *Employment Policy*, Cmnd. 6527, 1944, para.26.

4.7   Peter Hall, *et. al., The Containment of Urban England*, 2 Vols., Allen and Unwin for Political and Economic Planning, 1973. There was, of course, an economic side to Ebenezer Howard's garden city movement of the 1900's. But the cities in undeveloped countries are still 'exploding' in size with population moving in from the land.

4.8   E.g. in Professor Jones and others' Note of Reservation to the Barlow Commision Report, *op.cit.*, pp. 213-214.

4.9   Barbara M.D. Smith, *The Administration of Industrial Overspill*, Occasional Paper No. 22, Centre for Urban and Regional Studies, 1972.

4.10   The regulations on certificates and permits have varied over time and space and are no longer required in some parts of the country. Apart from the regulations themselves which are published as introduced in the *Board of Trade Gazette*, now *Trade and Industry*, see Barbara M.D. Smith, 'Industrial development certificate control: an institutional influence on industrial mobility', *Journal of the Town Planning Institute,* **57**, February, 1971, pp. 65-70.

4.11   Margaret M. Camina, 'Local authorities and the attraction of new employment', *The Planner: Journal of the Royal Town Planning Institute*, February, 1974, pp. 553-558.

4.12   West Midland Group, *Conurbation: A Survey of Birmingham and the Black Country*, Architectural Press, 1948.

4.13   For a long time, very little was known of the extent and pattern of total industrial movement, only longer and inter-subregional moves were collated in R.S. Howard, *The Movement of Manufacturing Industry in the United Kingdom 1945-65*, Board of Trade, HMSO, 1968. On local movement, see Notts./Derbys. Sub-Regional Management Committee,

Mobility of Firms: The Study Findings, Loughborough, 1972, and *A Developing Strategy for the West Midlands: Report of the West Midland Regional Study, 1971, Technical Appendix 3. Economic Study 3 (Industrial Mobility)*, 1972, pp. 11-14.

4.14   See, for example, *Town and Country Planning, England and Wales: The Town and Country Planning (Use Classes) Order*, Statutory Instruments, 1963, No. 708 (Ministry of Housing).

4.15   Barlow Commission Report, *op.cit.*, Appendix, p.283.

4.16   Critically discussed in M. Broady, *People and Planning*, Bedford Square Press, 1968.

4.17   G.C. Cameron and K.M. Johnson, 'Comprehensive Urban Renewal and Industrial Relocation – The Glasgow Case', in S.C. Orr and J.B. Cullingworth (eds.), *Regional and Urban Studies*, University of Glasgow Social and Economic Studies, Allen and Unwin, 1969, pp. 242-280 and John Holliday (ed.), *City Centre Redevelopment*, Charles Knight & Co., London, 1973.

4.18   County Borough of West Bromwich, *Structure Plan: Report of Survey: Industry and Employment*, 1972, p. 68 indicated that in 1970 16 per cent of local employment was in premises built before 1930 or 22 per cent in premises assessed as only fair or worse in condition. These figures can be compared with 1948 assessments in West Midland Group, *Conurbation, op.cit.*, p.148 where 34 per cent were considered to need replacing by 1980.

4.19   *City of Birmingham Structure Plan: A New Plan for the City: First Stage: Report of Survey: Employment and Industry*, 1973, p. 66 records what happened to these 1456 firms, 25 per cent of whom were relocated by the Corporation (20 per cent inside the redevelopment area); 29 per cent moved outside the city; and 21 per cent ceased trading; the remainder moving elsewhere within the city. There is no indication of the size of these firms but most were small, if not very small.

4.20   *Department of Employment Gazette*, October, 1973, pp. 1026-1027 and 1023. When the U.K. unemployment rate in September, 1973 was 2.5 per cent and the South-East rate 1.3 per cent, the rate in Londonderry was 10.5 per cent (Newry 14.2 per cent but Belfast only 4.6 per cent); Jarrow in Tyneside exchange district 5.3 per cent and Glasgow 5.5 per cent. Liverpool with a rate of 6.5 per cent is the only other group of exchanges with a rate of over 6 per cent outside Tyneside.

4.21   *Ibid.*, the Redditch rate was 1.5 per cent; Kidderminster 1.1 per cent; London 1.2 per cent; Coventry 2.7 per cent. There were ten exchanges listed with rates of under 1 per cent, eight being in the South-East and two in the East Midlands.

4.22   Margaret Roberts, 'Economic structure and employment: planning techniques 5-7', *Official Architecture and Planning*, November, 1970, pp.1003-1004 and 1007-1008; January 1971, pp.51, 53-54; March, 1971 pp. 212-215.

4.23   Basic industries were explained by Barlow, *op.cit.*, p. 28.

4.24   G.C. Cameron, 'Economic analysis for a declining urban economy (Scotland)', *Scottish Journal of Political Economy*, No.3, November, 1971, pp.315 *et seq.*

4.25   West Midlands Economic Planning Council, *The West Midlands: An Economic Appraisal*, Department of the Environment, HMSO, 1971.

4.26   Barbara M.D. Smith, *Employment Opportunities in the Lichfield Area of South Staffordshire*, Centre for Urban and Regional Studies, Research Memorandum No. 29, 1974, and Technical Appendices.

4.27   Ministry of Housing and Local Government, *Technical Memorandum No. 2: The Use of Land for Industry*, HMSO, 1955; Barrie Needham, 'The density of industrial estates', *Journal of the Town Planning Institute*, 53, December, 1967, pp.455-456; Greater London Council, *Greater London Development Plan: Report of Studies*, (no date), pp. 60-70. The Layfield Inquiry also discussed this, *op.cit.*

4.28   Bolton Committee of Inquiry on Small Firms, Cmnd. 4811, *Report*, HMSO, 1971.

4.29   M. Beesley, 'The birth and death of establishments', *Journal of Industrial Economics*, IV, 1955; G.C. Cameron, 'Intra Urban Location and New Plant', Discussion Paper No. 5, Urban and Regional Studies, University of Glasgow, 1972.

4.30   *Birmingham Abstract of Statistics*, 1969-70 and other issues; Edwin Hammond, *An Analysis of Regional Economic and Social Statistics*, University of Durham Rowntree Research Unit, Tables 2.5.2-3.

4.31   E.T. Penrose, *The Theory of the Growth of the Firm*, Oxford, 1959.

Further reading

Barlow Commission on the Distribution of the Industrial Population, Cmnd. 6153, 1940.

A.J. Brown, *The Framework of Regional Economics in the United Kingdom*, N.I.E.S.R., Cambridge University Press, 1972.

G.C. Cameron and A.W. Evans, 'The British Conurbation Centres', *Regional Studies*, March, 1973, pp. 47-55.

J.B. Cullingworth, *Problems of an Urban Society: Urban and Regional Studies No. 6*, Allen and Unwin, 3 Vols., 1973, especially Chapter 2 in Volume 1.

David Donnison and David Eversley (eds.) *London: Urban Patterns, Problems and Policies*, Heinemann, London, 1973.

D.E.C. Eversley, 'Rising costs and static incomes: some economic consequences of regional planning in London', *Urban Studies*, October, 1972, pp. 347-368.

A. Goss, *British Industry and Town Planning*, Fountain Press, 1962.

Peter Hall, *The Theory and Practice of Regional Planning*, Pemberton Books, 1970.

Report of the Hunt Committee on Intermediate Areas, Cmnd. 3998, 1969.

Jane Jacobs, *The Economy of Cities*, Jonathan Cape, 1970.,

Gordon Logie, *Industry in Towns*, Allen and Unwin, 1952.

Gavin McCrone, *Regional Policy in Britain*, University of Glasgow Social and Economic Studies, Allen and Unwin, 1969.

R.C. Riley, *Industrial Geography*, Chatto and Windus, 1973.

Barbara M.D. Smith, *The Administration of Industrial Overspill: The Institutional Framework Relevant to Industrial Overspill in the West Midlands*, Centre for Urban and Regional Studies, Occasional Paper No. 22, 1972.

P.M. Townroe, *Industrial Location Decisions: A Study in Management Behaviour*, Centre for Urban and Regional Studies, Occasional Paper No. 15, 1971.

5 The Search for Environment

Introduction

The problems of the man-made environment are diagnosed in different ways, depending on our perception of the urban physical world which we have created. Those who have protested at the grime and despoliation of an environment, looted in the search for natural resources and wealth, have often joined forces with those who have criticised the effects of rapid urbanisation expressed in the physical and social realities of our industrial cities. The physical *effects* are tangible and immediate; they are readily appreciated by the proverbial man in the street.

The diagnosis of *causes* – why the environment is like it is and the way in which it is changing – has been a relatively neglected field of study, with the result that problems of the physical environment have been tackled in a piecemeal and fragmented fashion. Once diagnosis of causes leads to the view that the physical *results* of our activities are fashioned by our social and economic system and its predominant values, we can begin to fashion more effective *policies* to remedy perceived ills.

Such policies would embrace forms of action, guidance, regulation and control that consciously and explicitly utilised *non-physical* measures on a scale much greater than hitherto. We would be practising a form of environmental 'preventative medicine' and we would progressively seek to treat the causes rather than the symptoms of the disease.

We might categorise such activity as future-orientated, anticipatory, comprehensive in its substantive concerns, and by definition innovatory. This would be planning activity, ideally comprehensive and qualitatively very different to the realities of contemporary practice. We would use scientific techniques and rational methods to deal with perceived problems. Activity would be justified for both scientific and normative reasons.

If C.P. Snow highlighted the 'Two Cultures' in our society by referring to the humanists on the one hand, and the natural scientists on the other, there is another comparison that may usefully be made in relation to the origins of urban design and town planning; namely between the verbal and social, and the visual and individual. These two parallel traditions may be identified in the literature of ideas about 'planning' which invariably were formulated in utopian terms.

Our perception of the physical environment has not only eschewed the need to diagnose *causes* in order to devise *means*, it has been conditioned by a cultural tradition which has generally clung to utopian concepts, and more particularly has been midwife to the birth of a 'physicalism' in relation to desirable ways of living in society. The expression of such ideas has been archaic, necessarily culture bound and time specific, and like all designed artefacts, detailed and finite. Design has been a response to perceived *effects* and has not yet begun to respond to causes. It has chased the shadow not the substance, the form and not the essence.

In so far as we have categorised our perceived environmental problems, we have recognised the need to safeguard amenity, conserve and make the best use of land, and protect the countryside; special concern has been directed towards the physical environment and the retention of buildings of architectural and historic interest. A body of law, enshrined in administrative practice and institutions, rationales for spatial and physical planning, emerged from practice by trial and error.

As new needs, and components of environmental degradation, have been perceived, society has reacted in disjointed fashion, taken initiatives with respect to resources such as wood, water or minerals, and latterly to the negative effects of increased motorisation and noise generally. Society's response has been fragmented and incremental. The architect and town planner has tended to be a hostage to the past and a prisoner of social, economic and political forces. Today there are some hopeful signs that this is changing. We have to ask whether this passive relationship between professional and society, archaic ways of thinking, and love affair with the past, should continue in the future. The context for planning and planning itself is changing. We need to explore what we mean when we talk about environment and try and understand its various interacting strands. Are we in fact taking actions that are appropriate to the real problems? How can we view and improve design skills? What constitutes environmental quality? These are some of the underlying questions discussed in this chapter.

We need *historical perspectives* in order to understand why 'planning' has been linked with, and was initially indistinguishable from, urban design, the appearances of things and transient aesthetic preoccupations. The poverty of historicism and the irrelevancy of much that has passed for urban design in the face of rapid change requires more systematic and integrated approaches to design processes. A new *framework of forms*, ways of restructuring and adapting our physical and social environment over time are needed. Institutional complexity and procedural difficulties, especially with regard to *land ownership and land assembly*, are related to the wider problems of *environmental quality, standards and objectives*. The environmental effects of traffic and movement in a pluralistic society require *new directions and horizons*. In the sections which follow these ideas are explored in more detail.

Historical perspectives

" . . . Things fall apart; the centre cannot hold;
Mere anarchy is loosed upon the world,
The blood-dimmed tide is loosed, and everywhere
The ceremony of innocence is drowned;
The best lack all conviction, while the worse
Are full of passionate intensity."

W.B. Yeats *(The Second Coming)*

Without a sense of history, an appreciation of the rival ideologies which move men in diverse directions, and an appreciation of culture, how can we make sense of our world? It is a paradox of some importance that an historical perspective is required to reject ways of looking at the contemporary world that are themselves archaic (5.1).

In 1945 the mushroom cloud heralded the arrival of a very different world to anything we had known before the Second World War. At every level of life and living, things were different, very different to what they had been. We believed that they would be, and wanted them to be, very different in the future.

After the holocaust came a renewed vision of our ideal future. Traditional ideas were modified, but the progress of mankind and the nature of his social existence, the cities and regions he would inhabit, were envisioned, fashioned in the image of the past. In politics, science, technology and art, in the sphere of town planning, there were indications, intimations of profound change, but our world view hardly reached out to the future, hardly embraced a vision of the seventies that was remotely like we know the seventies to be.

The peoples of Europe emerged from the shadows and looked around at what was left of their great cities. The First War had destroyed the illusions of a generation and Robert Graves could write "Goodbye to all that", and yet new blueprints for the future were being prepared by victors and vanquished in the second. Coventry, the Phoenix city was to arise from the ashes, Rotterdam and Warsaw were rebuilt. A new city, one of hundreds, was to emerge out of the destruction of Stalingrad. Out of the rubble that was Germany in 1945 new cities have arisen.

It was one thing to theorise about the nature of the social structure of a society which would allow the city organisation to give the fullest expression to life processes and the technology on which these processes depend, quite another to confront the practicalities and realities of contemporary life.

In the event, many of the new ideas and projects were watered down geometric fragments of Howard's social city, collectivised versions of the colonial settler town and suburban rationalisations of a garden city tradition. Whilst somewhat different visual and architectural statements were made by men as different as Le Corbusier or Frank Lloyd Wright, for the most part they remained unrealised utopian dreams, trapped within physical and ideological parameters, overtaken by the turbulence and tide of events.

It was not simply the crisis of imperialism and empire, or the revolution in physics, anticipated and mirrored in the arrival of cubism and much later kinetic art, it was a more comprehensive phenomenon of ever accelerating change accompanied by a transformation in our understanding of the world and its processes, so complete that the transition from the mediaeval world to the Renaissance world pales by comparison.

Out of the despair of the thirties and the Second War, the paralysis of will of the middle classes, and the loss of confidence in the future, came a revival of belief in the ideas of the Enlightenment. The advanced industrial nations experienced a dramatic increase in material prosperity. The conflict and strife, the economic and social instability of the thirties appeared to be a thing of the past.

The belief that we could plan and manage our society in accordance with ideals and principles derived from our own national ways of life gained ground. At the heart of this belief in progress lay the promise of the second scientific revolution, rapid scientific advances, economic growth and developments, a new world fashioned by technology, itself the dynamo of change.

In the event, the undoubted technological successes of the last quarter of a century, the results of close linkages between theoretical science and applied technology, has brought new problems. We have become obliged to concentrate on trying to understand the process of *social* change in order to manage and guide it more effectively and thereby avoid certain dangers and encourage developments that will resolve some of mankind's greatest problems.

If progress means the abolition of poverty and want, the check on diseases, and general mastery over man's environment, then an understanding of complex social organisation, and particularly large scale manufacturing, transport, research and development units is essential. Social science and social technology may together make their contributions to social progress however society defines that progress. At the present time the proposition that unlimited economic growth may be equated with progress is under fire from many quarters.

It now seems very probable that the idea of unlimited economic growth and

URBAN PROBLEMS—
Birmingham

One of the most imaginative and successful schemes to upgrade the environment and rescue the nineteenth century canal system from dereliction and dirt is the rehabilitation of Gas Street Basin and the renewal of the canal side sites in the civic centre of Birmingham.

The James Brindley Walk scheme (Cambrian Basin).

The same view before improvement and rebuilding.

(Photographs reproduced by kind permission of the City Architect, Birmingham).

Manchester

Of Manchester's comprehensive planning proposals, those for the civic area have aroused the most interest.

Aerial perspective of Civic Area, Manchester. Much of the area has been redeveloped. The advisory scheme, one of five prepared for most of the city's core, provides a three dimensional framework based on uses and accommodation requirements. Proposals are intended to serve as a brief to developers and as a basis for detailed design work. Inset diagram entitled: 'Comprehensive Planning Proposals'.

(*Reproduced by permission of City Planning Officer, Manchester, from City Centre Map Report*, **1967**).

Manchester

Of Manchester's comprehensive planning proposals, those for the civic area have aroused the most interest.

The famous Rylands Library has been given a new setting flanking the pedestrian way through the heart of the civic area to the Education Offices and Magistrates' Court beyond.
(*Reproduced by courtesy of Architects, Messrs. Leach, Rhodes and Walker*).
Magistrates' Court, Crown Square, Manchester.
Architects: Yorke, Rosenburg and Mardall in Association with S. G. Besant Roberts (City Architect). Acknowledgement: Brecht-Einzig Ltd.

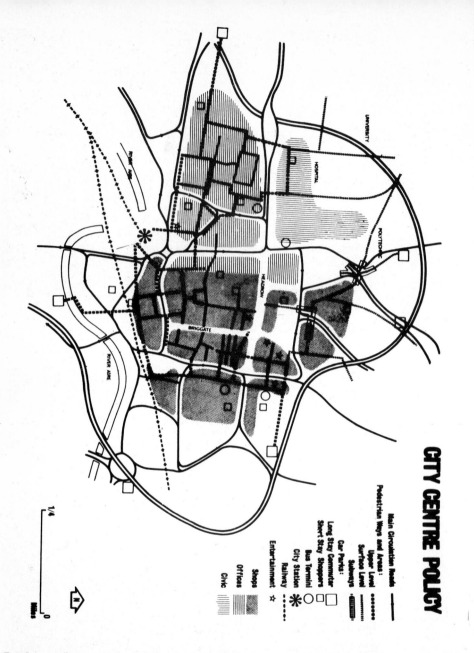

CITY CENTRE POLICY

Main Circulation Roads
Pedestrian Ways and Areas:
  Upper Level
  Surface Level
  Subways
Car Parks:
  Long Stay Commuter
  Short Stay Shoppers
  Bus Termini
  City Station
  Railway
Entertainment
Civic
Offices
Shops

Leeds

Leeds central shopping area reflects the city's integrated approach to circulation of vehicles and cars. Great emphasis is placed on the need to upgrade the physical environment and to improve public transport especially in relation to shopping and journey to work.

City centre policy diagram.

The County arcade — a **19th** century thoroughfare adapted to a new system of **pedestrian** movement in the central shopping area.

The central shopping area has been transformed by the introduction of foot streets and integrated environmental management measures. Buildings have been cleaned and spaces have been adapted to new activity patterns with attractive planting and well designed street **furniture.**

(Photographs and diagram reproduced by courtesy of the Director of Planning, Leeds Metropolitan District Council).

Newcastle-upon-Tyne
  Bank House, All Saints Complex.
  Grainger Street. Stone cleaning has transformed many older streets, but this does not remove the traffic and pollution.
(Photographs reproduced by permission of City and County of Newcastle-upon-Tyne).

The museum and art gallery once separated from the pedestrian promenade by ugly walls, overgrown hedges and unsightly benches, has now been given a much needed face lift.

Photographs reproduced by permission of the City Planning Officer).

Leicester
The New Walk area of Leicester has been attractively restored.
The Oval, with its attractive Victorian railings, provides an example of what may be achieved by judicious conservation and improvement.

development is an illusion. New problems consequent upon continued and rapid economic growth may not be equated with past experience. It is just not proven to assert that the U.K. or even the U.S. has the technical capability *at this time* to resolve them without serious losses in material welfare.

Whether we adopt an anthropomorphic view, and see history as progress or not, we can accept perhaps that man's social development, the level of technology, the economic and political organisation of society has shaped both the cities of man and man himself; a process of adaptation and innovation in the face of ecological pressures, changes in climate, population growth and scarcity of resources. The history of man may be interpreted as the invention of alternative technologies to solve pressing problems; it may also be viewed as the invention of culture, ritual and symbol as aids to the process of adaptation and change.

Early town builders and designers responded to fairly simple imperatives such as the need for defence. The range of building types was limited and the craft skills required were broadly predictable. Views about the nature of the world — rival cosmologies — were related to the design systems and shaped the aesthetic principles which guided building design processes. Over long periods of time, the structure of the town, the spatial distribution and relative accessibility of its parts, reflected the social structure.

But any framework for understanding change processes must go beyond the implied economic and technological determinism which characterises pre-industrial towns on one side of a balance sheet as static and all industrial towns on the other as dynamic (5.2). The processes of urban change differ from culture to culture, and over time. There are fundamentally different forces at work. The processes are producing different results in different world regions transcending any superficial similarities (5.3).

If the comprehensibility and imageability, even the continued existence, of the city is increasingly called into question, the inherited formal rules of town design become increasingly irrelevant in meeting the practical social and economic needs of societies that have called a new world into being. It is not simply a case of technological misfit, it is an even more deep-seated cultural incompatibility. It seems that there are no positive theories of urban design to be had for the asking or indeed for the researching. Theories which try to explain social change are likely to possess much more utility for planner and designer alike.

Indeed, it was the ideas of social reformers, philanthropists, men of action and the practical administrators of the 19th and 20th centuries who brought into being and then managed a system of government concerned, *inter alia* with health, sanitation, fresh air, sunlight and building. These self-same practical men attempted to create more humane urban environments in ways which have met with only limited success, because such theoretical insight that was brought to bear on the urban condition was derived from a culture that had passed into historical limbo, and was compromised from the outset by its social and political ambivalence. The apparent virtues and efficiency of the market place coupled with the primary objective of securing individual freedom of choice, took priority in the allocation of scarce resources and the good things of life. Intervention in urban processes was conditioned and limited by powerful social, political and economic constraints.

Whereas in the future more comprehensive planning may be a pre-requisite not only for the good life, but human survival, it has been generally viewed as little more than a peripheral activity correcting here and modifying there, the imperfections and blemishes of a market economy.

Urban planning has its roots in radical liberalism. The regeneration of town and country, the rebirth of region, were causes expounded with great conviction and fervour by Ebenezer Howard, Patrick Geddes and many others. Men such as Henry George began to study the problems consequent upon private land ownership. The image of the good life was the folksy mediaeval village or in the States the pastoralism of the early settler communities. Notions about economic planning as expounded by socialists such as G.D.H. Cole, Shaw and the Fabians, neo-Marxist ideas with regard to centralist planning and fundamental political change, all arrived on the scene later. If the origins and strands which have produced town and country planning have been reasonably well documented, there remains the need for an authoritative account of the genesis of complementary ideas about economic and social planning. Whilst the U.S. experience favoured limited controls on *laissez faire* suburban development, Howard's social city was a potential tool for social and regional regeneration. It was to be accompanied by public enterprise and public ownership of land. Its ideological imperatives assumed a collective responsibility for land. He was the one idealogue whose objectives could have been written as a manifesto for social and political action.

In the United States, the Whites (5.4) have fully documented the strong anti-urban tradition. The defenders of the city have had greater difficulty in the U.S. than in Europe. The scale of the European cities is different, whilst the historical dimension is much more in evidence – visually, spatially, architecturally in our memories and our feelings. Rural-urban conflict may still exist, but the reorganisation of local government, the planned containment of urban growth together with its guidance to particular locations, are just a few of the important differences between the U.S. and the U.K.

Nevertheless, the concern for civic design and the existence of a vigorous domestic vernacular building tradition deserves noting. The types of landscape preferred, preserved and reproduced by the English – the picaresque, the deciduous, the tidiness and antiquarianism – are regarded by them as uniquely English (5.5). As Britain faces its worst domestic crisis since the end of the

Second World War, Kingsley Amis' comment that "What is characteristically British is superannuated", assumes even greater point and poignancy (5.6). The genius of the place, the character of a site, its geography and history is all important. The passion for conservation is often predominantly non-aesthetic. There is a nostalgic but firm commitment to the old, the tried, the worn, and at times the ugly (5.7).

* * * *

Piaget has pointed out that:

"To know an object, to know an event, is not simply to look at it and make a mental copy, or image, of it. To know an object is to act on it. To know is to modify, to transform the object, and to understand the process of this transformation, and as a consequence to understand the way the object is constructed. An operation is thus the essence of knowledge, it is an interiorised action which modifies the object of knowledge" (5.8).

The quality or otherwise of our environment may well go relatively *unperceived* by a large proportion of the population. Part of the explanation lies in the visual impoverishment which is a built-in part of working class life (5.9). The inability of many of those who live in the inner city to perceive the particulars of their own environment should not come as too much of a surprise. We have all, in differing degrees, become desensitised and unseeing. It needs an environmental scientist or an artist of the stature of Dickens or Lowry to reveal the many sided nature of the environments we have created. It is not true that all white men look the same or that when you have seen one slum, you have seen them all. It is not always easy to perceive the environment of others and thus the image is characteristically dehumanised; buildings, categories of buildings, spaces unconnected or related to human beings, provide the basis of a generalised description. If one's chance in life largely depends on where one is born — then our environmental perception is largely conditioned by that environment. *In short, we need to recognise that the search for environment has a visual dimension which is also social.*

Do designers fulfil social needs, and how far should they be expected to do so? What is the theoretical basis for urban design?

It would be true to say that there is no 'body of theory'. What we do have is an ill-defined field of concern without too much theoretical under-pinning. Visual fashions are the rule rather than the exception and a simplistic social theory labelled 'architectural determinism' has tended to dominate the outlook of the design professions.

Much of the work on design methods and design processes has been made available only in the last decade or so and the substantial work that has been carried out on man—environment relations is scattered through many disciplines and is usually of little direct relevance to the designer.

We may distinguish three characteristic features in the evolution of urban design practice and in the ideas which have been held about that work.

(i)   The almost uniquely normative emphasis
(ii) The self-centred view of the designer
(iii) The absence of scientific method in the analysis, synthesis and evaluation of design problems and solutions.

The spirit which has moved town planning is born of the Renaissance, which with its passion for formality and regularity influenced all subsequent developments in Europe and America (5.10). The notion of the city as a work of art and the search for the ideal city in design terms is well documented (5.11). The predominant philosophy or aesthetic system held that the nature of the modern city was such that like a building structure, its design could be controlled by reference to a set of formal rules. This view has been shown to be erroneous for both the modern city *and* modern building. This traditional approach has led to a preoccupation with pattern making and formal exercises, to fabulous and frivolous architecture and the sterility of grand designs for cities such as Brazilia or Chandigarh.

The great designer-architect is as much a Renaissance concept as the grand design itself. The divorce between scientific engineer and gentleman architect was well-nigh complete by the year of the Great Exhibition in 1851. Paxton's Crystal Palace is a symbol of a new world and a new relationship between designer and society. As Bernal observed (5.12),

"It was from this period that the split between the humanists and scientists, which is such a feature of our own day, first became serious. Its immediate effect was to prevent the co-operation between the two branches of intellectuals without which no constructive criticism of the economic and social system was possible. The humanists never knew enough of how it worked to have other than ineffective emotions about it; the scientists were blunted by a quite deliberate turning from everything — art, beauty or social justice — that did not come within the purview of their, by then, highly specialised work."

The historical role of architecture and urban design does not reveal any marked positive social response to the social essence of industrialisation; its dehumanizing effects are neither articulated in *architectural* form, nor has there been any commitment or great degree of success in practice to *restructure* (as opposed to redevelopment) the industrial towns of Britain in accordance with explicit social objectives. By and large, architects, and this includes their employers, had other tasks. If and when they dreamed, it was to interpret ideal communities. Occasionally it was possible, as in the case of Raymond Unwin and Edward Lutyens, to produce designs which were watered down versions for the prosperous middle class; a Hampstead Garden Suburb or a Bedford Park.

Generally, architecture and urban design has only attempted to confront some of the environmental problems created by industrialism and the factory system in the period since the late thirties. There has been a significant development of public housing schemes, which with the exception of the New Towns, has been largely on an *ad hoc* basis, subject to and hedged around with all manner of political, economic and social constraints.

There are two consequences of the legacy of urban design:

(i) An undue reliance in practice on outdated rules of architectural design of a purely formal kind, the corollary of which was that such design would necessarily be socially beneficial.

(ii) Failure to recognise the complexity of the design process itself or the object of that process. This is equally true for a building structure or a new town.

In both cases, little attempt has been made to identify and analyse the nature of the problems to which a design synthesis should respond. Oversimplifying, we can say that scientific method was not the rule, but the exception. Art was substituted for life:

" . . . The modern designer relies more and more on his position as 'artist', on catchwords, personal idiom and intuition − for all these relieve him of the burden of decision and make his cognitive problems manageable. Driven on his own resources, unable to cope with the complicated information, he is supposed to organise, he hides his incompetence in a frenzy of artistic individuality. As his capacity to invent clearly-conceived, well-fitting forms is exhausted further, the emphasis on intuition and individuality only grows wilder." (5.13)

The legacy which we have inherited has undervalued the need:

(i)   to analyse and define satisfactorily the social needs to be met
(ii) to adopt techniques or strategies to assist designers
(iii) to distinguish between intrinsic design problems within the physical environment and the ongoing processes of planning (5.14).

A framework of forms

Christopher Alexander has described the design process as finding the right physical components of a physical structure (5.15), whilst a definition proposed by Mohr (5.16) suggests that design is the geometric realisation of concepts in response to a unique problem environment with the intention to achieve form.

Both these definitions suggest a view that goes beyond the traditional view that urban design is concerned with the relationship of buildings to spaces, producing an interesting townscape effect and peculiar to the local area (5.17). It has been suggested, with some justification, that a broader view would be concerned not only with visual criteria, but also with the comprehension and design of all activities considered urban and not exclusively with buildings and their physical linkages (5.18).

Perhaps the former view describes current practice and procedures whilst the latter posits the desirable. Certainly, complex structures such as transportation interchanges, airports or industrial plants, not to mention major shopping centres require the second approach if the design operation is to be remotely successful in practice. Empirical evidence would tend to support this view.

We need to adopt exploratory attitudes in solving current problems while supporting further research. As our environmental problems change so must our approaches to problem definition and resolution change too. It is worth reminding ourselves of Popper's advocacy of 'piecemeal social engineering' (5.19).

"The piecemeal engineer, like Socrates, knows how little he knows. He knows that we can only learn from our mistakes. Accordingly, he will make his way, step by step, carefully comparing the results expected with the results achieved and always on the look-out for the unavoidable, unwanted consequences of any reform; and he will avoid undertaking reforms of a complexity and scope which make it impossible for him to disentangle causes and effects, and to know what he is really doing."

One need not be an out and out empiricist to recognise the need for caution and a little scientific scepticism before moving to designs or plans that could have serious implications for people. We are far from satisfying social needs in much of our man-made environment. Designing for people increasingly means designing with them, otherwise we know not what we do. With the contemporary emphasis on social process, the paths and criteria for designers have begun to diverge.

In the modern metropolis multifocality must be an organising principle for structuring forms and ordering spaces in response to human needs. We are dealing with "motion, flux, changing relationships, growth, physical and psychological time . . ." (5.20). The concept of overlapping realms, if not replacing place, physical space and physical objects, at least adds another dimension to an understanding of the formal attributes of an urban region conceived as a structured process. The additional dimension must comprehend more effectively than hitherto both social structure and social process. The implications of this view are that what is needed for physical planning and design is an analysis of those human needs which are relevant to its subject matter.

We need a framework of forms which would translate needs into physical reality (5.21). Such a framework is the province of the design fields; it includes architecture, but comprehends many other professionals in the landscaping, physical planning and industrial design areas. In the context of the physical planning and environmental design field we are concerned primarily, if not exclusively with capital goods, i.e. the construction of durables. The framework of forms is concerned with the physical configuration and relations of what is being accumulated and managed. But without an understanding of the needs to which this panoply of forms is called upon to respond, it is impossible to formulate the objectives of the planning or design operation. This is precisely the deficiency which has been recognised in many recent plans and is the basic weakness in many a design scheme.

As Alexander has suggested, the city is not tree-like and the problems of synthesis are not analogous to a hierarchical tree-like structure, but rather to a lattice or network of interacting relationships. The historical legacy of architectural design, and the emergence of physical land use planning in its institutionalised form, prior to other generic forms of planning has tended to elevate the importance of technical, functional or visual attributes. The work of the constructivists revealed a love affair with technics that was sterile. It was a small step from constructivism and futurism to authoritarianism. The functionalism and formalism of Le Corbusier emphasised the importance of plan forms, whilst still in thrall to the new machine age, or as Rayner Banham has put it, the *first* machine age. Today, much so-called design is concerned almost exclusively with outward appearance, relying heavily on historical forms and formal principles of composition. We have to admit that little progress has been made in establishing efficiency criteria and no visual theoretical framework exists.

In the research literature concerned with man/environment relations, in the contribution of theoretical and practical scientists, physicists, and psychologists, there are hopeful signs. Increasingly, they are making a contribution to environmental design, and the solution of some environmental problems. The needs of people become the focus of study and behavioural response assumes great importance. Environmental planning and design is becoming a focus for interdisciplinary study and looks like providing a common framework for the solution of many physical environmental problems.

Any theoretical framework concerned with the physical environment has to take into account the relevance of both *unitary* and *adaptive* approaches. The physical environment is structured and adapted by man over long periods of time. For example, the rate of structural change in a city region is normally many times slower than the adaptive processes of its component parts. As Foley has explained in a seminal paper of great importance (5.22), the adaptive approach seeks to influence various aspects of the development forces at work and is less concerned for future metropolitan form as an *aim*. The unitary approach aims to create a future product, a physical environment for the city. The adaptive view concentrates on processes, recognises that the political economy of a city region is an allocative and decision making mechanism. *It is the processual context within which unitary or developmental activity takes place*. In this sense, the adaptive approach does not necessarily view the creation of a better physical environment as *the* major goal.

Moreover, it is not just a matter of scale. Goals for a relatively small community or neighbourhood may embrace many factors; desiderata relating to social life, to the economy, and wider environment; qualities that the urban designer has traditionally ignored or considered relatively unimportant.

If there appears to be tension between the unitary and adaptive approaches, it is because each tends to reflect different scales of activity, human skills, attitudes and values. The unitary approach was intrinsic to architectural design and development planning at local scale. The approach has been manifestly unsuccessful at city or regional scale. The British New Towns designers adopted a unitary approach initially. The newly created structures are now having to be adapted and in some cases extended to meet some unanticipated requirements.

"In a design sense, the unitary approach inevitably relies heavily on intuition and represents a synthesis . . . a predetermination to see things whole and to create a whole design. It reflects, too, a willingness to treat communities and planning units as independent, separate units" (5.23).

This is a non-systemic view perhaps. But what *form* of design is necessary for a new planning unit in a new town? What is the appropriate approach with respect to areas of old towns? In practice, products are created or emerge from both unitary and adaptive approaches. Perhaps we may conclude that adaptive approaches to large, highly complex dynamic structures like regions and cities are necessary, whilst unitary approaches must of necessity be partially adopted towards the design and implementation of physical components like buildings and elements of infrastructure. The extent to which we understand urban change processes, may perhaps influence the extent to which in practice we adopt a unitary or adaptive approach to the design of urban components; such wider knowledge must inform the brief to the designer and his response in terms of the artefact produced.

Structuring as an adaptive mechanism

Urban design then is more than architecture. It has to do with underlying concepts of the purposes of the city and concepts of visual order. Without such concepts the act of design is impossible.

If urban design has something to say in respect of the form and structure of cities, what that something is cannot easily be stated. Kevin Lynch (5.24) and others have analysed the critical aspects of urban form and contributed theoretical insights that the designer may find valuable, if the nature of his work is clearly specified. There are a variety of basic structures or design shapes, each with their advantages and disadvantages. But these prototypes are not readily applicable to the great urban regions of Britain or North America, though grid concepts or linear concepts may be extremely valuable in approaching the design of entirely new cities, towns or extensions to towns.

It is true that the future form of the polynuclear urban region has attracted considerable attention, but it is certainly arguable whether preconceived *design* forms are as critically important as more non-spatial considerations such as the nature and mix of policies related to the movement of people and goods (5.25). If we regard patterns and shapes as suggestive and no more, so far as the urban planning context is concerned, we will probably be on firmer ground. In this sense, as Lynch suggests, we do not seek *the* design; the form and structure emerges from a correct diagnosis of the problems to be solved and the identification of the physical and spatial components.

The search for macro-form or macro-design is to be seen in many urban physical plans. The Washington D.C. Plan for the year 2000 is just one example. But as if to underline the point, Washington's planners are finding it difficult to introduce internal order to the directional line of growth or to restrain the growth in the intervening open areas. The developing pattern is a reflection of economic and social forces where the powers of planning control at Federal, State or local level are not very great.

Even where planning powers are greater, in the U.K., Denmark or France, it is difficult to describe the form giving exercises in respect of urban growth and population movement as a design process, however much such exercises are necessary and innovatory. The difficulty is to know whether such spatial form plans are the product of close analysis of what is regarded as the best spatial and locational settlement, or whether they are simply rationalising past trends, taking the easy way of bowing to the inevitable in the absence of vigorous controls (5.26).

The most coherent attempts at form giving are to be found in Professor Colin Buchanan's three volume study of Southampton and Portsmouth, in which the idea of the *directional grid* would allow for progressive development, within a spatial frame composed of a hierarchy of routeways to meet the requirements of a population of 1¾ million by 2000 A.D. (5.27).

The most significant fact about the public housing effort in the 25 years after the end of the Second World War is that only 4 per cent went into the new towns and expanded towns programme (5.28). Contrary to popular belief the contribution of new towns has been relatively small. The norm has been peripheral development and massive suburbanisation. We have pursued social and economic policies which, whether we realised it or not, encouraged high rise, high density public housing schemes in London, Birmingham, Glasgow and other cities.

Directional macro-form giving exercises suggest advantages in respect of housing and employment, providing an economic base for manufacturing and service industries that are now located in the congested inner areas of cities. The evidence points to this approach being economical (5.29). Theoretical studies of the Mersey Valley in North West England, linking Liverpool and Manchester, have demonstrated the attractiveness of such a directional approach (5.30).

If form giving is part of an *instrumental* planning process at the macro-scale, can much the same be said at the micro or local scale? The answer is probably a qualified yes (5.31). But environmental planning is certainly not large scale architecture, though it may comprehend the need for groups of structures to be designed comprehensively and, therefore, require design skills. Designers are not always appropriately skilled to deal with urban problems at the local, any more than the macro-scale, though their skills may well be valuable in inter-disciplinary work teams tackling complex problems. Civic problems are not simply design problems. If this were the case, our cities would soon appoint our best architects as Chief Executives. In Jane Jacobs' words, urban design is not an occupation for 'taxidermists'. We should avoid attempting to substitute art for life; cities and neighbourhoods are not architectural problems, and hence are not capable of being given order by transforming them into disciplined works of art (5.32).

If social scientists have been quick to seize upon Jane Jacobs' powerful polemic and to use it to criticise architectural megolomania, giantism, formalism and the rest, they have not all been able to share her passion for the streetwalks of yesterday's New York. To embrace such a nostalgic and folksy view of the pattern of yesterday is in essence much more than an argument against a technocratic and dehumanised high rise modern architecture, it is a rejection of all forward looking attempts to plan, to manage and guide, to learn how better to live in society (5.33).

Lewis Mumford writes, "Nobody can be satisfied with the form of the City today. Neither as a working mechanism, as a social mechanism, nor as a work of art . . ." (5.34). He suggests that the time has come to reconsider the whole process of urban design; the professionals must consciously re-orientate themselves as part of a wider transformation; a new utopia must replace the discredited. If the diagnosis is persuasive his solutions are not. Mumford mourns the passing of the mediaeval world, its diminutive scale and traditions are viewed through as romantic a pair of pre-raphaelite spectacles as were ever worn by Dante Gabriel Rosetti.

He argues that sanitation, hygiene and communications had little effect on the visible city. The great mass of metropolitan buildings since the 19th century has been disorganised and formless. Urban progress is still identified with high buildings, wide avenues, long vistas; the higher, the wider, the longer, the better. Current suggestions for urban improvement still tend to fall into a purely mechanical mould; formless urbanisation has become well-nigh universal. The The individual identity of urban forms has disappeared and "therewith one of the main functions of architecture to symbolise and express the social idea" (5.35).

It is evident that architectural or urban design at the scale of the *community* needs reorientation. Governance needs to be considered at an early stage. Even at the micro-scale, rather than a master plan we need a more adaptive and responsive planning process that evolves with the community — designing, building and planning further.

The improvement in environmental design skills should make it possible for development to be guided to the most suitable location and designed according to performance criteria that recognised human as well as purely technical and economic needs. Such a style of operations would be conducted in terms of probabilities; contingency planning would be the *modus operandi* in respect of deciding alternative courses of action.

Unit or cellular growth concepts should be given greater attention by researchers and designers alike. The directional grid of Buchanan and the units comprising the diagram plan for Milton Keynes (5.36) are examples of design components which could be subject to major redesign prior to construction if the need arose. There are also possibilities in devising framework plans, the stages of which would be implemented over time in such a way that at each discrete stage more than one possible direction could be taken. *Such inbuilt strategic as well as tactical flexibility is becoming essential.*

Research findings point to the need for adaptability and open ended solutions capable of accommodating new functions at low economic or social cost. In this sense, Raymond Unwin's famous slogan 'Nothing gained through overcrowding' retains its relevance. Building at low densities leaves room for growth, change and adaptability; room for an additional traffic lane, or an additional bedroom. Architects have dubbed this approach as far as buildings are concerned as long life — loose fit architecture.

We guage the health of the economy through a set of 'economic' indicators, but we have no set of comparable 'social' indicators. There are few measures of the 'quality of life' and increasingly the utilitarianism of much economic thinking is being challenged even by some economists. Mishan argues that unless we can wrench ourselves free of today's dominant ideology in which the quality of life is but a by-product of the momenta set up by technological growth and business expansion, our civilisation will begin to fall apart before the year 2000 (5.37).

Disenchantment with a bright new technological future is widespread. Victor Gruen speaks for many architects and planners in suggesting that technology will subvert the search for an environment conducive to man *if we leave it to develop along its present course* (5.38). The condition of our cities, which expresses itself in different ways from near insurrection and riot in Northern Ireland to ghetto in Notting Hill, from pollution of air, water and land to the deterioration of the public environment in large areas of central and inner London, should be the point of departure for all thought on the future. Attention is increasingly being given to the next 5 to 10 years, as well as the year 2000 and beyond.

Our discussion on design and development, the shortcomings of our urban condition, should be capable of being assessed, if not measured, against the need for well founded criticism, positive and imaginative proposals aimed at shaping a better future environment. It follows that a coherent approach to design and development requires an equally coherent and consistent social context and social philosophy.

In this sense, many of the futuristic ideas which have emanated from architectural utopians have been not merely impracticable, but objectively disastrous to the cause of social reform and an architecture truly humanistic.

The immediate and longer term task of physical reconstruction demands a national effort greater than hitherto. Social priorities may change. It may be that the focus of activity will increasingly be in the inner areas of our cities. If this proves to be the case, it will require the reallocation and concentration of vast resources. We should be prepared to reverse or modify trends – this is the quintessence of planning. Development planning is one of the more important instruments necessary to solve existing problems and to achieve social goals.

The evolution of physical planning in Britain has been in practice part of the evolution of public housing policies. It has been most successful when it served as an instrument of social policy and change; when it assisted in re-allocating resources to deprived groups or regions and renewed its links with political reform movements. It could be said that effective environmental design, of which building design is an integral component, requires a public planning system which attempts a more positive restructuring of town and region and applies adaptive mechanisms at various scales of operations related to the institutional hierarchy of plan/policy making and urban governance.

Land ownership and methods of land assembly

Land is the most important resource for the environmental planner. In classical economic terms, it is not produced; it is fixed in amount; its price is fixed purely by demand, and it is limited specifically by its location in space. Every parcel of land is unique. The most enlightened of plans cannot be realised without land. The availability of sufficient land supply to meet demand is necessary if its value is not to escalate. Planning does not of itself create new values, it redistributes them in various ways between different groups of society. As we become more concerned with such distributional aspects and their social and economic effects on society, questions relating to the value, assembly and ownership of land are likely to dominate the planning scene, and in particular the political debate on the kind of environment we want.*

* The Labour Government's proposals to nationalise development land, details of which are currently awaited reflect the importance attached to the land question at the time of writing.

Planning control, and in particular policies preventing development on green field sites in the Green Belt — the key instrument of a comprehensive vision that supplied the rationale of post war British planning — have certainly prevented urban coalescence (5.39). With important exceptions, where the outward pressures of increased population growth and the need to decant inner area urban residents proved too strong, central government has generally resisted the demands of the cities for more land to rehouse those displaced as part of the residential urban renewal process (5.40).

We know all too little about the social and economic cost of the policy of *cordon sanitaire*, represented by Green Belt policies. What we do know is that whilst the policy of urban containment has been apparently successful, the pressures on urban land have been such as to have decidedly negative financial and environmental effects. In so far as the outcome of planning represents an allocation of land for development, it may become a more effective instrument of social policy providing that it makes the positive control of land by the community possible.

From a planning point of view, positive control should mean the allocation of land for housing and other activities in desirable locations of a city, town or village. It should be possible to allocate a central area site, perhaps presently part of an area of obsolete cotton warehouses in a northern city, for an opera house and arts centre. But allocation is one thing, acquisition whether by agreement or by the use of compulsory purchase powers quite another. No planning committee is likely to countenance land allocations required for public purposes on any significant scale unless financial resources are likely to be available to pay for the subsequent acquisition and servicing of the land when required. This is as true of land needed next year as of land judged likely to be needed in ten years' time. *This is a key issue in urban planning today and the most significant constraint on public expenditure and effective locational and development policies. The environmental implications deserve the most careful study.*

The difficulty here is not *in principle* as complex as is sometimes made out. Land in short supply and in critical locations where competition for its use is considerable, is likely to be expensive. If in addition 'betterment', i.e. the increase in land values which arises purely from the ownership of a piece of land in a particular place, and not from any direct actions or improvements which the owners undertake, accrues to the private owner and not the community, the value of private land and property in areas of public activity/expenditure tends to rise accordingly. The value of a private or public site in a good central location increases if its accessibility is improved. This might be a new underground station or a road widening or extensive pedestrian areas from which through traffic has been excluded; in each case 'betterment' accrues to those who benefit. (If planning redistributes values created by economic activities and betterment is created in some locations, it should be remembered that 'worsement' is also experienced by someone, somewhere.) Of course, if a city already owns much of its centre and all the 'plum' sites, it will recoup any betterment that results from any improvements it carries out and its own land and property interests could be benefitted by private developers, not only on public, but also on private land.

We are not concerned here with the ramifications of the betterment issue so much as the physical and environmental effects of present financial and institutional arrangements, generally agreed to be inadequate from a planning point of view. For this reason, public ownership of land is often seen as being directed towards planning and in the process as a way of collecting betterment in an equitable fashion. The Uthwatt Committee of 1942 was principally set up to consider the problem of betterment. Even so, it concluded that a large degree of public ownership of land was inevitable for an adequate solution (5.41). Since 1954, when the financial provisions of the 1947 Town and Country Planning Act were dropped, and despite the brief existence of the Land Commission set up in 1967, it has in practical terms been impossible to subordinate the question of development values. Similarly, it is impossible to discuss environmental quality and urban design in purely technical terms, as simply a failure which reflects upon professional competence, important though this may be in many instances.

Any planning officer who has had to negotiate with private developers in respect of central area redevelopment schemes, knows the practical environmental implications of the institutional and financial climate within which his local authority and the developer, together with his technical and professional advisers, have to work. Apart from the speculative nature of much commercial development and the limited number of prime sites, there has been a shortage of public finance for land acquisition and development. If the private capital has existed* – despite high interest rates and the rest – the local authority has not always had the resources at the time when they were needed to effect road and other environmental improvements that would make the development proposed a worthwhile proposition.

Similarly, the problems of either providing improved public transport facilities or private car parking facilities has often impeded the private developer in making progress. High interest rates has made delay costly. In practice, the major development schemes have been carried out by the larger property companies that have the necessary expertise. Often a development company, despite the compulsory powers available under the comprehensive development area procedures of the 1947 Town and Country Planning Act, has systematically and discretely gone about the difficult task of buying out existing land and property owners in order to unify existing fragmented ownerships in an area, to enable a scheme of an appropriate size to get off the ground.

* Large sums have been made available from Pension funds and invested in property.

The scale of modern commercial or retail development, responding to modern functional changes and requirements relevant to commercial and retailing activities, and to the planning and highway proposals of an Authority attempting to restructure its mediaeval street system to the needs of the motor vehicle, demands much larger sites. Hence the competition for prime sites for shopping and the escalating costs, in part the result of such competition, makes it necessary for developers seeking profitable returns on investment to attempt to secure as intensive a development as possible. Existing users of the old buildings are inevitably squeezed out as redevelopment takes place, simply because they can no longer afford the new rental levels being asked.

Market forces tend, therefore, to squeeze out those uses which have least need to be in the prime positions to peripheral positions. The variety and mix of activities found in the high street is fast disappearing. There is a social and visual impoverishment of the town centre.

If intensive development is the rule, overdevelopment is not the exception. There are many badly sited high buildings. Minimal open space is provided for the use of the public. Perhaps most serious, there is an all but universal use of nasty and cheap looking building finishes, especially in many commercial schemes (5.42).

Private developers have only partial knowledge of the economic situation, the planning proposals, and the various developments going on in parts of an urban region. In order to prevent useless and wasteful competition and the possible decline and disastrous effects on rateable value which would result in parts of a city, city planners have produced town centre maps, of a non-statutory kind to attempt to provide a rational context or framework within which development decisions may be made and environmental control measures may be operated.

Prior to the 1968 Town and Country Planning Act, various *ad hoc* attempts were made to overcome the defects of the 1947 Development Plan System, not least the environmental problems produced by *ad hoc* development in towns. The Town Map, a statutory requirement of the 1947 system was grossly inadequate as a tool for pursuing environmental design objectives and there was literally no guidance for town centre development other than the *Design of Central Areas* handbook, published by HMSO in 1947. Accordingly, the Ministry of Housing and Local Government published its most influential and useful Bulletin No. 1, *Town Centres and Approach to Renewal*, in 1962. In many ways, this handbook was a model rule book for local plan making and the designation of action areas.

In every case, city centre plans have attempted to come to grips with the environmental problems resulting from the conflict between vehicles and pedestrians, but land costs and site assembly have remained serious and intractable problems.

The traditional approach has been to design a transport system strongly oriented towards the city centre, allowing major environmental improvements for the benefit of the pedestrian to take place in the central core (for example, in Leeds and Birmingham). Nevertheless, the emphasis on road building can bring its own special problems with rising car ownership; traffic congestion is simply transferred from core to inner city areas and car parking problems become even more difficult and expensive to solve. The greater the accessibility provided to the central area, the greater the cost of acquiring the adjacent fringe sites needed for multi-storey parking. Indeed, some sites are more profitable to the local authority for car parking than for a civic and cultural use, notwithstanding the fact that such sites may be excellently sited and needed for such public purposes.

If there are environmental problems stemming from speculation, ownership patterns and difficulties of land assembly, we should bear in mind the problems arising from the need to release land for development beyond the urban fence. Future development will require the release, assembly, and servicing of substantial areas of new land, at least on the scale of the present new towns (5.43). Two main conclusions may be drawn. First, long term comprehensive land assembly, in accordance with effective regional strategies and on an adequate scale, is a pre-requisite, if not a guarantee of effective environmental planning. Second, due consideration must then be given to detailed environmental factors, siting, layout, landscaping and design.

We may see major changes in the planning process as a result of changes in ownership. It is likely that local government will progressively own and manage more land, carry out more development on its own account or in partnership with financial and property consortia. The implications of such changes would be considerable and could lead to a much more effective and positive attitude towards local planning and design.

If changes do not occur, then the task of environmental planning and the attempt to improve the quality of life will become even more difficult. Indeed, such powers as planning possesses will be eroded. Public dissatisfaction with its claimed results will be confused with the underlying reasons that have been briefly touched upon here. Planning must not be characterised as a process which is inevitably and for all time little more than an *ad hoc* response to economic and market forces. Such trend planning and deterministic thinking is defeatist and unimaginative, and completely ignores the dynamic role which planning could play.

Unfortunately, it is the potential of planning that we continue to talk about rather than its reality. The environment we inherit is not the result of planning as such; this is a myth. The man-made environment is the creation of many variables and planning has a relatively limited umpire role in relation to the land, the main resource for which it has some responsibility. This is as true at the strategic as at the local scale. The planning system is characterised by negative control and regulation, its practitioners finding themselves increasingly acting in administrative capacities, rather than in creative and innovative roles.

Environmental quality

Attention and public concern has shifted from pollution and participation to the overt and concealed inequalities which exist in Britain today. 'Social planning' and 'positive discrimination' have become fashionable slogans and part of our political and social vocabulary.

Certainly, pollution of the physical environment has been recognised as of international as well as national concern. The International Conservation Year, legislation and annual report by the United States' President on Pollution and the State of the Environment, the Stockholm Conference, and Architectural Heritage Year 1975 are indicative of the attention now being directed towards environment. In Britain we have had reports from the Standing Royal Commission on environmental pollution.

But inexorably, world events and the energy crisis have underlined a wider range of problems; the evaluation, use and control of resources for the benefit of present and future generations. Pollution and conservation, important as they are, are only facets of our contemporary dilemma. Resource planning is indeed a much broader activity and frame of reference than traditional town and country planning. The key issues which relate to environmental quality are:

(i)   Resource allocations
(ii) Equity and choice
(iii) Acceptable standards.

The interaction between the social and physical environment is well illustrated by London's problems. The plight of the London public services is aggravated by staff shortages made more serious by the shortage of appropriate housing. Problems of allocation and tenure, the disappearance of unfurnished homes for rent, underline the massive social problems of London and help to explain the process of *physical and spatial* environmental change in London's inner boroughs (5.44).

". . . The crush in the city centre drives anyone who can afford it to move out into the suburbs. Deprived of revenue from the well-off, the central area cannot afford to improve its services, and people become more anxious than ever to escape to somewhere less dreary. There is no one left to drive the buses, so office workers come in by car, increasing the dirt and congestion." (5.45)

In short, 'environmental quality' is lower in densely populated regions; though it is argued that there are advantages in living in such areas which in conditions of relatively free choice are *trade offs* for poor environmental quality — some compensation for the noise and grime and the uncared for appearance of the houses.

Widespread, pervasive and insidious pollution, components of environmental degradation that adversely affect or threaten our existing environment or sterilise and blight areas which otherwise might be prime redevelopment areas; aircraft noise or motorway noise, noxious industry, areas where tipping or dereliction is extensive—all are factors that tend to result in development decisions being made by authorities on behalf of those without choice. In this sense, problems of the physical environment and the quality of life are essentially environmental planning problems, part social, part physical, requiring coordinated policies and action.

Certainly, providing dwellings without the necessary ancillary amenities in an uncompromising environment, huge tower blocks and slab blocks in the midst of dockland and dereliction, or in areas already densely populated and without adequate space for schools, hospitals and other essential public services is the antithesis of good planning (5.46). But unfortunately, inadequate housing policies, the rising cost of land, inflationary pressures and speculation in land and property has increasingly made it more difficult for local authorities to formulate positive strategic and coherent policies, let alone implement them.

In the six English metropolitan regions — Tyneside, West Yorkshire, South East Lancashire, Merseyside, West Midlands and Greater London — slums have been cleared or closed faster than new houses and flats have been erected at a time when house purchase has become a receding vision for most young people. In the five major metropolitan regions outside London, demolition and closure of slums in the twelve months up to June, 1972 was running almost 3000 ahead of new home completion rates. For the year ending June, 1973 the excess of clearance over construction rose to just on 14 000. The problem is that the number of re-lets becoming available to former occupants of dwellings declared unfit is stabilising and the waiting lists for houses are steadily growing. The process of 'gentrification', sometimes the results of improvement paid for by the taxpayer, was not the intention of planned action.

Those with an adequate income can exercise effective choice. Increasingly, choice is denied to the newly married, the elderly, and those whose relatively low incomes renders them ineligible for a mortgage. Such choice as is exercised is effectively circumscribed by economic necessity. Environmental quality in relation to housing and community presents major problems for architects, landscape architects and environmental planners generally, problems over which for the most part they have little control.

The quality of design, particularly in the private sector, leaves much to be desired. The small number of housing design awards are a symptom of the situation. Housing standards in the private sector often fall below Parker Morris and often the council house in certain significant respects is the much more satisfactory product. A few local authorities like Lambeth and Camden or a New Town Corporation like Runcorn, have shown what can be achieved. A few private builders have produced good design and shown great sensitivity to consumer preferences; Eric Lyons' designs for 'Span' showed what could be achieved with urbane lower middle class housing, particularly when owner occupiers ran their own estate committee and landscaping fund. Urban landscaping or townscaping is a little understood and even less practiced art. We need more imaginative treatment of the space between buildings, great simplicity in detailing and choice of materials. Above all, the *quality* of materials is an essential component of environmental quality.

The residential area known as the Barbican in the City of London designed by Chamberlain, Powell and Bonn, has taken about 15 years from conception to completion; every aspect of the physical environment has been carefully designed. The clients choose to live there. They choose to rent de-luxe accommodation and pay for the quality of physical environment among other things. The tenants are self-selecting. There is an absence of 'problem' families, hooliganism, 'old bangers', washing, scruffy children and prams. The social environment appears as frozen as the architecture and as antiseptic as the original drawings and perspectives. It seems that people and their activities interact with the physical environment – use the environment, adapt its spaces and channels of movement – in ways not fully understood.

Housing accounts for about two thirds of the total land used for development of one kind or another so it is important to understand much more than we do how to manage residential areas and estates, as well as to design and lay them out in the first place. Belatedly, we are now giving greater attention to this and the housing 'consumer', whether out of choice or not, is being encouraged to indicate what he or she would really have liked, what he would have preferred and indeed what other opportunities he would be prepared to forego.

Environmental standards and objectives

It has been said that a city without old buildings is like a man without a memory. But environment is not just a question of old buildings. Cities must be made environmentally attractive. The essential qualities of all towns requires sensitive conservation of the building fabric and relationships which give positive character. The inroads which the motor car all too easily makes can soon destroy that illusive quality we refer to as identity. Landscaping and open space, high standards of design and splendid buildings, freedom to walk about in safety are now recognised as essential components of good urban environment.

Despite the determined attack that has been made on the image of grime and obsolescence associated with the towns and cities of the first industrial era much remains to be done. So far as air pollution is concerned, the application of the Clean Air Acts has now almost removed pollution from domestic heating in London and other cities and has made a striking contribution to the atmosphere and appearance of their central areas.* The large scale cleaning of public and other buildings in many cities has revealed hitherto unappreciated architectural gems.

Nevertheless, smoke and fumes from the engines of motor vehicles presents a nuisance. There is considerable apprehension at the possible health hazards from carbon monoxide, lead and other components of fumes from vehicles.

But so far as physical planning is concerned, there is little doubt that pollution from traffic, and in particular noise pollution, is of particular importance because the reduction of noise nuisance is something about which planners and environmental designers can do a great deal. It is also appropriate to refer to the problems caused by aircraft noise. Fear of increased noise from traffic, particularly in residential areas, is undoubtedly the reason for many objections to road proposals in the first structure plans considered at inquiries (5.47).

We know little about the effects on people of noise from traffic, but it obviously causes stress and anxiety. Much research work is under way by Government agencies and within the Universities into aspects of the noise problem. Stopping or reducing traffic noise at source is obviously the most desirable solution of all, but these matters are all outside the direct responsibility of local government (5.48).

It is evident that traffic noise will become worse with increased volumes of traffic, if no remedial measures are taken. Many people are sceptical about the extent to which environmental standards and remedial measures will be adopted and applied in the design of new roads. Nevertheless, changes extending the number of those entitled to receive compensation in connection with urban motorways, a growing public recognition of the need to consider roads and the environment, and the prospect of further legislation on noise abatement all suggests that Government is far from complacent.

There has been a steady stream of new vehicles regulations and the five years sponsored research programme for the development of a quiet heavy vehicle and a similar programme for motor cycles deserves mention. But it is obvious that good environmental planning and design of roads together with appropriate remedial treatment can make a major contribution (5.49).

The objectives of urban transportation plans are increasingly being framed in environmental terms. This has resulted in part from the knowledge that the transportation system can be manipulated to achieve desirable patterns of urban development and in the more negative sense from growing awareness of the

---

* The Clean Air Acts and the making of smoke control orders will make 95 per cent of Greater London smoke subject to control by the end of 1974.

disamenity that stems from urban road traffic (5.50). Methods of measuring the physical environmental impact of road traffic in terms of noise, pedestrian delay and hazard are operational, whilst research is proceeding into less subjective ways of assessing visual intrusion and severance. Although a good deal of emphasis has been placed on the effects of traffic on urban motorways, as well as the impact of motorways on the townscape, there has been a marked reluctance to face up to the environmental effects and planning problems that will result from increasing traffic on 'secondary and local roads' (5.51).

Whilst there are still many buildings that are physically and functionally obsolete, there are many existing streets and buildings, areas of cities and towns, with a character that is worth retaining and here the challenge is to integrate the new with the old; to conserve is not to freeze areas of the city as museum pieces. As the Civic Trust has pointed out:

"The marriage of the new and old — so that new construction pays due regard to the character, scale, proportions and materials of its neighbours — is an integral part of the conservation process."

The Civic Amenities Act, 1967 and the 1968 Town and Country Planning Act (Part V) has given greater legal protection to buildings and areas of architectural character and historical importance. The real difficulty in conserving many listed buildings is to find an appropriate and economic use, and for the local authority, even with financial assistance from Central Government, to accept the financial burden which results from rigorous conservation policies. In historic centres like Bath, the resulting economic problems are in sharp conflict with environmental and social objectives so that the case for national assistance for the conservation of a unique historic core of international fame is a strong one. Bath also illustrates the fact that the successful conservation of an historic centre depends on a sensitive resolution of conflicts between environment and vehicular traffic.

In the absence of any control over development, the older areas of our cities were developed very intensively and the whole or most of the site area was covered by buildings. Apart from the poor lighting conditions, the minimal loading or servicing arrangements, the street system was a maze of narrow alleys and the result today is appalling congestion and physical structures that are rendered obsolete by virtue of their inadequate interrelationships as much as by any structural or internal deficiencies.

The measure usually adopted today for the control of density is the 'plot ratio', and represents the relationship of the total floor space in a building to the net area of the site to be developed. In the City of London plot ratios of about 5:0 are not atypical. Much the same could be said of the older and more intensively developed areas of Manchester's commercial core; these are the areas where the intensity of traffic generated, correlates approximately with the intensity of development. Given the mediaeval street system, it is little wonder that without stringent traffic management, congestion would be even more serious than it is.

For new development in Manchester's central area, a plot ratio of 3:5 has been used in areas where development is primarily for offices. The plot ratio figure is considered essentially a measure of congestion and the standard adopted represents the results of experience and is related broadly to the capacity of the secondary street system to carry traffic generated. There is little doubt that generally redevelopment densities have been too high. The scale of Wren's London has been destroyed and Lewis Mumford and others have lamented its passing. If plot ratios of 3:5 are exceeded, it becomes very difficult to generate building forms and site layouts that relate in scale to the general character and grain of existing city centres in the U.K. Not that plot ratio is an attractive 'design' tool; it is a crude control over the intensity of building development and attempts to achieve some degree of equity as between developers. Unfortunately, a good many schemes are designed simply to achieve the maximum plot ratio allowed.

"It is frequently contended that limitations on density inhibit redevelopment by not permitting the economic potential of expensive sites to be exploited. If this argument was to be accepted and density control relaxed, it could only mean that site values would rise even further in those very limited parts of the central area that are particularly attractive to developers. The result would be that uses would be even more concentrated and adequate servicing could not be provided. Serious over-development of a small part of the central area, apart from presenting insoluble design problems, in relation to scale and amenity, would also tend to deprive the remainder of the centre of its development potential; in the long run it would be self defeating" (5.52).

In many central business districts there are examples of development which illustrate the dangers of excessive building bulk and traffic congestion. The overriding need to improve the physical environment and conditions for the pedestrian in London and other cities, suggest that lower ratios than are currently permitted would have advantages, especially in the most congested areas. The Layfield Report comments:
"We certainly do not accept that a higher ratio may be justified in exceptional cases in Central London . . . on the contrary, we think they should be strictly applied and that consideration needs to be given to see whether they ought to be lower" (5.53).

Plot ratio 'bonuses' could be given to encourage developers to locate in particular parts of a city or region or to provide residential units as part of the development or in exchange for land needed for road widening. Other suggestions have been made that extra plot ratio could be sold to a developer, the proceeds from such transactions going to pay for the costly infrastructure that has to be provided at public expense to serve such schemes. The central role of plot ratio as a planning standard in commercial development underlines how much the urban development process is shaped by market forces.

Finally, it is perhaps germane to this chapter on the physical environment to note the range of broad environmental objectives that are currently found in statutory and non-statutory plan/policy statements. At best, alternative futures for regions require to be judged against certain criteria or broad objectives (5.54).

(1) A high quality of physical environment — which plans should preserve and enhance.

(2) Wise use of economic resources — particularly in providing public services, transport and main drainage.

(3) Conservation of physical resources — agricultural land, quality of the landscape and townscape.

(4) Freedom of choice in respect of jobs, housing, shopping, recreation, and social facilities for the individual and in the choice of industrial and commercial sites for the developer.

(5) To provide a clear identifiable form for the area.

(6) Mobility — choice of public and private transport, minimum congestion and restraint.

(7) Flexibility.

Levels of investment have become the critical factor, if not in the generation of strategies, then certainly in the choice of a preferred strategy — in the case of South Hampshire, not to mention the Greater London scene, based on the maximum realistic use of public transport.

New directions

New forms of corrective action have become necessary to prevent progressive deterioration of the quality of the physical environment. (For example, outdoor noise levels in central areas of large cities are of the order twice the perceived level in the residential areas of those cities, in turn twice the perceived level in suburban areas or small towns.) Further legislative measures, including noise abatement zones, are needed which may be viewed as incremental and valuable extensions of existing piecemeal regulatory techniques, including conventional land-use and building development controls. It may also become necessary to introduce legislation prohibiting outright, activities or industrial processes that impose on the community substantial external costs, whether by atmospheric, water or noise pollution.

By raising the price of impairing amenity through measures designed to internalise such external costs of production, the demands made upon the environment might be significantly curtailed; more drastically, the same result might be achieved by means of policies designed to stabilise or even reduce in size the population that generates these demands.

The solution of many so-called physical problems requires institutional solutions as well as physical remedial measures. The increasing importance of publicly provided goods, both in terms of quantity and quality, emphasises the importance of political choice. If the market is not the measure, then tests and criteria to assess the effectiveness of policy instruments will become of critical importance. The need to forge sensitive instruments or market surrogates is now widely recognised by policy makers and professionals alike.

We have yet to devise more effective ways of identifying and measuring the effects of policy programmes on the conditions that they were designed to correct. Information systems and monitoring or review techniques have to be made operational if we are to make much progress in this direction; at present, analysis and quantitative evaluation takes second place to political and social subjectivity. Information problems, the frailty of statistics, and the difficulties of prediction, require policy makers to make value judgements which often reflect their prejudices and 'gut' feelings.

The generation of alternative courses of action or policies is constrained by the limited powers and possibilities conferred by the political process at local government level and by the availability of central government finance. Public policy is formulated in a political, social and technological context of complexity, uncertainty and risk; and with inadequate and incomplete information about the resources available and the preferences and requirements of individuals and groups.

Planning decisions have both a resource and political dimension. Myriad decisions help shape the physical environment in special and particular ways. Costs and benefits are created for different groups. There are different ways of dealing with economic growth and developmental change. It would seem that it costs more to protect the environment and that the taxpayer, you and I, defray such social costs from which the private developer or some particular group is set to gain differentially to the public at large. What is in the public interest, therefore, is debateable (5.55).

Planning disputes certainly include a component which represents an uncertain amount of cost value that will either be borne ultimately by the developer or the public sector. This is the crux of the matter, albeit highly simplified. The price of amenity is determined within the institutional framework of political decision making (5.56).

To conceptualise the process is one thing, to quantify quite another. The distinction is crucial precisely because in practice the exercise has proved formidable whenever it has been attempted. What the economist argues may be quantifiable in principle, may be quite impossible in practice.

Attempts at measuring disamenity are being made, but whatever one's view of the social costs of such research efforts and the possible pay-offs, it remains true that there are not yet generally accepted techniques for converting units of environmental degradation into monetary values.

Health, safety, convenience and efficiency have been traditional considerations at the heart of the public planning process. Control mechanisms have attempted to secure the acceptance and guarantee of the implementation of minimum standards; they are the tangible results of social progress. There is a fifth consideration known as 'amenity', a much used and abused word. Like the term 'the public interest' the word 'amenity' means different things to different people; it means different things at different times and places; amenity is the least easily defined or measured factor of the five considerations listed. The range of variation in people's tastes may explain the difficulty. Our notion of what is good or bad, our aesthetic pre-conceptions, our images and models are culturally derived. It is a question of values.

The planning conflicts which increasingly arise today are not conflicts between the forces of 'light and darkness', but between competing goods which are differently valued by groups or individuals; a price is paid for amenity. The results of progress — motorways, gas holders and refineries — are unwanted by those adversely affected by their environmental impact. The inescapable conclusion is that the price to be paid for public goods — for amenities — must be valued by politicians, measured and guided by experts wherever possible.

It follows that in addition to actual physical measures and institutional changes brought about by political action, there is the need to redefine social goals so that their context goes beyond so-called efficiency criteria. It is only through stimulating greater articulation of values which are sensitive to environmental considerations, that pragmatic social goal criteria can be defined in terms of survival, flexibility and *satisfaction* and so be weighted according to human evaluation rather than to the nature of the criteria themselves (5.57).

Growing environmental problems arising from vehicular traffic have undoubtedly influenced approaches to transportation. Problems are being redefined and econometric techniques are making a major contribution to approaches to urban transport planning, characterised by the increased emphasis given to human values and social considerations.

Engineering and systems design efficiency, 'demand' for personal mobility and the criterion of profitability applied to only one — the public — mode of transport, no longer provide the major tests in making investment decisions. There is a growing recognition of the need to take social, economic, environmental and aesthetic needs of the community into account (5.58).

Planning, concerned only with the effects on transportation itself, or planning which is seen merely as an appendage to building roads and relieving traffic congestion will make little contribution to urban problems and social well-being. The transportation planning process has to be viewed in the context of the larger urban social system.

Within the past year or so, a decade after *Traffic in Towns* was published, we have had the Report of the Urban Motorways Committee, the Second Report from the House of Commons Expenditure Committee on Urban Transport Planning, and the Report of the Panel of Inquiry into the Greater London Development Plan. These reports (5.59) highlight three interrelated areas of concern:

(1)   The environmental effects of traffic and road building in urban areas.
(2)   The need for public transport and its improvement in urban areas.
(3)   The need to adopt measures to restrain private cars in urban areas.

Taken together and now viewed in the context of the energy crisis, these reports suggest the urgent need for a transport policy review. The Commons Report suggests a new approach in urban transportation studies, while the White Paper, *Putting People First* has been translated into legislation which promises a more equitable compensation code for those whose properties are affected by major road proposals, but which are sited outside the highway limits.

Authorities are taking another look at existing schemes which are in the pipeline to assess their environmental impact. The additional costs of remedial treatment will need to be taken into account, and the justification for major road proposals at public inquiries are having to include information and costs for such treatment.

The two underlying assumptions in *Traffic in Towns* (5.60) were freedom to use the motor car and the feasibility of large scale reconstruction of our cities.

"We accept the motor vehicle as a potentially highly beneficial invention. It is implicit in this that we reject, as an initial standpoint, a currently held view that the traffic problem in towns would take an altogether different complexion — that it might indeed almost disappear — if motorists were obliged to pay the full economic costs of running their vehicles, including the rental of roadspace. We think the public can justifiably demand to be fully informed about the possibilities of adapting towns to motor traffic before there is any question of applying restrictive measures."

The ambivalence that has been noted in *Traffic in Towns* arises in part from the assumptions made. The public could also be justifiably expected to be informed about the *resource cost* of adapting the city to the car and the alternative 'goods' which could be traded off in lieu of urban motorway building and the consequential physical and remedial measures required. Whilst it is right to highlight the contradiction between good environment and accessibility to urban areas by car, it is equally necessary to adopt a strategy to resolve this contradiction which takes both the environmental impact and resources available into account. It is no longer satisfactory to attempt to overcome such conflicts by spending larger and larger sums of money and expending increasingly scarce and limited resources on physical solutions. Moreover, the acceptance that measures to reduce environmental degradation will be necessary both in the case of new roads and existing roads carrying high volumes of traffic, will undoubtedly have the effect of making new urban road schemes much more expensive. It has been argued that *Traffic in Towns* tended to emphasise the wrong problems attendant on rising car ownership and underestimated the practical difficulties in making the Alker Tripp precinct idea operational, over-emphasised physical solutions and tended to play down the need for econometric concepts and tools.

If the effectiveness of the design concept of environmental areas as an organising principle, is measured by the number of such areas, then little has been accomplished on the ground. The concept of environmental areas and a hierarchy of roads, it is claimed, puts highway capacity and the capacity of buildings to generate traffic into an understandable relationship on a calculable basis. However, in practice, most of our larger cities have road networks which are extremely limited, in extent and capacity, and were never designed as part of a hierarchy.

Environmental conditions in central and inner areas are in many cases deteriorating. This is no more than a way of saying we know there is too much traffic there already. The so-called environmental capacity of central and inner areas, is difficult to establish. What is needed are models for measuring what would be acceptable environmental conditions on particular links of a road network as a tool for adopting appropriate restraint policies over discrete areas of towns and cities. In such a model, the notion of longer and shorter distance movement of vehicles is perhaps of less importance. The environmental area concept has been difficult to apply because there has been a failure to really limit accessibility by private car, to establish clear policy objectives and priorities for movement systems in cities.

Restraint policies on the one hand and levels of traffic generation on the other are critical factors which relate to conflicting objectives and conflicting desires by different sections of the public. In the absence of adequate restraint policies for the private car and particularly where new road space has been provided there has been an intensification in the use of land with higher buildings, commercial ousting residential uses, and hence more traffic generated than previously. The traffic likely to be generated would outstrip the capacity of any planned network and tend to lower still further the quality of the environment without accompanying expensive remedial measures.

The objective of improving the physical environment in our cities must be seen in the context of:

(1) The growth of an increasingly militant and informed environmental conservationist lobby, which questions the wisdom of road building and the growth in the use of the private car in the inner and central parts of cities.

(2) The corresponding growth of a vocal public transport lobby together with a growing acceptance and understanding of the need to conserve and improve the public system.

(3) Recognition that economic growth, whether desirable or not, is likely to be much lower than has been assumed, inhibiting the scale of investment in urban reconstruction. The adaptive approach is seen as both more desirable and realistic. Changes in the structure of great cities over 20 years, for example, tends to be at the margin. Transportation planning strategies must, therefore, be robust enough to meet a range of future situations with regard to population and employment levels.

(4) A growing acceptance of the need for restraint policies and for the private motorist to pay the full social costs of his journeys. Similarly, that employers must pay the extra social costs of public transport required to support their activities in preferred locations.

(5) Car parking policies and physical restraint measures need to be applied together with newer as yet untried measures such as area licensing and ultimately possibly road pricing, though these require further research and development. Other measures such as staggering working hours, bus only lanes, lorry routes and lorry parks are currently the subject of experimental schemes, research and development.

The next ten years will be critical. A decade has gone by since *Traffic in Towns* advanced a model of urban traffic which, for all its limitations, marked a significant advance. Nevertheless, there has been little action. The environment has deteriorated, and public transport has been the loser. Dynamic change has become the norm and the excuse for our collective failure to provide a context for coherent design policies.

The utility of long-term master plans, which treat the distant future as certain, have proved inadequate in both conceptual and practical terms. The virtue of flexible, adaptable, sequential planning, which allows for feedback in order to learn from the changes we bring about, and from unanticipated change in the system, is increasingly recognised. This is leading to an acceptance of the need for decision making to be informed and justified by evidence and expert technical appraisals. Such evidence as we have tends to suggest that policies designed to obtain maximum benefits from social overhead investment (the existing street systems and buildings), increasing the capacity of some streets and compensating those affected, may be more effective and represent better value for money than large-scale demolition and reconstruction (5.61). The strategic implication of such a policy for our great urban areas demands not merely an integrated transport policy, which is a separate problem in itself, but more selective road improvement, and relatively fewer miles of new urban roads.

The implications of such a policy should not be under-estimated. The environmental problems of selected primary and other roads will increase without effective restraint policies. Even then, the environment will be unlikely to improve without improvement in environmental management techniques and decisions taken on the location, intensity and character of many other activities which take place in our urban regions.

Such decisions are not necessarily directly part of the transportation planning process, but they are certainly essential components of an effective planning strategy, without which environmental objectives and transport policies have little social, economic or aesthetic meaning.

In conclusion, a word of warning. Value for money is an essential test in assessing proposals of any kind, and certainly proposals which commit us to spending large sums of public money. Accountability is an essential element in public decision making, but not everything in the physical environment is clearly marked and priced. It is certainly not possible, as I have tried to show, to find a simple economic criterion against which to evaluate alternative courses of action. The possibility of extending economic cost benefit analysis, for example, until it can be used for the complete evaluation of projects, must be rejected and other methods found for extending rationality in decision making (5.62).

Values are in conflict. Consensus valuation, which implicitly accepts interpretations of the 'public interest' is not necessarily wrong as an activity of Government, but it does create its own methodological difficulties and the important fact is that the results are increasingly subjected to criticism by various sections of the public, particularly those adversely affected and articulate. They question conventional wisdom and their questions demand clearer answers from policy decision makers and professionals.

Postcript

The attitudes we strike and the causes to which we adhere reflect disenchantment with the environment of the city. Those that can, appear to have been following the advice of Henry Ford about solving the problem of the city by leaving it.* Our attachment to the market town and village may be seen in the character and scale of our district centres and in the conflicts which arise over redevelopment proposals in the centres of many towns and cities. The inner-eye or aesthetic system has tended to reflect the idealised socio-spatial structure of the European city; social and spatial differences are seen as substitutes for one another.

As in the city states of Hellas, architectural monuments and the symbolic role of building types in specific relationships and locations legitimated social relationships, providing in the process an aesthetic pleasure derived in part from the illusion of permanence conferred by such architectural magnificence on the prevailing social order. Little wonder that the bourgeoisie aped the architectural fashions of the nobility or that the new middle class of England built their modest town houses with so much ingenuity that a score of them might just conceivably have been mistaken for the facade of a much grander stately home.

The resistance to change is witnessed by the resurgence of preservation campaigns, especially during periods of acute land speculation when the competition for land and desirable sites is at a premium. The most powerful have tended to win, though the struggle to prevent the erosion of existing activity patterns has been a permanent feature of the English city. In the inner city, the struggle for space has been the fiercest, the lack of security of tenure for the poorest most characteristic. The price of land has always tended to force up the density of housing schemes in inner areas.** Housing has historically been particularly affected by the process of competition, for it is one of the least profitable urban land uses. It is apparent that it is the high cost of land – the result of urban concentration in the conditions of a free market – which presents not merely the greatest economic disadvantages to economic organisation and enterprise in the big city, but which also tends to perpetuate the present density patterns. High densities are sometimes the effect of, at other times the cause of high land values (5.63).

We are at the parting of the ways in more senses than one at the present time. There is a seemingly widespread disenchantment with historical models and urban design utopias. Whilst the negative and regulatory approach is inadequate *in itself* to anticipate, let alone invent the future, it remains a necessary *concomitant* of policies directed towards the creation of humane environments.

So far as urban policies are concerned, the lessons of the energy crisis should be clear. We can no longer be satisfied with a planning style that relies on problem solving and trend regulation alone. Effective positive development

* Not only is Birmingham's resident population – like all other major western cities – falling, more traumatic still, the number of employees working in the central business district is falling. The foundations of the region's strategy, such as it is, are in danger of collapse.

** Undoubtedly exacerbated by the ruthless pursuit of the green belt policy by successive governments.

planning and leadership must be viewed in terms of public or social progress, moving the urban system or parts of it in the direction of the desired future.

Berry (5.64) suggests that many urbanists realise the need for new intellectual frameworks specifically applicable to different socio-political circumstances, within which the guidance of urban process may be studied. Such a framework would need to comprehend the developmental or design process since its products affect and interact with both the physical environment and our perception of that environment. The man-made or built environment is the result of conflicts between those with different degrees of power. As ideologies rise and fall and the balance of power changes, so the built environment is modified. It has been suggested that the social structure is the key to the spatial structure and that until we understand how a given socio-economic system places people with regard to fundamental scarce resources, we are unable to make predictions about (and hence effectively design) future spatial structures in a given society.

Nevertheless, in the meantime, life goes on and there are environmental problems to be solved. We must seek to define such problems, decide the range of policies which may be available for their solution. We have concentrated on the physical environment in this chapter. It must have become obvious to the reader that this cannot be considered in isolation from the social environment, from the institutional structures and values which exist in society. We have to recognise that an increasing number of 'experts' are coming to a similar conclusion.

References and Notes

5.1   Sidney Pollard, *The Idea of Progress, History and Society,* Pelican, 1971.
5.2   Gideon Sjoberg, *The Pre-Industrial City,* Free Press, 1960.
5.3   Brian J.L. Berry, *The Human Consequences of Urbanisation,* Papermac, 1973.
5.4   Morton and Lucia White, *The Intellectual versus the City,* Mentor, 1964.
5.5   David Lowenthall and Hugh C. Prince, 'English Landscape Tastes', *Geographical Review,* 55, 1965, pp.186-222.
5.6   *Ibid.,* quoted from 'What's left for Patriotism?', *Observer,* January 20th, 1963, p.21.
5.7   *Op.cit.*
5.8   Quoted from 'Cognitive Development in Children', in *Generations,* Clifford Adelman, Penguin, 1973, p.157.
5.9   R. Hoggart, *The Uses of Literacy,* Chatto and Windus, 1957, Penguin, 1968.
5.10 "A Renaissance painting was a most exact diagram of the concept that God was the focal point through which integration took place. All forms, all acts and all spaces were directed, ordered and understandable on the basis of this single focus of relationship. It was the general plan for the early mediaeval thought structure, social structure and metropolitan structure," Reichek, *A.I.P.J.* **XXVII**, May, 1961, p.141.
5.11 H. Rosenau, *The Ideal City in its Architectural Evolution,* Routledge and Kegan Paul, 1959.
5.12 J.D. Bernal, *Science in History,* Watts, 1965.
5.13 Christopher Alexander, 'A City is not a Tree', *Design* (London), 206, February, 1965.
5.14 Roy Adams, *Urban Design,* unpublished Postgraduate dissertation, 1973, University of Aston in Birmingham. Permission to include references and a number of important points made by its author is gratefully acknowledged.
5.15 Jones and Thornley, 'The Determination of Components for an Indian Village' in *Conference on Design Methods,* Pergamon, 1963.
5.16 Ed. W.J. Mitchell, *Environmental Design: Research and Practice,* Conference Proceedings, 1972. L.A. University of California (2 Vols.)
5.17 See, for example, G. Shankland, 'New Role of Urban Design', *R.I.B.A.J.,* 72, 2, February, 1965.
5.18 J. Thomson, 'Urban Design: What is it? Who does it?' *Zoo Magazine,* Heriot Watt University, Edinburgh, 1969.
5.19 K.R. Popper, *The Poverty of Historicism,* Routledge and Kegan Paul, 1972.
5.20 Reichek, *op.cit.*

5.21   A. Benjamin Handler, 'What is Planning Theory?'*J.A.I.P.*, **XXIII**, 1957.

5.22   D. Foley, 'An Approach to Metropolitan Spatial Structure', in *Explorations in Urban Structure*, Pennsylvania University Press, 1964.

5.23   *Ibid*.

5.24   See, for example, Kevin Lynch, *The Image of the City*, M.I.T., 1960, pp.91-118, also, 'The Pattern of the Metropolis' in *The Future Metropolis*, Braziller Inc., 1961.

5.25   See, K. Lynch, 'The Possible City' in *Environment and Policy, the Next Fifty Years*, E. Wald Jr., Indiana, 1967.

5.26   J.R. James, 'A Strategic View of Planning', *R.I.B.A.J.*, October, 1967, pp.419-429.

5.27   *South Hampshire Study: report on the feasibility of major urban growth*, HMSO, 1967.

5.28   See Peter Hall, *et. al.*, *The Containment of Urban England*, Vol. 1., George Allen and Unwin, 1973.

5.29   See, for example, *The West Midlands – an economic appraisal*, West Midlands Economic Planning Council, 1971.

5.30   The three strand structure which embraces existing settlements and linked townships, developed in *Central Lancashire: Study for a City: Consultants' Proposals for Designation*, HMSO, 1967, represents an application of this approach on a north south axis; its attractiveness ensured the eventual designation of Leyland Chorley City.

5.31   Consider ecological and landscape problems. Introduction and design of clusters of low rise family housing, interrelationships with activity nodes and open space/open air leisure activity systems; relationships between urban components at local scale with structural elements that are essential structural and form elements at the larger strategic sub-regional scale, e.g. rapid transit station interchange or an urban motorway; climate control, lighting, heating, noise control areas. How would one bring to such an exercise, a sense of place; convey an identity and generate symbolic form relationship? Two short and inadequate answers, which do no more than point the direction, are:
(i)   specify the environmental characteristics and standards to which one will design
(ii) specify the social objectives to be achieved.

5.32   Jane Jacobs, *The Death and Life of Great American Cities*, Random House, 1961, also Penguin Books, esp. pp.372-376.

5.33   Indeed, this New York centred view ignores the fact that perhaps some of the most attractive opportunities to create new environments of quality are at the edge of the urban region. Given effective mechanisms for land assembly, and effective public and private arrangements for implementation the prospects are not unpromising. What is lacking more than anything is the positive regional strategy for such development.

5.34   'The Future of the City', *Architectural Record*, 132, October, 1962.

5.35   To programme a complex community twenty years in advance, the planner must pretend to a knowledge and power that he does not possess. "In such fluid times a 'plan' is tyranny and no planning is madness." D.R. Godschalk, 'Reforming New Community Planning', *A.I.P.J.*, September, 1973.

5.36   See, for example, Milton Keynes, 'Software versus Hardware', *R.I.B.A.J.*, July, 1970.

5.37   See, 'Thinking for the Future', ed. J. Mishan, *Europe 2,000*, Volume 1, The Hague, 1972.

5.38   *Resources for the Future: The Next Fifty Years*, E. Wald, Jr., Indiana, 1967.

5.39   M. Ash, *T. & C.P. Journal*, September, 1973.

5.40   See, for example, Peter Hall *et. al., The Containment of Urban England*, Vol. 1, George Allen and Unwin, 1973.

5.41   See, for example, Barras, Broadbent and Massey, 'Planning and the Public Ownership of Land', *New Society*, 21st June, 1973. Also paper at 1973 Town Planning Summer School by Desmond Heap.

5.42   Under the heading, 'Money motive blamed for cities littered with anti-environment buildings', the *Times*, Planning Reporter, January 17th, 1974, writes:

"Except for would-be owner occupiers, the sole motive behind almost every planning application was money, Alderman Stanley Crowther, Chairman of Rotherham Borough Council, told a conference . . . in London . . .

'The difference between an application for Centre Point and an application for a bungalow in somebody's back garden is only one of degree' . . . 'both are motivated by financial gain and neither applicant makes any pretence to be improving the environment.'

"Our towns and cities were littered with buildings that no planning committee liked, but they were there either because the applicant won an appeal or because the committee was convinced that he would appeal if opposed.

'We are not really planning authorities at all in this field,' he added, 'we are merely part of a machine for making personal fortunes.'"

5.43   Andrew Thorburn, 'The Difficulties of Land Assembly by Local Authorities', *T.C.P.A. Journal*, September, 1973.

5.44   *The Report of the Inquiry into the Greater London Development Plan* HMSO, 1973, Chapter VI, see pp.176-180.

5.45   The *Times*, Leader, October 30th, 1973.

5.46   David Eversley, 'Problems of Social Planning in Inner London', in *London: Urban Patterns, Problems and Policies,* Heinemann, 1973.

5.47   River and water pollution, the problem of water resource planning generally, comprise a vast field with its own professional expertise. It is worth emphasising in passing just how important the recreational and leisure aspects of water resources, whether the Thames or canal, lake or pit flash, can be. Birmingham has shown what may be achieved with its Canal Basin at Gas Street and Manchester's splendid Rochdale Canal waterway landscaped linear park is a model of planning opportunities taken.

5.48   See, Cmnd. 2056, Committee on the Problem of Noise: Final Report, HMSO, 1963.

5.49   There is a growing literature on the subject, much of it sparked off by work carried out for the Urban Motorways Committee, e.g. 'Motorways in the Urban Environment', Llewelyn Davies, Weeks, Forestier-Walker and Bor and Ove Arup and Partners.

5.50   J. Roberts, 'Impact', *Official Architecture and Planning*, 2, 35, pp.85-91, February, 1972; and F.E. Joyce and H.E. Williams, 'Assessing the Environmental Impact of Urban Road Traffic Noise', *Int. J. of Env. Studies*, 3, 1971, pp.201-207.

5.51   See, for example, 'Proposals for Secondary Roads – Illustrative Examples', Greater London Council, G.L.D.P. Inquiry, Background Paper, No. 443, February, 1971.

5.52   See, for example, Manchester City Centre Map, 1967, J.S. Millar, City Planning Officer, pp.39-53.

5.53   G.L.D.P. Report of the Panel of Inquiry, Vol. 1, p.609, para. 22.16.

5.54   For example, The South Hampshire Plan Advisory Committee, First Interim Report on South Hampshire Plan, Winchester, 1970, p.111.

5.55   R. Gregory, 'Conservation, Planning and Politics', *International Journal of Environmental Studies*, IV, pp.33-39, 1972.

5.56   *Ibid.*, "Both developers and conservationists, are intent upon minimising the costs, financial in one case and environmental in the other."

5.57   'Toward a Concept of Strategic Resource Planning', G.A. Norton, *International Journal of Environmental Studies*, 1973, Vol. 4. pp.189-199.

5.58   For example, *The Urban Transportation Planning Process*, O.E.C.D., Paris, 1971.

5.59   All HMSO publications. See also, *Traffic Limitation in Urban Areas*, Report of Working Party, Association of Municipal Corporations.

5.60   *Traffic in Towns*, Report of the Working Group, HMSO, 1968.

5.61   See, for example, 'Economic Evaluation of Urban Transport Projects: the state of the art', Professor K.M. Gwilliam, *Transportation Planning and Technology*, 1972, Vol. 1 pp.1-20.

5.62   See, for example, N. Lichfield, 'Evaluation Methodology of Urban and Regional Plans: a Review', *Regional Studies*, 4, 1970, pp.151-165.

5.63   "A large concentration means a large number of men on a limited area of land. As men compete for this land, its price and rent go up. These high prices or rents give priority to uses of land that profit from a central site . . . They drive out uses which find this centrality relatively less profitable." Sargent Florence in *The Metropolis in Modern Life*, Doubleday, 1955.

5.64   Brian J.L. Berry, *The Human Consequences of Urbanisation*, Macmillan, 1973, see 'Four Modes of Planning', pp.172-178.

Further reading

Sidney Pollard, *The Idea of Progress: History and Society*, Pelican 1971.

Brian J.L. Berry, *The Human Consequences of Urbanisation*, Papermac, 1973.

Morton and Lucia White, *The Intellectual Versus the City*, Mentor, 1964.

R. Hoggart, *The Uses of Literacy*, Chatto and Windus, 1957, Penguin, 1958.

H. Rosenau, *The Ideal City in its Architectural Evolution*, Routledge and Kegan Paul, London, 1959.

Christopher Alexander, 'A City is Not a Tree', *Design*, (London), 206, February, 1965.

K.R. Popper, *The Poverty of Historicism*, Routledge and Kegan Paul, 1972.

A. Benjamin Handler, 'What is Planning Theory?' *J.A.I.P.*, **XXIII**, 1957.

D. Foley, 'An Approach to Metropolitan Spatial Structure', *Explorations in Urban Structure*, Pennsylvania University Press, 1964.

Kevin Lynch, *The Image of the City*, M.I.T., 1960, pp.91-118. Also, 'The Pattern of the Metropolis' in *The Future Metropolis*, Braziller Inc., 1961.

Kevin Lynch, 'The Possible City' in *Environment and Policy: The Next Fifty Years*, E. Wald Jr., Indiana, 1967.

Lewis Mumford, 'The Future of the City', *Architectural Record*, 132 October, 1962.

R. Gregory, 'Conservation, Planning and Politics', *International Journal of Environmental Studies*, **IV**, pp.33-39.

G.A. Norton, 'Toward a Concept of Strategic Resource Planning', *International Journal of Environmental Studies*, **4**, 1973, pp.189-199.

K.M. Gwilliam, 'Economic Evaluation of Urban Transport Projects: The State of the Art', *Transportation Planning and Technology*, **1**, 1972, pp.1-20.

N. Lichfield, 'Evaluation Methodology of Urban and Regional Plans: A Review', *Regional Studies*, **4**, 1970, pp.151-165.

6   Transport and Communications

Introduction

This chapter examines the extent to which problems really do exist in relation to urban transport and concludes with the suggestion that, for better or worse, communications will play a key role in transforming those problems. Above all is the vital necessity to recognise the interdependence of transport and communications. This is not the conventional wisdom which insists that the interaction of transport and land use be recognised − a wisdom on which the present art of transportation planning is based and has been for the past ten years since the Buchanan Report was published. The argument advanced here is not that the convention is wrong, but merely that it is too limited. For, by concentrating on physical land use as the fundamental determinant of trip-making, the much more important patterns of social activity are overlooked in the forecasting of future demands for transport and in making the best use of the systems we have.

The importance of distinguishing between transport and communications
Transport, by which we mean the physical conveyance of people and goods, is sometimes confused with communication, which suggests rather the interchange of ideas and information. Even where they are not regarded as synonymous, they are often taken to be direct substitutes for one another; that is to say, it is assumed by many people that by conveying an idea or a message one can obviate the need for providing for physical movement. Although this is obviously true in the case of telephoning a friend instead of going to see him, it is rather less obviously true in the case of (for example) ordering groceries by telephone since the journey to the grocery is not made, but the groceries themselves nevertheless have still to be delivered. This will encourage the physical movement of goods, possibly from far afield.

What is universally true, however, is that communications and transport always complement one another. For, unless journeys are to be entirely speculative, some sort of information must always precede the physical undertaking of a journey. This will be information about possible destinations, about conditions likely to be encountered on alternative routes, on alternative modes of transport and so on. Conversely, when communication is established between two people, very often decisions about the transport of people and goods ensue. The relevance of this to what we might regard as transport problems in urban areas is evidenced by the situations which arise due to inadequacies of communication. Few people contemplating journeys in urban areas would actually seek congestion, but on many occasions and increasingly, they find it. This suggests that the intending traveller often has insufficient information about the conditions he is likely to encounter on his journey and certainly insufficient information concerning alternative destinations, modes or routes of travel which he could use. Choice is rarely based on anything but an accumulated experience of conditions on similar journeys undertaken previously. The mere fact that these historic data do not relate to the conditions he will find on the journey he now contemplates, means that the probability of forecast inaccuracy is high.

The implication is, therefore, that many of the situations we construe as urban transport problems could be overcome if we were to devise ways of improving the level of information on which individuals' decisions are based when contemplating journeys in urban areas. Unless this turned out to be a hollow presumption, it may well reward further investigation — since to ignore the role which communications play in determining the patterns of demand for transport may be to preclude a highly effective way of remedying an apparent problem and is certain to preclude a relatively cheap and simple way of solving such a problem. This is because where improvements in the physical supply of transport require heavy material investments, corresponding improvements in communications require relatively little. In terms of social disruption, the difference between the effects of investment in physical movement of persons and goods and in the transmission of ideas and information is very great indeed. Perhaps, more importantly, the changes in infra-structure which are needed to accommodate shifts in the patterns of travel demand, even within a fairly static land use framework, are far more obtrusive and far more irreversible than comparable changes in the networks of communication. Throughout the history of the industrial revolution, transport has been regarded as one of the great determinants of urban growth and development; certainly during this century, with the rapid growth in urban economy and the exploitation of private transport, its influence on land use can be clearly seen. Although often exaggerated claims are made for transport as a fundamental force in the process of urban growth, the fact of its physical imprint on urban development is undeniable. By contrast, communication networks do not have the same physical form and therefore act as 'hidden' forces in the process of urban growth and change.

What makes urban transport a problem?

The acceptance of traffic congestion in urban areas as an inescapable fact of life has persisted for a remarkably long time and it is only since the Second World War that the idea of an objective study and forecast of demands for road space has been translated into what we now refer to as a 'transportation study'. Prior to that, the analyses of traffic problems were confined to the measurement of traffic flows and their extrapolation into the future on the basis solely of past trends. Incredibly, the use of growth factors as the basis of traffic forecasting was not abandoned officially until 1965. Nevertheless, a decade before that, some serious attempts had been made to base forecasts of demand for travel more soundly by relating them to patterns of activity and the use of land. Since the mid-1950's when one can identify the origins of the present day land use transportation study, just about all the major urban areas in Britain have been subjected to a process of data collection and analysis for the purpose of determining future travel needs. Yet despite this vast programme of study and analysis the precise nature of the problem, either now or in the future, was very rarely identified whilst plans, strategies and investment programmes, most of them costing millions of pounds, were invariably the output of these land use transportation studies. It seemed to be sufficient that a consultant's advice had been sought for him to assume confidently that a problem existed.

Arguably, the identification of the problems is the toughest part of any investigation of this kind and yet, in nearly every instance, it was the part that received the least attention; since, in transportation studies throughout the 1960's, there seemed to be an obsession with the techniques of analysis and forecasting and an aversion to the fundamental job of defining what problems, if any, existed within the area of study. This grave imbalance can be seen in the sequence with which a transportation study is conventionally carried out whereby the phase referred to as 'evaluation' usually comes towards the end of the process. The declared aim of this evaluation phase is to find out how well the various alternative solutions which have been proposed will perform either operationally or environmentally and above all in economic terms. To compare the performance of solutions presupposes the existence of a problem. Simply to compare what might be with what exists and to conclude that a change of the kind proposed would be beneficial implies finite, deterministic, static thresholds between what is adequate and inadequate, between what is acceptable and unacceptable − thereby inferring some absolute measure of what is a problem and what is not a problem. Unfortunately, for those whose living is made by undertaking transportation studies, problems are multi-dimensional, highly variable and set in continua. Their definition must relate, therefore, to degrees of dissatisfaction that exist in a community towards the way in which its transport systems function and not merely to the more obvious symptoms such as congestion, vehicular delay and accidents.

One of the earliest cases where the definition of urban transport problems was seen in terms of dissatisfaction was in the book *Motorways in London* (6.1) which was severely criticial of the largest land use/transportation study ever undertaken in Britain, namely the London Transportation Study. Its opening chapter was devoted to the definition of the problem and its opening words were:

"Londoners, like the inhabitants of most cities, are dissatisfied with their transport facilities and are likely to become increasingly dissatisfied if the trends of recent years continue. The transport policies of the city must be related to the task of overcoming this dissatisfaction and in particular of removing its root causes."

In none of the massive volumes of the London Transportation Study can one find so clear a definition of the problem that faced Londoners at that time and to which the whole costly and elaborate exercise was supposedly devoted.

Sources of dissatisfaction
If we are to re-define problems in terms of the degree of dissatisfaction which exists within a community to the way its transport systems function, we may well be led to consider solutions other than crude frontal assaults on the obvious symptoms like congestion, vehicular delay and traffic accidents. We will certainly be led away from the amassing of huge amounts of 'objective' data and towards more intricate data on attitudes and subjective responses; not just from the users of transport, on the qualities and performance standards that they experience when travelling, but also from non-users of transport, such as residents and workers, on the conditions imposed on their environment by the provision and operation of transport. In this way, we would begin to identify what are the sources of dissatisfaction with the way the system works at present. These sources may well be many and varied as between individuals, but they should be capable of analysis broadly within and between communities of different characteristics — the important characteristics being size, occupational structure, age and income structure, car ownership etc., in categories similar to those used in a conventional land use/transportation study.

The main difference arises from the fact that changes in land use and the renewal of physical fabric are relatively slow to occur, whereas changes in activities and in popular aspirations are remarkably rapid. This merely acknowledges that a structure designed for one purpose at one time becomes ill-suited to a markedly different one at another time. Thus it is with trip-patterns for people and goods that they are intimately related to activities and the *social* organization, but only indirectly related to buildings and the *structural* organization of towns. It is when the characteristics of transport are measured up to the various dimensions of trip-making that the sources of dissatisfaction are revealed; for, to be ideal, the transport system must match the needs of trip-making in all its dimensions. These dimensions are legion, but include purpose, volume, destination, direction, mode, timing, frequency, routing, combination and linkage. Even if a transport system could be devised that would be flexible enough to satisfy the needs of a group of trip-makers in all these dimensions, they would still be concerned with such overall characteristics of the system as its performance in relation to cost, its safety, its comfort and its impact on environment.

It is clear that for comparatively few trips made in, say, a small town, no *one* transport system is going to be able to satisfy all the demands made on it due to its inherent limitations, both morphological and functional. Given the ability of human beings to adapt to imperfect surroundings, these short-comings of the transport system in meeting the demands of trip-makers, need not necessarily give rise to dissatisfaction. Nor may serious dissatisfaction arise from the fact that patterns of trip-making vary at different times of the day or different days of the week in a particular area to a greater degree than the limited flexibility of operating the transport system can accommodate. Peak-period commuters, for example, in big cities, acclimatise themselves to travelling conditions which other people in other places (or even they at other times) would scarcely tolerate.

The real sources of dissatisfaction arise because of the fundamental changes that can take place in the pattern of trip-making over relatively short periods of time which defeat entirely the ability of the transport system, either structurally or functionally, to adapt to the change. This would not present a problem if the shifts in the pattern of trip-making had occurred simultaneously with, and in response to, structural changes in urban fabric because this would give the opportunity of making the necessary changes to the transport system. However, even if a transport system provided *ideally* for the pattern of trip-making at some stage in the past, subsequent changes in demand caused by changes in activity within the same land use framework could cause the transport system to become increasingly ill-adapted to meet those demands. How else can one account for the demise of once well-patronised suburban bus services, whose schedules remain unaltered over the years?

There are really only two ways of avoiding this problem. Either, a massive amount of spare capacity and redundant equipment could be built into the transport system within towns so as to meet every foreseeable pattern of demand, or a corresponding amount of flexibility would have to be built into the physical layout of the town such that buildings and land uses could be changed as rapidly as shifts occured in the demands for trip-making associated with the activities of the town. These alternatives may well provide for a high degree of trip satisfaction but the physical and economic implications of building either into even green field urban development may be unacceptable from many other points of view. Certainly in the inherited (historic town) case these attributes were never thought to be of sufficient importance, even if accurate forecasts of the change in trip-patterns over the years were possible, and yet in these inherited towns and cities, where the vast majority of the population live and work, increasingly there is a gap between what people have come to expect of transport and what, with its physical limitations, transport is able to provide. This is the problem in its essence.

Trends in trip-making

The patterns of trip-making associated with an agrarian way of life are straightforward and readily determinable. Even after industrialisation trip patterns remain fairly simple mainly because the majority of the population still live within walking distance of their work. Only when employment has diversified and urban areas, served perhaps by commuter railways, have begun to expand do trip patterns become more complicated. Only during the last half-century, a period marked by unceasing suburbanisation and a relentless rise in private car ownership, have the patterns of trip-making begun to alter either markedly or rapidly. Yet, ironically, we now pretend that we can forecast future changes with more certainty than ever before! The contrast is between, on the one hand, an unsophisticated, economically undeveloped community, whose wants are simple and whose spatial horizons are limited and whose generated demands for travel are relatively easy to satisfy; and, on the other, an expanding, economically developed, highly urbanised community whose demands for travel are not only complicated but increasingly dependent upon other aspects of consumer choice. The contrast is between a comparatively stable situation where a symbiosis exists between urban form, a predominant mode of transport and a high degree of satisfaction of travel demand and a complicated, unstable situation with rapidly changing patterns of demand for trip-making and rapid shifts in the choice of mode of transport.

To illustrate this over the last 30 years in this country, Figure 1 shows the persistent rise in the proportion of household expenditure devoted to transport and Figure 2 shows the growth in car ownership within the population and by household. These two Figures together suggest that the increased real expenditure by the community on travel does not necessarily mean a huge increase in the number of miles travelled but certainly reflects an increase in the use of more costly and flexible forms of transport. In many transportation studies there has been a temptation to conclude from the results of surveys that the number of trips made by a household increases with the level of car ownership.

Figure 1   Amount and proportion of total expenditure devoted to personal travel (1946-1975)

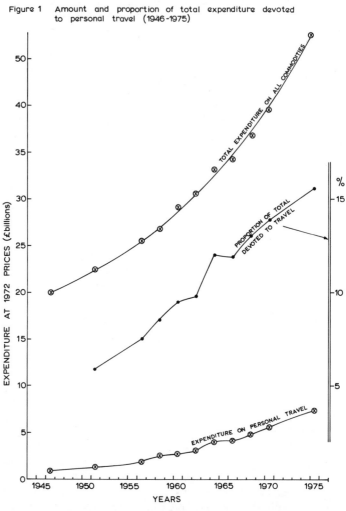

[Source = Annual Abstract of Statistics (1972)]

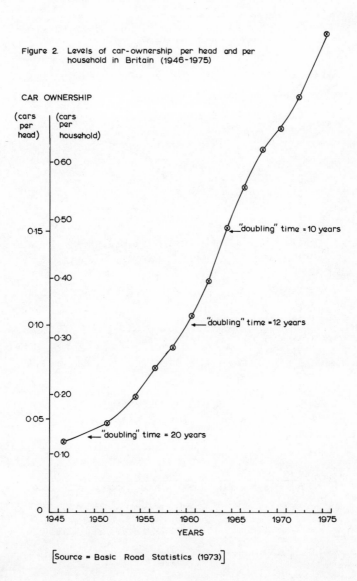

Figure 2. Levels of car-ownership per head and per household in Britain (1946-1975)

[Source = Basic Road Statistics (1973)]

Figure 3 Daily trips for car-owning and non car-owning households
of various income level (London 1962).

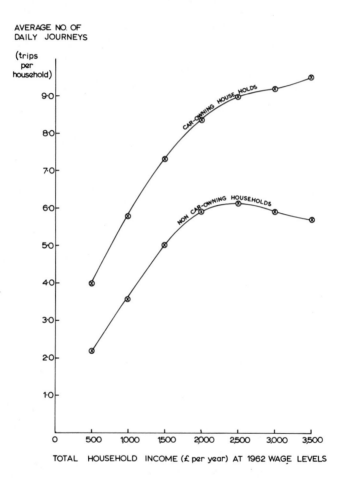

AVERAGE NO. OF
DAILY JOURNEYS

(trips
per
household)

TOTAL   HOUSEHOLD   INCOME (£ per year) AT 1962 WAGE LEVELS

[Source ▪ London Traffic Survey - Vol I (1964)]

One of the best examples of this was the London Traffic Survey published in 1964. Figure 3 shows the average trip rates determined for car owning and non car owning households with various income levels. The apparent difference in trip-making is largely accounted for by the fact that walking trips were not included in the survey. What is significant between the two types of household is, of course, that those without cars undertake many trips on foot; thus, even if trip patterns were constant, the consequence of a mode-shift occurring (within a given trip pattern) caused by the rise in car ownership would have important consequences for urban areas — particularly when this happens rapidly over the span of a few years.

The influence of car ownership
An individual, who can afford to buy a car, acquires a flexibility in his transport which is otherwise lacking in the public system which previously provided for his trips. This flexibility, this ability to match the supply of transport intimately and uniquely to the pattern of demand, is the inherent advantage which private transport has to offer. So highly is it valued by those who seek to acquire private transport that it overcomes the perennial disincentive to car owning, namely cost. The dream of Henry Ford, whereby there would emerge a universal car-owning democracy, seemed to entrance everybody until the end of the 1960's. Now the realities are beginning to be apparent, for mass car ownership would not achieve the freedom and satisfaction for all to anything like the extent that it is enjoyed at present by the privileged few. On the contrary, a point would be reached when the marginal private gain from increasing car ownership would be massively outweighted by the resulting marginal costs to the community. This does not mean that the rise in car ownership would cease at that point, because the gain would still be to the private individual while the loss would be to the community as a whole.

This argument, revolving around increasing marginal social cost, is at the basis of the road pricing controversy, the technical case for which was made clear in the report of the Smeed Committee in 1964. More recently, arguments by conservationists and others have taken a rather longer-term view about the impact that mass car ownership could have on the consumption of resources (6.2). Others (for example, Hillman *et al* (6.3)) have argued that higher levels of car ownership can be appallingly divisive within a community since although car ownership per household may rise, car availability does not necessarily rise with it. This distinction is more profound than it may seem at first sight. Even the highest saturation levels which were forecast in *Traffic in Towns* (6.4), were for only four or at most five cars per ten persons. This would mean that the majority of households would still only have one car. Thus for a household where the car is used by one of its employed members for the work journey, then the rest of the members of that household would be deprived of the car for the whole of the working day. If, meantime, the growth in car ownership has caused the demise of all forms of public transport, then those people belonging to a car *owning* household, would in fact be as bereft of transport as are the old, the young and the infirm.

Consequences of contructing urban morotways
What has dawned during the last five years is the realisation that we are entering a crucial period. It is crucial not just because we are reaching the mid-point on the progression towards saturation level in car ownership but because, for many European cities, the decision to commit themselves to a car-orientated way of life is at hand. Urban motorways are the tangible expression of this decision and the decision to embark on a programme for constructing urban motorways, even when it is a conscious political decision, can have very far-reaching consequences. At the recent Greater London Development Plan Inquiry a great deal of odium appeared to attach to the GLC proposal for a 'ringway' system of motorways in London. It was argued that these are nothing more than high-capacity special roads; but, in fact, a motorway has certain characteristics which make it more than a special road. Indeed, a great deal of the evidence against the ringway proposals was not necessarily against road building *per se* but against the notion that these roads should be built to motorway standard.

This argument was spelled out most clearly in the book *Motorways in London* (6.5) ". . . the definitive feature of a motorway is its highly restricted access, both as regards the number of access points and the exclusion of pedestrians, cyclists and slow-moving vehicles. The advantages have been proved on rural motorways in terms of traffic capacity, speed and safety, but in urban areas where journeys are shorter and more randomly distributed, there may be a case for more access points in order to draw traffic more conveniently from surrounding roads, even if this lowers the performance of the motorways themselves. Although the proposed access frequency on the ringways is already much higher than on rural motorways, there will nevertheless be many areas on the line of motorways with poor access to them, whilst other areas possessing an access point will attract heavy concentration of traffic wishing to use it." The cogent point here is that urban motorways are influenced by engineering fashion, where design standards are rigidly set to satisfy traffic engineering criteria of efficiency on the motorway itself, "with too little regard to the implications for other roads or for the environment". As a general conclusion, there seems to be a greater reluctance to lower traffic standards than environmental standards. "We suspect that the case for conventional motorways may be too much taken for granted and that slightly lower classes of road may sometimes be preferable whilst adhering to strict control of frontage, development and access." *(op. cit.)*

The recent report of the Urban Motorways Committee (6.6) has dealt with the objections, or many of them at least, to urban motorways in terms of their own environmental impact by recommending that substantial improvements are made in terms of three-dimensional design to urban motorways in future. But what that report did not deal with was the more subtle objection to the design of motorways, namely the effect that a system of urban motorways would have on the patterns of trip-making, inferring that there is something inherent in the characteristic of a motorway which causes it to be self-defeating in its function. In fact, the consequences of introducing a system of urban motorways into a city are very complex but sufficiently important to be worth exploring in some detail: ". . . the reaction to more roads is yet more traffic and the full implications of this interaction, between the amount of road space and the amount of traffic, are not adequately realised. New roads alter the pattern of accessibility provided by the network on which they are imposed; that is to say, travel by road becomes faster between certain origins and destinations within a given disposition of activities . . . (with) short, medium and long term effects." Thomson's group identified six effects in the short term:

(1) The new roads will relieve those congested streets that lie closely in parallel with them, i.e. from the day they open there will be a straightforward diversion of traffic from the old road to the new.

(2) Before long, other car users (already making trips within the area) will find that alternative destinations have become more accessible to them on account of the new roads and they too will be encouraged to divert.

(3) There will then ensue a general reassignment of traffic over a relatively wide area of the street system as road users adjust to the new pattern of accessibility.

(4) In practice it is often found that the possibility of fast free-flow on new roads induces road-users to make longer journeys through diversions of route and/or changes of destination. (Longer journeys mean more traffic, of course, for the same number of trips.)

(5) The improved journey times and reduced journey costs of road transport relative to rail may lead to some switching of mode-choice from rail to road.

(6) The performance of private road transport will sometimes be improved relative to that of buses and this may lead to switching from public to private road transport.

In fairness nearly all of these effects are accounted for in the evaluation phase of any transportation study undertaken since the days of London Transport Study Phase III (6.7). Techniques for handling the cross-elasticities of demand by mode were introduced here, although too late to aid the GLC Ringway Plan they were so valiantly testing.

What are still not satisfactorily modelled in the land use/transportation planning process are these three further effects which will begin to be felt in the medium term:

(1) People will gradually learn that certain destinations are more accessible than before and that various trips formerly not contemplated are now worth making, including some by bus.

(2) The enhanced advantage of having a car will accelerate the growth of car ownership and hence the use of cars in place of public transport.

(3) Increased car ownership will itself stimulate more trips.

In practice the magnitude of these short and medium term effects, together with the growth in demand which may have occurred anyway, is often so great that not long after the roads are open they become congested and traffic conditions on the other streets are little better than before. "It is easy at this point to assume that the rapid growth of traffic is solely the reflection of greater activity and affluence and the new roads were built just in time to avert chaos and that further road construction is necessary to meet the needs of similar growth in future." (6.7)

To refer to these as short- and medium-term effects is misleading in the context of the 35 years which is usually taken as the useful life of a motorway, or the 20 years which is often taken as the basis of a planning period. In this context it is the long-term effects which are perhaps the most important:

(1) New roads tend to induce people to live farther from their work or to work farther from their homes.

(2) The inducement towards greater dispersal created by new roads tends to take people to areas less easily served by public transport – resulting in an added inducement towards higher car ownership and a further shift away from public transport.

(3) The steady erosion of demand for public transport commonly leads to higher fares and a decline in the quality of public transport manifest by reduced services and financial stringency. In turn these lead to a further shift from public to private transport thus exacerbating the difficulties on both sides.

(4) Since individuals do not make major changes in location of their home or their job very frequently, increasing road congestion and deteriorating conditions of public transport gradually trap some people in locations which they would not have chosen (had they forseen these unfortunate developments). This leads to discontent and to demands both for better roads to fulfil the expectations of motorists and for better public transport to restore the quality of service expected by public transport users.

The conclusions from this are dire, since it would seem that a commitment to a car-orientated way of life could be an open ended one – open ended both in the sense that, without planning control over suburban growth and development, a motorway building programme could become self-defeating and in the sense that one would have to commit more and more resources to accommodating private car use whilst at the same time propping up public transport (for example by means of subsidies) in order to maintain a minimum service for up to 40% of the population for whom no car will be available. Other worrying conclusions emerge. First of all, the major environmental problems in future might well be associated with the generation of car trips in residential areas, whereas now the environmental problems are thought to be associated with motorway structures themselves (*cf.* Urban Motorways Committee Report 1973). Secondly, the units in which any transport problem should be measured is in *vehicle miles* per hour and not just trips – that is to say, the function that governs trip length is crucial when considering the total amount of movements to be accommodated in a city. Thirdly, the inequity implied by a community divided from top to bottom, between those who have a high degree of personal mobility and those who are 'captive' to a basic minimum public transport service, would suggest that transport policies leading to such a situation would be acting in the opposite direction to many of the policies in the welfare sector. This in turn suggests that the impact that transport investments have on the distribution of wealth between different sections of the community is an important consideration which we must allow for when assessing the desirability of those investments. Fourthly, there must be an awareness from this of that basic interaction between the supply of road space for vehicles and the demand for vehicle trips that results.

In a demand-elastic situation such as this the principles that govern consumer choice are psycho-economic in nature and are far removed from engineering. Thus, although engineers may be uniquely fitted to undertake the layout and design of motorways in urban areas, they are far from fitted to assess the desirability of their social and environmental impact. And yet, for predominantly historical reasons, advice on transport policy and decisions on transport investment have been almost the exclusive preserve of engineers hitherto. If material prosperity is going to continue to rise and options open to the individual to continue to expand, the realm of consumer choice in transport will increase and we have to find new ways of predicting what the outcome of increasingly free and increasingly complex choice-situations will be. At the same time we have to be on guard against the possibly serious social outcome of trying to provide for unfettered freedom of choice. This basic dilemma is shown up most clearly by the consequences of a wholesale commitment to urban motorway construction.

What has it to do with planning?

Control of car use: a crucial planning objective
As we have seen many of the strands of dissatisfaction can be traced back to private car ownership and use, not just actively through congestion and the impact on environment, but reactively through its effect on attitudes to other modes of transport, through raised expectations of comfort and journey speed and through widened social horizons which car ownership make possible. Thus, the very instrument which seems capable of liberating people is capable also of tyrannising them. Indeed, justification for intervening in the seemingly inexorable progress towards 'saturation' car ownership, is to institute some control which will ward off this tyranny and to maintain social equity in our transport arrangements.

The problem this poses for planners in relation to car use is a challenging one; for, where almost every aspect of change with which planners have had to deal has been geared to population or real income growth, perhaps 2% or 4% per annum, car ownership has surged ahead at 8% to 10% per annum, without respite for the last two decades. If one were trying to provide for the doubling in numbers of some stationary artefact every ten years, it would be hard enough. More perturbing still is the persistence of this growth. In the Buchanan Report (1963) forecasts of the future vehicle population were given which (in terms of vehicles per head) are still valid ten years later and this is despite the relatively poor performance of the British economy during those years. Nevertheless, during the 1960's, with a steady fall in the real costs of vehicle ownership reinforced by a modest rise in real incomes and a growing propensity for car use, the numbers of cars registered in Britain has doubled in the ten year period 1963-1973. Current inflation and the aftermath of the oil crisis could cause doubts to be raised about Buchanan's forecast of vehicle numbers trebling within twenty years. However, in 1973, the year of the oil crisis itself and a year which marked the onset of severe inflation (in excess of 10% per annum) where the GDP per head remained virtually constant, between 100 000 and 150 000 new registrations were recorded each month. This suggests an enormous propensity for car use and that the ingredients for further growth in car ownership may still be present in the 1970's and 1980's, even though economic prosperity may not be so assured.

This is not just a reflection of the inherent flexibility of private transport to fit the changing travel patterns, it is also fuelled along by the wide mis-perceptions that exist about the real cost of car operation. We continue to pretend that public and private modes of transport compete with one another where the ground rules under which the so-called competition operates are profoundly inconsistent, and where glaring differences exist between the perceived and actual value of costs and time for travellers choosing car use as opposed to other modes. The failure to introduce road pricing as well as the failure to recognise fundamental and generic distinctions between cars and all other forms of transport has led us to the present grossly-inflated reliance on car use with all the problems that we now foresee. In order to offer realistic and socially acceptable options in future, within a framework of consumer choice, we have to try to unravel the complex attitudes of individuals towards car ownership. It is becoming increasingly evident that the acquisition of a car alters an individual's attitude towards all other modes of transport; not just buses, which he may still see as a possible substitute for car trips, but to walking, cycling and motor-cycling as well.

Hidden within the overall growth of car population, amounting to some 2000-2500 per day in Britain, is the corresponding growth of 200-250 cars to already car owning households. These second and third cars, whether they are bought of necessity or by choice, reflect the dissatisfaction with other available modes of transport that is felt by households with relatively high incomes. As the years go by with continued prosperity, more and more people will find themselves in this situation. As a research task, it will be vital to find out the nature of the interaction between the choice of residential location, the choice of mode for the journeys to work and the trip patterns that are generated for non-work purposes, and it may well be that the availability of a car in a residential area is crucial to this set of choices.

Dangers inherent in dispersal

Where widespread car availability exists in a comparatively free-for-all climate of competition, the result in the long run tends towards a lowering of residential densities and the more widespread dispersal of land uses. Considerable evidence is to be found in the USA of the powerful impetus given to dispersal by rising car ownership and by implementing vigorous inter-urban highway programmes, both of which are now happening here. The vital difference is that we have a much greater inherited regard for compact towns with fairly high residential density and much stronger planning legislation for controlling the use of land. It will be our preparedness to stand by these two commitments which will be crucial in the next decade if dispersal is not to occur in Britain.

The case for relinquishing planning controls is a plausible one, for it is based on the assumption that new urban forms should be generated which are symbiotic with mass car ownership and use. By assuming that the transport mode should determine the form of the town rather than the other way round, many would see this as a plan for the millenium. One major problem, however, even if this policy were agreeable to the population as a whole, is the acute disparity between the rate of achievement of planned dispersal and the growth of the forces that propel us towards it. For, whilst it may be difficult not to achieve a doubling in the number of car owning households in the next ten years, it will be very difficult to achieve a replacement of more than about 20% of our dwelling stock in the same period. If we allow for the expected growth of population, perhaps as many as one million more people, only one ninth of the existing urban dwellings could be 'dispersed' in that ten year period, even if *all* the effort of construction were devoted to it. In practice, of course, only a proportion of the nation's constructive effort could be devoted to such a programme and that would mean that less than 1% of the building stock could be dispersed in a year. So for those who see the millenium in terms of a vast low-density suburban sprawl, even under the most favourable circumstances, they may have to wait for a substantial part of a millenium for it to be achieved.

The danger of dispersal lies not in its feasibility on a large scale — for that is as impractical as it is impolitic — but rather in the fact that it can be feasible on the fringe of large cities as a virulent resource-consuming development tending to generate more problems than it solves. For the mobile, car owning, relatively rich, environment seekers take with them, as they disperse, a large share of the benefits which are generated from employment within the city where they formerly lived and worked. It is not just a question of the sad loss of countryside caused by dispersed development, it is the effects of a permanent shift towards the privileging of a minority, the consequent undermining of the economy of the city they leave behind, of its public transport and of its employment opportunities. The inequities in this situation arise from the fact that those left behind in the city still depend on public transport, whose performance is impaired and declines, whereas those who flee the city do so with their own private transport with all its inherent flexibility.

In the extreme limit, however, this car dependence can itself become divergent; for, as densities fall and car ownership rises, the trips that could previously be undertaken on foot are now made impossible owing to the distances involved and as public transport in the dispersed areas collapses in the face of competition, it will no longer offer a scheduled service but revert to a purpose-specific organisation. It may, in the end, cease to operate in any 'public' sense at all. Further car ownership beyond this, to reduce the isolation for those who depended on those public transport services, will further add to the congestion on the highway system. In these circumstances, dispersal on the fringes of urban areas can generate over a very wide area a congestion that the act of lowering densities was supposed to prevent.

Reactions to comprehensive development

If dispersal poses a threat on the fringes, an even more potent threat is posed at the core by the attempt to provide for a high level of car use in the very heart of cities. The argument established in the 1950's and promoted in nearly all the transportation and planning studies of the 1960's hinges on maintaining a high degree of accessibility for vehicles to central areas so as to counter the incentive towards dispersal. In many ways, the most developed line of thought and resulting source of encouragement on this was the Buchanan Report *Traffic in Towns*. Although wrongly regarded by many people as *advocating* wholesale redevelopment to accommodate car use, the report did clearly see a virtue in the comprehensive approach and it was eloquent in its demonstration of the consequences of failure to plan comprehensively.

Nevertheless, one of the more important conclusions which emerged from *Traffic in Towns* was that, however much redevelopment may take place, there was likely to be a physical limit to the degree of motorisation that could be planned for in any city. Indeed, it was suggested that for towns of typical layout and form in Britain the maximum size for which '100% motorisation' was feasible is about 200 000 population and that for any larger city size restraint within the central area would be inevitable, regardless of the rate of redevelopment or the amount of resources devoted to it. In practice, the limits may well be imposed by economic or environmental constraints for cities of a lower population even than this. In an extreme case such as Bath, which Buchanan himself has come rather bitterly to realise, popular pressures for the retention of existing forms of development may prevent often well-designed proposals to increase the degree of car use within relatively small cities of around 100 000 population. Other larger cities where Buchanan has faced difficulties in getting comprehensive plans accepted (for example, Cardiff and Edinburgh) have been subject to an increasingly vigorous campaign against major urban road construction. The irony lies in the fact that the campaigners, although probably a minority, have an effect disproportionate to their numbers and espouse the same basic environmental arguments as those put forward by the Buchanan Report in 1963, but couple them with a number of strenuous disbeliefs, notably in the alleged advantages of comprehensive redevelopment.

Since this issue represents the primary point of departure of public opinion from the *Traffic in Towns* philosophy, it is worth exploring in some detail. Acknowledging that the "issue of comprehensive redevelopment . . . raises so many controversial questions of procedure, finance and the pooling and redeployment of ownerships" (para. 121) the report was unequivocal in arguing the need for the comprehensive approach. The design solutions of Chapter 3 and the pleas for wider planning powers and more comprehensive redevelopment testify to this. Para. 63 which is headed 'A Problem of Design' makes this quite clear: ". . . how can these agglomerations of houses, factories, shops, offices, warehouses etc . . . be adapted to meet the wishes of people seeking to use motor vehicles . . . these questions indicate a problem of design in the actual layout and form of buildings and access ways". With hindsight, one might conclude that this was the Achilles' heel of the Buchanan thesis, since further on (in para. 121) the report warned that ". . . unless the public accepts that there has to be comprehensive redevelopment over large areas, any opportunities for dealing imaginatively with traffic will all be lost . . .".

As I see it now the public by and large do not accept the need for comprehensive redevelopment for reasons not just of sentiment, in the retention of old buildings, but much more profoundly of social equity, in the retention of areas of mixed use and of heterogenous population. However, the report managed in the same paragraph to redeem itself by adding ". . . in the end this (the failure to redevelop comprehensively) will severely restrict the use that can be made of motor vehicles in built up areas". So far, it is hard to predict what the public reaction to traffic restraint is likely to be since the issue has yet to be presented in terms of valid political options and, even if it had, a workable and democratic procedure for choosing between these options has yet to be devised. At the same time, many professional planners are beginning to doubt not just the wisdom of designing for saturation car ownership conditions, but also the wisdom of allowing these conditions to occur at all.

A profound shift in public attitude which can be seen clearly in the weight of objections now presented to public inquiries into anything but the most modest investment proposal cannot be passed off as hysterical, whimsical or merely un-informed (whatever the outward signs may be) for not only has the shift been steady and prolonged in the case of rehabilitation versus comprehensive redevelopment, but it also has been widening and encroaching upon moderate opinion, as in the case of conservation versus consumption of resources. Present predictions of world-wide oil shortages, even if they turn out to be alarmist, are bound to sustain the opinion that massive investment in elaborate design solutions which encourage high car ownership and use (therefore implicitly increasing oil consumption) would be better deployed in some other way.

This has brought together two important but quite separate bodies of opinion and has led both to argue from their different standpoints, the need for traffic restraint. On the one hand, there are the 'moderates', basically self-interested, content to accept the advantages of a car-orientated way of life and increasingly able to afford them, who dimly perceive a threat to their future convenience and economic well-being arising out of world oil shortages and sharply rising costs of private transport. On the other hand there are the 'radicals', perhaps more socially conscious, who equate provision for continually growing demands for car use with the continuous decline in public transport and of the areas served by it and who perceive rather clearly the consequences of wholesale road construction in urban areas in terms of further equities in housing, jobs and income distribution. Spanning these two groups, and in many ways providing a meeting ground for what would otherwise be diametrically opposed views, is the conservation argument. It ranges from a sentimental nostalgia for old buildings and the existing scale or form of urban development, through confused notions about the real as opposed to the market value of land for different purposes, to the genuine fears of environmental pollution and the regressive effects this can have on the quality of life. Overall there is a brooding unease that our present rate of consumption of resources — not just oil but gravel, clean air, pure water, open space and so on — is exceeding our present ability to regenerate and recycle these resources. That, in the nature of growth and expansion, cannot go on indefinitely, and that restraint of all highly resource-consuming activities is inevitable sooner or later. Given a preference for gradual rather than catastrophic change, the restraint ought to be sooner rather than later.

On these global issues the Buchanan Report had little or nothing to say. If it were to have been published now rather than ten years ago, these issues would have been central to its theme. The fact that they were scarcely touched upon was partly to do with the terms of reference chosen for the report but mainly due to the complete absence of public and professional awareness of the problems at that time. The disturbing trend in the intervening years, however, has been the growing awareness of problems by the public unmatched by a corresponding shift of professional opinion. For despite the inexorable march of public reaction to the social and environmental impact of urban transport schemes, there still seems to be a strong emphasis placed by the professional on the technical and design aspects. They may be forgiven a failure in 1963 to appreciate the vital consequences of transportation plans (especially those providing for a high degree of car use) in terms of income redistribution and the relocation of employment, but it is quite inexcusable to ignore these now.

Shortcomings of conventional transportation studies
The origins of the now-conventional five-stage transportation study lie with American studies in the mid-1950's, notably those of Detroit and Chicago, whose concern was primarily with forecasting the need for more urban highway capacity. The link with land use in these studies was a simple recursive one, whereby 'planning inputs' provided the basis on which the forecast of future trips produced and attracted by various zones, were made. A straightforward model analog was used to distribute these trips between origins and destinations in a way which would match either the observed traffic flows on the existing highway system, or the results of home interview surveys where questions relating to the origin and destination of trips were asked. The question of modal *choice* did not really arise, since it was assumed that as car ownership increased in the future, in line with a trend already established, the proportion of trips for which cars were used would rise in a corresponding way.

The last two stages then involved the testing of alternative highway systems which were put forward for the urban area concerned. The first, that of traffic assignment, was concerned to test the operational efficiency of the network and the second, an economic evaluation, was concerned to test the return on capital to be invested in the highway programme. The procedure was wholly recursive, since at no point was there any feedback between the forecast demand and the costs of supplying the system to satisfy it. With hindsight, we are now able to see that this five-stage process was incredibly naïve in its attempt to model trip-making behaviour and to differentiate between alternative plans to satisfy it. Not only were there no feedbacks, but the idea of choice as being fundamental to the determination of demands for trip-making, did not seem to be represented at all in the process. In essence, the whole thing is to do with choice; trip generation is to do with whether or not a trip is undertaken, trip distribution is to do with the choice of destination, modal split is determined uniquely by modal choice and traffic assignnment is to do with the choice of route. So too is evaluation which might at first sight seem to be 'objective', where the worthwhileness of a scheme is measured against some detached economic criteria, but choice enters here on the basis of the preferences which determine the values that are placed on costs and benefits by different sections of the community. Finally, there will be the choice between alternative investments when resources are scarce.

Where we are faced with a multiple choice situation, it is vital to determine what influences choice and to attempt to model the behavioural mechanism of choice. It is this which the transportation planning process has consistently failed to do. Of course, throughout the 1960's, as city after city undertook its own transportation study, the techniques of data collection and analysis and the sophistication of the models improved both here and in the USA. The first few transportation studies undertaken in Britain, e.g. the London Traffic Survey (6.8) and the West Midlands Traffic Survey (6.9) did not benefit from some of the methodological improvements that were taking place in some of the contemporaneous American studies, e.g. the Puget Sound Study and the Penn-Jersey Study. The London Traffic Survey and the West Midlands Study were little more than carbon copies of their American precursors; indeed American consultants were brought in on the plausible grounds that insufficient expertise for such studies existed in Britain at that time.

Arguably, the theory and methodology of transportation studies have advanced more rapidly on this side of the Atlantic in the last ten years and recent transportation studies in Britain, notably the SELNEC Study, have endeavoured to tackle some of the behavioural shortcomings that are inherent in the process. More recently there have been other shortcomings concerning the highway-mode bias of conventional transportation models and the failure in earlier studies to allow sufficient participation by the public and by politicians in the task of objective-setting and the making of value-judgement that are inimical to such studies. Great efforts are now being made, e.g. with the New Greater London Transportation Study (GLTS) and the Sheffield/Rotherham Study, to try to rectify these weaknesses. However, so complex is the situation that these studies are endeavouring to reveal, and so politically-charged have the issues themselves become, that great difficulty is being experienced in trying to improve the transportation planning process in these directions. Some argue for further elaboration and sophistication of techniques (6.10) as a way of progressively making the transportation model more behaviourally-responsive and the process itself more politically-responsive; while others argue for a massive simplification of the model and of the process (6.11) in order that many more and possibly radically different policies can be tested, and a great deal more public awareness generated, of the social and environmental implications of alternative plans.

As with many apparent differences of opinion in life, there is in fact room for both and the common ground amongst people concerned to improve the transportation planning process is considerable. In particular, it is widely agreed that models must incorporate considerations of all forms of urban transport and they must endeavour to replicate the mechanism by which choices are made by trip-makers. Above all, they must be capable of testing out wide ranges of policy option, not only in relation to transport but also to land use, employment and so on. Increasingly, they must allow for the effects of restraint on car use in urban areas which is rapidly ceasing to be an option and is beginning to force itself on policy makers as unavoidable.

The essential mechanics of restraint
The recognition of the need for traffic restraint in the denser parts of urban areas is now widespread amongst professionals, politicians and public alike. The report of the Select Committee on Urban Transport (6.12) contains evidence collected from a wide spectrum of informed opinion on the problems. This report leaves little doubt that restraint policies are going to be of great importance in the next decade and yet, as transportation planners, we know precious little about the effectiveness of any restraint measure apart from congestion (which of itself is a wasteful and debilitating condition). Pressures are mounting for pedestrianisation, for parking controls, for pricing, for permits and priority for buses and many other means of positively restricting the use of private cars in city centres; and yet the techniques we have for modelling the consequences of these policies are sadly inadequate.

It may be that if car owners are given a good environment and a markedly superior public transport service than the one they are now deserting, they would accept restraint on car use in certain places at certain times with equanimity. In these circumstances, policies of restraint will achieve their purposes magnificently. On the other hand, it may be that car owners, when faced with controls on car use of this kind, will react by exercising the remaining options open to them. In seeking to evade restraint they could undermine the economic well-being of city centres and transfer the problems of congestion and social cost to other areas, to suburban centres and so on, which are no better equipped to provide for a high degree of car use. Restraint measures in these areas as well, to which car users might react in the same way, could set off the chain reaction of urban sprawl which we have discussed previously. It is imperative, therefore, that we seek to understand the basic behavioural mechanism which underlies all the choices that are available to trip-makers (particularly car owning trip-makers), so that we can begin to predict in a way which is not possible at present what the consequences of traffic restraint policies are likely to be.

What can technology do?

The specification is socio-economic

In a developed economy where technology has played a vital part in achieving economic development, it is common place to regard the problems that arise as being capable of solution by further applications of technology (If technology has served us in the past, there would seem to be no reason why we should not rely upon it to serve us in future) especially when the problem is apparently one of inadequate physical capacity to meet our need — in this case for movement) In fact, although many people argue that the present problems have been brought about by technological advance, it would be quite unrealistic to turn our backs on technology as a source of solving these problems, but what we must recognise is that the specification of the problems which we seek to solve is socio-economic in nature and not technological.

Failure to overcome the expressed dissatisfaction with our urban transport systems, when we attempt to apply technological solutions to them, is not really the failure of technology but is rooted in the attitude of the technologist and his failure to comprehend the nature of the problem. For throughout the history of transport there are graveyards strewn with relics of transport systems devised to solve transport problems that were never adequately defined. A vast amount of research and effort goes into engineering the more elegant *hardware* of new transport systems and precious little by comparison into the sources of dissatisfaction with the primitive systems that we presently have. The inclusion of disciplines other than engineering within the transportation planning field is very recent indeed. Although the participation in the transportation planning process of economists, geographers and town planners is welcome there are still precious few applied psychologists and behavioural scientists and yet, as we have seen, the nature of the problem with which the transportation planner has to deal is essentially behavioural. As the demise of numerous exciting technological discoveries testifies, there is little point in designing a brilliant machine and then trying to sell it to a confused and sceptical public.

If this means that urban transport has little to offer highly trained but otherwise redundant aerospace engineers then so be it. The scope for technology in urban transport is likely to be very considerable at a relatively unsophisticated and distinctly unglamorous scale, as it will involve patient application of well-tried, well-established techniques to solve specific problems which have been identified by those best fitted to identify them. By the nature of the problems these people are unlikely to be technologists. There will be three main areas of importance for the application of technology. First, there will be the need to make the vehicles that are used in towns more civilised; secondly, there will be a need to make those vehicles more compatible with the scale and structure of urban areas; and thirdly, there will be the need to make the utilisation and the productivity of those vehicles better and the system within which they operate vastly more efficient than at present. These are the ways in which our technological inventiveness can be brought to bear on urban transport problems.

Making vehicles more civilised
Although the Buchanan Report spelled out in some detail the environmental consequences of wholesale car use in urban areas, it is only really in the last five years (since conservation became a major political cause) that concern for the pollution and environmental damage that can be caused by road vehicles has been studied with any seriousness. The most detailed and comprehensive study of the problem has been carried out by OECD (1972) where the major sources of atmospheric pollution as well as the chemical hazards that are released through the combustion of petrol and other fuels have been determined quantitatively, and work is going on in many parts of the world into the clinical consequences of different degrees of exposure to pollution for plants, animals and human beings.

Whilst it is true that the majority of the hazards can be traced back to the internal combustion engine, it is also fair to say that at no stage in the development of cars and trucks has any concerted attempt been made to preclude these hazards. The mere act of stipulating design criteria for safety or pollution-free exhaust could cause a dramatic improvement in these respects in the space of a very few years. The perennial argument that these improvements can only be made at exorbitant cost can be put to the test by legislating for change and thereby giving encouragement to the more inventive designers and manufacturers. Already many pollution control devices, whose development has been stimulated by various laws passed in the USA in the last three years, have fallen dramatically in price through mass production and the economies of scale that result. In any case it is tempting to suggest that pollution control devices will always be relatively expensive so long as they are regarded as mere appendages to an otherwise 'dirty' engine design. If someone were brave enough to redesign the internal combustion engine with pollution-free exhaust as a prime objective, then in the long term the cost of achieving environmental improvements could well be less than they are today. However it is achieved, the scope for refining and adapting existing engines is very great indeed. Sustained, if not actually stimulated by public opinion, the best way to produce these improvements is to alter the legislative framework for vehicle construction and use as rapidly as possible. Legal necessity will come to be regarded as the mother of automotive invention.

Many fears are now voiced about the depletion of resources, particularly of fossil fuels, through the profligate use of internal combustion engines and it may well be that within a generation or so we will be forced to seek some other form of propellant if private transport is maintained at the present or currently forecast rates. Once again, many tempting technological solutions seem to lie just over the horizon; ranging from the fuel-cell to sophisticated forms of battery and even to various kinds of *external* combustion including closed-system steam engines. The trouble is that none of these seemingly attractive alternatives are without their own resource implications or their own pollution problems. For example, the fuel-cell which, by relying upon the combination of hydrogen and oxygen to give off energy and water, would appear to be ideal, but in fact, it also gives off hydrogen peroxide and ozone, both of which could be serious sources of pollution for an urban population. In the case of conventional batteries, even if the power-to-weight ratio could be increased sufficiently to make these power units efficient, the implications for the world's resources of lead could be staggering. Other promising forms of battery, e.g. the zinc/air or the sodium/sulphur cell may seem more promising but they could take at least 20 years of further research. Lack of efficiency also hampers the Sterling Cycle and other modern developments of the external combustion steam engine. The contribution of technology in this sphere can at best give us cleaner, quieter and less dangerous machines; although this in itself will be very valuable during the next 10 or 20 years.

Making vehicles compatible with towns

To the extent that congestion is perceived as a source of dissatisfaction and to the extent that congestion is a function of the size of vehicles that we use, there are some limited gains to be made by improving the control over the flow of vehicles using the street network. Advances in computer technology and the increasingly widespread use of simulation techniques will enable us to improve the control of street traffic over wide areas just as developments in monitoring equipment will enable us to control the interaction between vehicles through progressive control on speeds, headways and so on. Unfortunately the objectives that the technologist sets to effect these improvements often militate against environmental objectives that a planner might set; thus, by maximising the use of a network by vehicles, one may well be causing serious environmental disruption through severance of one area from another, through pedestrian delay, through noise and (perhaps most pervasive of all) through intrusion on the visual scene. This is likely to limit rather severely the gains that can be made from network control systems of the kind which we are beginning to see in the central areas of cities.

The idea of smaller, impact-resistant vehicles packed into all the available spaces between buildings is not a particularly appealing one. Even if the visual and severance problems associated with this kind of strategy could be overcome, it is unlikely that personal mobility could be achieved for all. This is mainly due to the fact, as the government report *Cars in Cities* (6.14) found, that the amount of protective space required for a small vehicle is little different from that of a large vehicle and consequently it is only in the storage of vehicles where considerable gains can be made in space. However, it may be possible by adapting the vehicles in size and speed and manœuvreability to the conditions that prevail on an ordinary street system, that the degree of restraint on the use of these vehicles would be less severe than would otherwise be the case. To the extent that there will be a continuing demand for this kind of private transport, then the development of a 'car' which is more compatible with existing urban form will represent an improvement.

Making the system more productive and efficient
Although both control over emissions from vehicles and control over the operation of vehicles are both desirable in themselves, the gains are likely to be modest compared to the benefits of improved information flow. If we were to apply the technology which has arisen on the basis of information science we could enable much more accurate and up-to-date information to assist the decisions made by people contemplating journeys. This is the concluding theme of this chapter, but it can also react favourably on those decisions taken by transport operators in their attempts to match the supply of transport to the prevailing patterns of demand.

We need to bring technology to bear on what Beesley (6.15) refers to as the 'product-differentiation' of buses so that we bridge the increasingly yawning gap between the fixed route, fixed time, fixed fare, fixed destination, scheduled bus services and the go anywhere, go anytime, go anyhow flexibility of the private car. The range of public transport services must be expanded to meet the changing patterns of demand evolving through greater ranges of choice. Key to success in this direction lies in making bus services 'demand-responsive'. For this a central control is required into which information about trips people are wanting to undertake can be fed in and analysed so that the routes and timings of buses can be optimised within a set of constraints (like bus capacity, maximum waiting time, maximum excess travel time per trip, limits of operating area, and so on). Several experiments of different systems of varying sophistication are already in hand — for example the Stevenage 'Superbus', the Harrogate 'Chauffeur-Coach', the Milton Keynes 'Dial-a-Bus', and numerous car-pooling schemes.

If technology has any hope of offering radical solutions to the problems of consumer dissatisfaction with public transport it will be in this vital area of making systems more demand-responsive. This will require great improvements in information transmission and control. Another beneficial outcome will be the marked increase in the productivity of both staff and vehicles. Bus operation is incredibly labour-intensive and, given the relatively uncongenial nature of the work, labour productivity will be increasingly important as a way of keeping unit costs down. By allowing all possible flexibility in the system this can be achieved, but in very few cases to a level that will enable bus operating costs to be met out of revenue. The lingering adherence to the notion of 'profit-making' public transport as the prime criterion for efficiency, indeed as the only criterion for continued operation, is linked to the assumption of competitiveness between modes. As more and more empirical studies of modal choice are undertaken, more obvious it becomes that provision of public transport must, in future, be justified on social cost benefit grounds alone, where the subsidy limit is determined by the costs the community has been saved by avoiding further provision for private transport.

Information can reduce dissatisfaction

Despite the growing tendency towards 'flexitime' – the introduction of variable starting and finishing times – in many places of employment, most of the transportation plans drawn up in recent years have assumed that the distribution of travel-demand over the day will remain constant and have concentrated their forecasts for some peak period which is assumed to occur in 20 years' time in much the same way as it does today. Given the unpleasantness of congested peak period travel, individuals would, in their own interests, adjust the patterns of their trip-making if only they had reliable and up-to-date information about the conditions that they would have to face. This calls for much more widespread use of monitoring equipment on transport systems and the establishment of reliable means of feeding this information back to intending travellers. If bus stops, for example, were to display information, not about the times at which buses were supposed to run, but the times at which they were actually running, this could be of much greater use to the traveller in planning his route or the mode that he would use. If car drivers, for example, were able to telephone to some central point to find out in which parts of the town congestion was occurring, they would be able to plan their routes more intelligently. In fact, if we were able to make all the 'static' direction and information signs into 'dynamic' ones, we would be going a long way towards an optimum redistribution (in time, by mode and by route) on the systems that we have at present.

As things stand at the moment it is the lack of this kind of information presented to the trip-maker in a form from which he can modify his decisions which results in the staggeringly low level of efficiency with which we use what we have. There would, of course, be an important premium to be placed upon accuracy and reliability, since the confidence with which the trip-maker would use the information would crucially depend on these factors, but once he had gained confidence in the reliability of the information he used, the level of satisfaction that he would achieve without any capital having been expended in the physical improvement of the system could be very great indeed. The real promise that technology holds for dealing with our urban transport problems, lies in the humble multi-core cable and not in the glamorous magnetically-levitated train. For the cost of each failed experiment to install some 'personalised rapid transit' we could carry out literally hundreds of experiments in relaying and displaying information to travellers. That may not be the transport technologist's dream, but in the reality of the waking world we have suffered enough already from technologists' dreams.

Conclusion

Transport as a link between social activities

In this chapter some of the conceptual and methodological weaknesses have been revealed in current thinking on urban transport problems — not least in the actual definition of the problems themselves. These weaknesses are largely attributable to the historical evolution of transportation studies and to the professional stranglehold until very recently exerted by engineers on the formulation of transportation plans. No-one doubts the skill of a qualified surgeon but few people would think it wise to consult him *first* especially if they were uncertain as to whether there was anything wrong!

Expanding the range of disciplines involved in transportation planning has helped enormously but some conceptual weaknesses persist. Two that spring to mind are: (i) conceiving the provision of transport as an 'industry', when it produces nothing and consumes a great deal; and (ii) conceiving travel as a 'commodity', where it is in fact an inescapable cost of moving from one beneficial activity to another. The transport (so-called) industry produces dissatisfaction in terms of generalised cost to its 'customers', destruction in terms of lives and limbs of its victims and disfigurement to the environment within which it operates. The majority of 'benefits' we ascribe to transport are merely *reductions in cost* to the community, either as users or non-users of the transport facilities provided; that is to say apart from joy-riding, there is almost no *intrinsic* benefit from transport *per se*. The benefits derive from the enhancement of social activities that transport, as a means, may make possible at the ends of each trip.

To construe progress in terms of ever-increasing the size, complexity and physical structure of transport facilities is to endow transport with the status of universal benefactor; when, in fact, it is often a disruptive, profligate and socially-divisive way of achieving greater scope for human contact and social activity. Not only that, but the strong *physical* links required by transport impose a rigidity on towns and cities, where these human contacts and social activities thrive, which is ill-fitted either to evolution or to purposeful adaptation. As Oscar Wilde once said of New York: "I shall refuse to go and live there until they have finished it!"

For Britain, these are the crucial years. We can either commit ourselves to costly programmes of urban motorway construction which will lead to a car-orientated and ultimately car-dependent way of life or we can endeavour to retain more genuine options through the planned restraint of car use in urban areas. Above all, there is an urgent need now for rethinking between related activities in towns. Even if the present pattern of activities were to be left unchanged, the efficiency of our present physical links could be greatly increased by improving the quality and flow of information to the users of transport. Further than this, we can improve the efficiency of existing transport systems in a host of ways (other than physical reconstruction) to improve average journey speed, reliability, safety and amenity — the great prospect here is for 'demand-responsive' systems.

Potentially, the really large gains in reducing dissatisfaction with urban transport lie in altering the social time-table. Readjustments and the making of more flexible arrangements in working times, shop hours, working days of the week, holiday periods and so on offer enormous scope; as do numerous technological developments in communications. The miseries suffered by urban commuters arise almost wholly because of the rigidity with which the community adheres to the traditional pattern of working times. Investment in telecommunications, on a tenth of the scale required for new urban transport systems, could transform the effectiveness of business and commercial contact. This should be the new frontier for planning. We should go beyond the recognition that the demand for transport is a function of land use and grasp the more fundamental truth that the demand for *communication* is a function of *activities*. Hopefully, in a few years' time, the formulation of plans for investment in urban transport will be based not on land use/transportation studies, as we now know them, but instead on *activity/communication* studies. With hindsight, we will wonder why our blinkered obsession with the physical movement of persons and goods as the promotor of social welfare took so long to be dispelled.

References

6.1   Thomson, J.M., *Motorways in London*, Duckworth, 1969.

6.2   Bendixson, T., *Can We Kill the Car?*, forthcoming.

6.3   Hillman, M., Henderson, I. and Whalley, A., *Personal Mobility and Transport Policy*, PEP Broad Sheet 542, London, 1973.

6.4   Buchanan Report, *Traffic in Towns*, HMSO, London, 1963.

6.5   Thomson, J.M., *op.cit.*

6.6   Urban Motorways Committee, *Report of the Urban Motorways Project Team*, DOE/HMSO, London, 1973.

6.7   Greater London Council, *London Transportation Study – Phase III*, (unpublished), London, 1969.

6.8   Thomson, J.M., *op.cit.*

6.9   Freeman-Fox, Wilbur-Smith and Associates, *London Traffic Survey*, Vols. I and II, 1966.

6.10   Freeman-Fox, Wilbur-Smith and Associates, *West Midlands Traffic Survey*, Vols. I-III, 1968.

6.11   Bayliss, D., Wilson, A.G., Blackburn, A.J. and Hutchinson, B.J., 'New Directions in Strategic Transportation Planning' from *Urban Transportation Planning Process*, OECD, 1971.

6.12   Plowden, S.P.C., *Towns Against Traffic*, André Deutsch, London, 1972.

6.13   Expenditure Committee of the House of Commons, *Second Report on Urban Transport Planning*, HMSO, London, 1973.

6.14   Ministry of Transport, *Cars in Cities*, HMSO, London, 1967.

6.15   Beesley, M.E., *Urban Transport – Studies in Economic Policy*, Butterworth, London, 1974.

Further reading

Independent Commission on Transport Report, *Changing Directions*, Coronet Books, London, 1974.
London Amenity and Transport Association – London Motorway Action Group, *Transport Strategy in London*, evidence presented to GLDP Inquiry during 1971-72, 1971.
Pharoah, T., and Collins, M., *Transport Organisation in a Great City – the case of London*, Allen and Unwin, London, 1974.

7   Recreation

One of the outstanding features of planning over the last ten years or so has been the emergence of recreation as a major element in both urban and countryside planning. It is already evident that the requirements of a motorised society, with its increased free time and higher disposable incomes, will more and more exercise the attention of planners and administrators alike in the decades leading to the 21st century. Recreation planning is in its infancy and the professional and administrative organisation is weak and confused. Town planners and others have taken up the many challenges in this developing field, but inevitably their responses have been *ad hoc* and fragmented. Hopefully, however, we are on the threshold of a much more coordinated and purposeful attack on the problems and opportunities that are presented.

This chapter brings together the major issues with which urban recreation is concerned. We begin with a number of general matters with regard to the use of leisure time and the principles underlying the provision of facilities. We then turn to the main areas of recreation service: sport, the arts and community activities. Of these three, the first is expanded to include sections on swimming pools, indoor sports centres, open space, specialist facilities and water. Finally we note the significant developments which have taken place in the administrative framework of recreation planning, consequent upon local government reorganisation.

General issues

Recreation and leisure* are not new phenomena, nor has their importance

---

* For the purposes of this chapter, 'leisure' is taken as referring to 'free time', that available to the individual when the disciplines of work, sleep and other basic needs have been met. 'Recreation' is used to describe the total range of activities which may take place during leisure time.

only recently been revealed. Leisure as a 'quality of life' was as highly regarded by the Greeks in ancient times as it is today. Over 100 years ago, Disraeli referred to "increased means and increased leisure" as "the two civilisers of man". But the contemporary factors associated with the mass use of leisure time and the planned provision of facilities on an unprecedented scale are significantly different from previous generations or civilisations. Michael Dower has referred to the challenge of leisure as "the Fourth Wave", likened to the three great waves that have broken over England since 1800 — the industrial revolution, the growth of the railways and the sprawl of car-based surburbia. He suggests that in its impact this fourth wave, 'leisure', could be more powerful than all the others (7.1). The signs in the 1970's are that we are moving only slowly towards this state, but there can be little doubt that the demand for leisure activities, and for the facilities to accommodate them, is increasing and will continue to do so.

It is sometimes suggested that planning for leisure is inappropriate on the grounds that, to most people, leisure is the time during which they are free to do as they choose, whereas planning implies direction. Recreational planning is not, however, intended to inhibit freedom, but to enable such choice to be exercised. Without opportunity, there is little chance to exercise any choice.

The two main objectives of recreational planning could, therefore, perhaps be summarised as:

1. To provide a range of opportunities for people to spend their leisure time in meaningful, purposive or simply pleasurable ways.

2. To remove constraints upon people seeking opportunities for leisure by overcoming deficiencies, on the basis of demand, and bearing in mind the particular requirements of all sections of the community, young and old, active and handicapped, car owners and non car owners, and rich and poor.

Forecasts have been made of greatly increased leisure, on the basis of the increasing trend towards the automation of manual work, but the move towards this leisured state is far from rapid. Evidence, based largely upon official employment statistics would suggest that given the opportunity for choice between increased leisure and increased earnings, the individual is inclined to opt for the latter in the form of overtime or a second job. Thus, while the official working week has shortened over say the last 20 years, the number of hours actually worked has remained fairly constant.

Official statistics reveal the general trends, and are the only comparative data available over any reasonable time series, but they are incomplete and hide the very marked differences that exist between men and women of different ages and in different types of occupation. These differences have been clearly demonstrated in the national surveys of leisure that have been undertaken (7.2, 7.3). They have shown that while the male, manual worker, may choose to work long hours for increased pay, and that equally long hours are worked, in some cases for less tangible rewards, by those in managerial and executive roles, and by mothers and housewives (whose committed hours are often the most demanding of all) an increasingly large group, mainly in non-manual, secretarial and junior executive positions, are benefiting from much shorter working hours than in the past. Furthermore increasing opportunities for leisure are materialising in other ways. Working hours are becoming more concentrated. The general acceptance of a five-day working week, and the increasing numbers of workers now entitled to a three-week paid holiday, enable leisure to be enjoyed in longer and uninterrupted time sequences.

The availability of leisure time is only one of the constraints upon an individual's choice of recreation. Various studies both in America and in Great Britain have tended to confirm that leisure activity is strongly influenced by a number of factors, of which disposable time and income, personal mobility, educational exposure and population trends, appear the most significant. The statistics in Table 1 confirm that each of these determinants of leisure activity is increasing, suggesting that participation in leisure activities will be even greater in the future.

Table 1   Trends in factors related to the demand for recreation

	1951	1966	1971	2001
U.K. population (millions)	50.3	54.5	55.6	72.0
Average working week of manual workers (in hours)	47.8	46.0	44.7	35.0
Income (1963 = 100)	70.7	106.5	115.4	205.4
Car owning households	33.0% (1961)	40.0%	54.0%	82.0%
Professional and managerial occupations	16.0%	20.0%	22.0%	33.0%
Semi skilled and unskilled occupations	33.0%	29.0%	27.0%	16.0%
Working population with holidays of 3 weeks or more	1.0%	4.0%	67.0%	100.0%
Completion of full time education at 16 years of age or under	82.1%	71.4%	63.8%	55.0%

Given that people are becoming more highly committed to take part in leisure activities, the chief influence upon participation is likely to be the provision of an environment to allow such activity to take place. A recreational environment is composed of two main elements, that which is resource-based and dependent upon the natural resources of the countryside, (rivers, the coast, mountains etc.) and that which is man-made (the built environment). Although technological developments, such as artificial ski slopes and man-made canoe slalom courses, can extend the natural facilities, there is relatively little that can be done about the distribution of natural resources. However, good management can ensure the optimal use of scarce resources. The built environment on the other hand can be planned to contain those facilities best suited to meet the needs of the people and it is the role of the recreational planner to ensure that these are made available.

The choice of recreation among so many activities will, to a great extent, be determined by opportunity. Without the facilities to accommodate any one activity, a demand may be suppressed or an alternative activity substituted. This is one of the many difficulties in measuring demand. National surveys have attempted to quantify the demand for various leisure activities. In effect, they have only been able to measure the existing or 'effective' demand. Attempts to measure latent demand by asking the respondents to surveys what activities they might like to do in the future have proved only partially reliable. However, national surveys have helped to quantify present levels of demand and, to this extent, they act as useful indicators, but their usefulness is limited. A study group of the Sports Council considering research priorities in this field concluded that: "General studies based on small national samples are of little direct assistance in planning except in giving general information as to the balance between one type of recreation and another." They concluded that "any future national survey must be large enough in sample size to be capable of yielding useful regional data and adequate representation of specific pursuits" (7.4).

The shortcomings of national surveys, particularly their failure to provide reliable yardsticks on which to base decisions at local level, has encouraged regional and local studies. These can be seen to be of direct relevance to the planning situation because they have been geared to the needs of specific geographical areas. A number of regional surveys has been completed, of which the most comprehensive is *Leisure in the North West* which sets out both to measure the effective demand for recreation in the Region and to attempt to relate this to the existing supply of recreational facilities (7.5).

None of these surveys has yet provided an effective measure of latent demand and it is doubtful if such a measure exists. Experience of the use of recreation centres has shown that demand for new facilities is largely created by supply. This does not mean that measurement of demand is not necessary as there are saturation levels that commercial promotors of tenpin bowling and cinemas have found to their cost. It does mean though that reliance should not be placed solely upon demand surveys, but should also take account of relevant experience. It is essential to monitor carefully the use of new recreational facilities and to assess the impact they make upon community recreation. Ideally such study should take place both before the provision of the facility and also at periods following its opening. A number of studies of specific facilities has been undertaken by the Sports Council and Countryside Commissions.

National surveys of demand have their value in providing guidelines on which to base planning decisions and, when repeated over a reasonable time series, these can give useful indications of trends, but as a Select Committee of the House of Lords has commented, "if suppliers rely on the appearance of demand and on conclusive proof from demand studies before they take action, then they will take action too late . . . The best possible attempt should be made to predict demand and this will reveal both major deficiencies and cases where demand is satisfied. But one must go further than that and act on inspiration as well as proven facts" (7.6).

If one looks at those that have been among the pacemakers in leisure provision during the past decade, facilities such as the Harlow Sportcentre, the Midland Arts Centre, Billingham Forum, Bletchley Leisure Centre and Beaulieu Abbey, it is apparent that inspiration, initiative and faith has been a marked characteristic exhibited by those responsible for their development.

Although there has always been considerable private and commercial involvement in recreation, and it is hoped and expected that this will grow, the main provider of recreation facilities is the local authority. It seems clear that because of high capital cost of both land and buildings and because facilities are unlikely to be commercially viable, local government will continue to be the main source from which recreation provision of the future will stem. This has both advantages and disadvantages. Commercial companies can often act more swiftly than local authorities and frequently with greater flair and imagination, but emphasis upon commercial objectives can mean the exclusion of activities of doubtful viability or the introduction of pricing controls which may put their use beyond the means of some sections of the community. Commercial facilities tend to be more vulnerable to changes of fashion than public facilities and a slight decline in demand may lead a company to look to alternative uses for the facility, or the site which it occupies, with little thought to those who will be deprived of a recreation they have grown to value highly. Indeed, in some recent cases, a facility with a proven demand has been replaced with another solely because return on investment of the alternative was more rewarding. While local authority recreation provision is less dependent upon commercial considerations, and can operate through a degree of subsidy from the rates as a social service, it has always been something of a 'Cinderella' service within local government and liable to be the first to feel the effect of the treasurer's axe when cuts in expenditure are taking place. The priority needs of housing, education and the social services can be recognised, but it has been apparent from experience that facilities for recreation are an essential element in total planning that can be excluded only at cost to society. While difficult to quantify, this cost, whether in terms of increased vandalism, criminal activity, or impairment of mental or physical health, is obviously very considerable. The aim of the recreation service within local government should be to obtain a satisfactory mix between the various providing agencies, private, commercial or local authority itself. Constraints upon provision, of shortage of land and capital, make it imperative that careful planning should take place to ensure that resources are used to best effect.

Although many local authorities are now beginning to look comprehensively at their recreational requirements, the concept is relatively new and as yet there have been few attempts to co-ordinate information on which the requirements of these various components can be planned. As a general guide, however, we might suggest a number of important principles of provision that apply throughout. Six basic principles can conveniently be remembered by their common initial. They are:

> accessibility
> availability
> adaptability
> attractiveness
> augmentation
> awareness

Accessibility. Facilities for recreation should be provided within reasonable access of those likely to use them. In following this principle, it is important not to forget the considerable proportions — 46 per cent — of non-car owning families, and the equally high proportion of young people not yet able to drive who may wish to use the facilities independently of their parents. Access to public transport services may, therefore, be as vital a requirement as parking space. Basic community facilities, such as small open spaces, branch libraries, community halls and district swimming pools, should ideally be within reasonable walking distance of the population they serve.

Surveys of recreational facilities have tended to show that users come from within a fairly restricted catchment area. To provide an adequate coverage, a hierarchy of facilities should be established. Those most widely and generally in demand should receive priority in provision and should be distributed within easy reach of the public who will make use of them. Facilities that cater for specialist and minority interests can be justified only at sub-regional or regional level, and it must be expected that the devotees of these activities will be required to travel rather further for opportunities to participate.

Availability. In order to obtain maximum value from capital investment in facilities, these should be readily available, at reasonable charge, throughout the time during which most people will want to make use of them. The majority of people have most of their leisure hours in the evenings and at weekends. It is essential, therefore, that the facilities are available at these times. While this can be achieved by good management, there are implications for facilities themselves. An open space, for example, even if available for use on a winter evening, is of little value to the users if it has no floodlighting or if its surface cannot withstand the additional wear that extended use will imply.

Adaptability. Although the provision of purpose-built specialist facilities is the ideal, limited resources of both land and capital require that facilities, where possible, should be sufficiently adaptable to satisfy more than a single set of demands. Multiple use facilities not only provide a range of activity, but also safeguard against possible changes in taste. Even where specialist facilities are essential for specific activities, there will almost certainly be common require-ments for services, such as plant, social facilities, meeting rooms, and car parking, that can be provided more economically by careful grouping of elements within a single complex. Moreover, sharing of management facilities can effect a reduction in recurrent costs with benefits throughout the organisation from the highest level of management to that of the most humble cleaner or receptionist.

Attractiveness. The attractiveness of the environment in which leisure activity takes place has become a central issue of recreational planning in recent years. Perhaps led by the example in the commercial field, there has been a pronounced move away from the institutional image of publicly operated facilities towards a warmth and ambience of recreational environment felt to be of more appeal to users from a wide cross section of age and social groups. This applies throughout the range of provision, but is particularly relevant to those areas devoted to social activity. The specialist facilities of a sports centre in which the activity takes place may well be functional, but in the main areas where people mix, including circulation, refreshment, and reception areas, the introduction of a general warmth of environment, by use of colourful furnishings, comfortable and elegant (even if hardwearing) furniture, carpeting, and soft music can have a big influence upon its appeal and the extent of use. Studies of swimming pools and public libraries have revealed that many users have passed by nearer, older and less attractive facilities on their way to a new facility. It has also been shown that the newer and more ambient facilities, both

in swimming pools and sports centres, have tended to cater for a wider age group
of the population and for increasing family use.

Augmentation. Recreation facilities are provided by a number of agencies, both
public and private. Many public authorities indeed have a statutory duty to
provide these facilities. Where these facilities can be augmented to cater for
additional use, this should be encouraged. Co-ordinated planning of requirements can not only bring savings in capital works, but also ensure more effective
use. In some parts of the country, notably Nottinghamshire, Cheshire and
Monmouthshire, considerable progress has been made in co-ordinating the
requirements of school and the community. By augmenting the facilities in new
school building, centres suitable for full community use have been provided.
Capital funds are injected into a project from local authority sources to boost
those available for the school building programme. Thus both school and
community benefit from better facilities. As important as the actual facility is
the provision of a management structure capable of co-ordinating the interests of
both public and school and of ensuring their availability throughout the long
hours during which they will be in demand.

   This principle of dual provision has been applied mainly to schools and largely
to facilities for physical recreation, but some experiment is now proceeding in
providing facilities in this way for a wider range of leisure activities. It need not
of course be confined solely to school and community. All possibilities of
co-ordinating the requirements of various sections of the community should be
explored. School building has offered most opportunities to date, possibly
because the scale of the building programme, and the complementary demands
placed upon the facilities, by the school during the day and by the public in the
evening, have presented the fewest problems. There are, however, excellent
facilities for recreation, many provided out of public funds, in universities and
colleges, service establishments and industry, which by dint of careful planning
and negotiation might be augmented to cater more effectively for a wider
community than that for which they are primarily intended.

   Apart from providing new and purpose-built facilities for the community, it is
also necessary to ensure that existing facilities are adequately used. Indeed, the
very first stage in planning the future requirements for recreation facilities must
be to examine the existing stock. This will almost certainly reveal opportunities
that would contribute effectively to demand if only they could be made
available to the general public at reasonable cost. The problem for members of
the general public of gaining access to facilities for whom they were not
primarily intended, can be considerable, and unless tackled energetically, not
only is expensive capital plant ineffectively used, but opportunities to the public
are denied. The cost implications of increasing the caretaking establishment of a

school building to allow its use from 8 am to 11 pm on seven days a week are far less than the alternative costs of providing a duplicate building.

Awareness. It is of course no use providing opportunities for recreation if the public is unaware of their existence. Many opportunities for recreation currently exist but are insufficiently well known. In order to ensure the maximum use of the facilities provided, public awareness must be ensured and this implies that careful attention must be given to the siting of facilities, the advertisement of opportunities, and the use of sign posting. No recreation budget should be without provision for publicity to ensure that the public at large are well aware of the opportunities.

Sport and physical recreation

There are a number of agencies involved in the provision of facilities for sport and physical recreation. The main providers are local authorities, though their efforts are considerably supplemented by private sports clubs, and to some extent, by commercial provision. The fragmented nature of this provision at local level is mirrored at national level where within government a number of departments have specific responsibilities and there is, in addition, a number of voluntary bodies and governing bodies of sport all with an interest. In order to achieve some co-ordination between these agencies the Sports Council was established in 1965, with a subsequent network of Regional Sports Councils throughout England. These Councils, representative of local authorities and sports bodies — the main providers and the users — have made a start in providing a framework from within which the planning of sports facilities can take place.

It was apparent before the days of the Sports Council that there was little rationale behind the planning of sports facilities. One of the tasks given to the Sports Council by the Government was to establish criteria upon which the provision of sports facilities could be based. A working party was set up to "consider and to make recommendations on the scales of provision to meet the leisure time needs of urban communities in regard to sports grounds, swimming pools and sports halls". Its work was handicapped by the lack of information on which to base decisions, and time did not allow for the completion of research projects to overcome this deficiency. The report of the working party, *Planning for Sport* (7.7) therefore recognised that its conclusions would need periodic review and amendment as experience and research increased the stock of knowledge. The basis of their approach remains valid, but the availability of fresh data and the experience gained from new types of facility has enabled some revision to take place. Details of some of this fresh thinking is included in the Sports Council's subsequent publication, *Provision for Sport* (7.8), but developments have been rapid and there is already, only some 5 years after publication of *Planning for Sport* a need for substantial further revision.

The 'Planning for Sport' working party did not in the event recommend scales of provision for different sizes of community, feeling that regional variations in demand and the differences existing in opportunity to provide, in varying urban situations, invalidated rigid standards. Instead, the working party attempted to devise methods by which authorities could assess their own requirements.

The adoption of absolute standards, such as exist on the Continent, and of which we in this country have had some experience with the long standing National Playing Fields Association standard of open space, is not felt realistic in the light of the very different circumstances that obtain between one part of the country and another. The requirements of the small town may be very different from those in the heart of a conurbation and for each individual treatment is necessary. There are, moreover, many ways in which the same recreational needs can be satisfied and much can be gained from allowing flexibility to enable fresh initiative and innovation in recreational provision. This is not to say that broad standards of provision are unnecessary for they can give guidance in ensuring an equitable distribution of facilities or in safeguarding against over provision. Experience has, however, confirmed the advisability of allowing a flexible approach to planning.

The problem of assessing the requirements for recreation facilities varies from one area to another. Towns with a clearly defined catchment area present relatively few problems and Sports Council criteria provide a reasonable means of arriving at a scale of provision. The main problems emerge in the major towns or cities and in the conurbations. In areas with the greatest concentration of population, catchment areas will be much smaller, for within relatively short distances sufficient demand is generated to justify a modest scale of provision. As travelling within cities tends to be more difficult, the argument in favour of local neighbourhood provision, on a modest scale, is strong. There may also be a need in inner urban areas to provide indoor and intensively used facilities on a more adequate scale in order to compensate for deficiencies in open space. Recently, the House of Lords Select Committee has referred to the need to establish Recreation Priority Areas and to make separate and special financial provision in order to allow development of recreational facilities to compensate for general social deprivation in these areas.

In addition to basic community facilities, there is a need also for some specialist provision to cater for minority interests and to provide opportunities to stage events and performances that will attract large numbers of spectators. Between these two extremes, there can be intermediate levels of provision. The adoption of a hierarchical approach to provision such as, for example, that adopted for open space in London, may help to meet these varying requirements. The nature and extent of any hierarchy will vary in each area and can only be the subject of separate and individual study. It will depend not only upon the physical environment, on what already exists in the area, but also what is planned for the future. It must equally take into account the administrative structure of local government within which any developments will be implemented.

At the base of the hierarchy will be essential community facilities. These will be expected within easy access of all but the smallest communities. The extent of the catchment area may vary from a 20-30 minute car journey in a small semi-rural community to a half mile walk in an inner city situation. Among the facilities to be provided at this level will be swimming pools, indoor sports facilities and recreational open space. The requirements for these facilities have been treated at some length in the Sports Council's publications and the following paragraphs summarise the key features in the light of recent developments.

Swimming Pools. Of all recreational activities, swimming is perhaps the most universal. Both national and regional surveys have shown a large percentage – at least 15 per cent – of regular participants. As an activity, playing in water has considerable appeal to youngsters and is a popular family activity. Sixty-six per cent of participants are under 15 and 42 per cent attend in family groups. Apart from the sheer enjoyment of the activity, the challenge of learning to swim and the desire of parents to see that children accomplish this skill, ensures that facilities are well used.

There has, in recent years, been considerable interest by local authorities in pool building, but there are still major deficiencies. A study undertaken in 1966 showed that 56 authorities with populations of over 50 000 had no indoor swimming facilities. The Sports Council in *Provision for Sport* estimated a need for 447 new pools by 1981. This is partly accounted for by the large proportion of existing swimming pool stock that is outdated and in need of replacement. Over 250 pools built in the 19th century are still in operation, and in terms of modern standards of attractiveness and service, these cannot be expected to meet present day, not to say future, requirements.

Increasing costs of swimming pool provision make it essential that pools are designed only to meet essential needs. Post war pools with large areas of deep water and extensive diving and spectator provision have been costly and uneconomic in performance. In more recent developments, shallow water areas have been extended and this has brought the dual benefit of reduced capital costs and increased capacity. Such measures can contribute to more viable economic performance. Nor should the merits of the outdoor pool be forgotten. These are cheap to provide and to run and can supplement indoor provision in summer months when demand is at its peak.

Although surveys have shown that over 90 per cent of swimmers are intent only upon recreation, the needs of the competitive swimmer have until recently had a disproportionate influence upon the design of pools. Within a hierarchy of swimming pool provision, there is a need for some of the pools to be of an adequate specification for competition and training, but the majority of pools should be provided to meet recreational needs and this may necessitate a completely new approach to design.

The future may indeed see a concentration upon the leisure pool where the intention is to recreate the seaside and beach indoors. These free-shaped, shallow water areas with sandy beach entries, plastic rocks and shutes, and expensive, attractively furnished surrounds in which the patron can relax in colourful beach furniture, beneath an artificially created sunlight, or sit at the poolside bar under exotic palm trees, are far removed from the traditional approach to pool provision, but are already emerging in modern leisure provision. These pools are likely to be developed in increasing numbers in the future and their attractiveness may well increase substantially the total demand for swimming opportunities. Nor indeed will the leisure centre of the future concentrate wholly upon swimming activities. In recent years multi-sports centres combining both swimming and indoor activities have become popular and, as suggested earlier, these combinations can result in economies in planning and in capital cost.

The planning of swimming pool provision varies between different authorities. In areas where the population is barely sufficient to support a swimming pool, consideration may have to be given to an outdoor pool or a smaller pool, perhaps with overall shallow water. In small towns more extensive provision may be possible but still within a single establishment. In these circumstances, the pool should be a multi-purpose facility capable of catering, as far as possible, for the needs of recreational swimming, teaching and competition. The pool should be situated centrally and close to public transport facilities. In larger towns and conurbations, a hierarchy of provision can be established. This might be based upon a network of neighbourhood pools, possibly associated with schools and incorporating also other sports facilities. These pools should ideally be within walking distance of the population they serve. Within the hierarchy should be specialist provision designed to allow a good standard of competition in swimming and diving and capable of accommodating spectator events. Not all the pools within the hierarchy need to cater for competitive requirements and the case for one or more pools to be of a high environmental quality to cater, particularly for the more critical requirements of adults, could be justified. Between these extremes may lie many alternative means of satisfying the overall needs of the community that can only satisfactorily be determined by detailed study at local level.

Indoor Sports Centres. The concept of the indoor sports centre is still new. The first of these centres to be widely available to the public, at Harlow, opened only in 1964, and in 1966 when the Sports Council working party came to consider this area of provision, there was insufficient evidence to devise a method of assessing appropriate scales of provision. In 1967, when five such centres were in operation, the Sports Council supported a research project on the basis of which broad guidelines to enable an assessment of overall requirements were formulated (7.9).

These have formed the basis for the 1981 target figures of the Sports Council in *Provision for Sport* which estimates a need for some 815 centres in England and Wales. In the 10 years since the Harlow centre was established, the indoor sports centre has begun to be popular and there are well over 200 centres of various types now in existence; many are under construction, and even more are planned. As was noted when considering the indoor swimming pool, many of these combine 'wet and dry' facilities and a large number have been provided in concert with school building.

Judged by the experience of these early centres, the demand for indoor sports facilities is very considerable, but as with all facilities in which demand is supply-induced, there is a considerable problem in assessing the latent demand. While no single activity has itself a substantial demand, collectively the activities associated with indoor centres produce a total that is as significant as that for swimming. The Sports Council survey clearly indicates that the centres have uncovered a considerable latent demand — almost one in three users first participated in their sport at the sports centre. In the absence of firm evidence of demand, the Sports Council's initial assessment of requirements was based upon a modest figure of 5 per cent demand. While this may seem to be an under-estimation, it should be recalled that there are many existing indoor facilities of various types in schools, in small public and church halls, all of which can contribute to the total supply of facilities. It is evident, however, that an increasing amount of study of these facilities is required in the future to enable more precise assessments of the total requirements to be made.

Because of the inadequacy of the section on indoor sports facilities in *Planning for Sport*, the Sports Council has recently completed a revision of this section which it will publish separately in advance of a total revision of the remainder of the report (7.10). The revised report, based upon the experience of the early sports centres, makes fresh recommendations on sports hall sizes that represent a significant change. A hierarchy of provision is suggested and further, but still unrefined, advice is given upon the method of assessing overall requirements.

The multi-purpose nature of the sports hall, apart from making possible a flexible programme of sporting events, has enabled a wide variety of other uses. Conferences, concerts, dances, exhibitions and many other events, have been accommodated in existing indoor sports centres, and a positive policy to cater for the wider aspects of leisure has often been encouraged. Such policies are designed to make more effective use of the facilities, particularly at slack, off-peak times, but if introduced on any substantial scale, may make it necessary to rethink methods of assessment which have been based solely on sporting requirements and do not take into account the scale of need for the wider aspects of leisure.

In terms of land use, indoor sports facilities, accommodated on small areas of land and capable of intensive use, are a particularly attractive means of satisfying recreational requirements in densely populated urban areas. The case for this provision has been well made by the Sports Council and the need has been largely accepted by local authorities. As the increasing stock of knowledge becoming available from indoor sports centres helps to quantify this need more precisely, it is anticipated that indoor sports centres will have an increasingly important part to play in recreational provision in the future.

Recreational Open Space. In general, in this country, recreational facilities outdoors have been generously provided over the years and there is a large stock of existing playing fields, golf courses and other forms of recreational open space. Many of these facilities have been provided by local authorities in public parks and recreation grounds, but a large percentage, possibly in the order of 40-50 per cent overall, has been provided privately by sports clubs and by industrial or commercial organisations. While the overall provision of outdoor facilities is good, there are severe deficiencies in the conurbations and particularly in the most densely populated inner urban areas. An analysis of Development Plans in urban areas reveals that in conurbation towns, existing playing field provision is on average 2.6 acres per 1000 population, but this average disguises the range which extends from 0.1 to 6.0 acres per 1000 (7.11).

The problem of providing sufficient open space for recreation is not new. Nearly 50 years ago the National Playing Fields Association recommended a standard of 6 acres of playing fields per 1000 population. Although based upon assumptions of the age structure and estimated demand in 1925, this standard was recommended by the Ministry of Housing and Local Government in 1955, and more recently has been confirmed by the NPFA. In practice, the standard has been impossible to achieve in most urban areas, and changes in the intervening years in the demographic structure and playing habits of the population, to say nothing of such determinants as pitch drainage, the use of artificial surfaces and the style of management, make it of doubtful validity.

Although many have criticised the NPFA standard, relatively little research has been undertaken to enable a more satisfactory alternative to be adopted. The bulk of studies of open space have concentrated upon aspects of supply and relatively little has been done to study demand. A few attempts have been made to arrive at more realistic means of assessment and a suggested method of approach was included in the Sports Council's publication, *Planning for Sport.*

With improved data on demand now emerging from a number of national and regional studies, it should be possible to arrive at more positive recommendations.

The deficiencies in open space in urban areas call for a positive approach. Where it is impossible for supply to meet demand, alternative methods of supply have to be considered. Authorities have for many years been experimenting with alternative playing surfaces capable of more intensive wear. Various hard surfaced facilities have been used and a considerable number of hard porous pitches, floodlit to allow an even greater extent of use, have been provided. The most significant recent development has been the introduction of the synthetic turf surface. Two of these surfaces have been installed in London. The advantages are both practical and economic. The surfaces are expensive, but they more closely resemble grass both in their appearance and their playing characteristics than previous alternatives, and are capable of extremely intensive use. The capital cost of a complete installation – around £200 000 – must be seen in the light of the alternative costs of land acquisition to allow an equivalent amount of play. Land costs for a single football pitch in some inner urban areas could amount to £½ million and this puts the capital expenditure on the artificial surface into a different perspective. In practical terms, the average of 30 games a week now being played on these pitches is well over 10 times that experienced on grass pitches, and during the first two seasons there has yet to be a cancellation due to ground condition.

The advent of alternative surfaces opens up a completely new dimension in planning open space. Acreage per 1000 population is no longer a satisfactory measure. Spatial requirements need expressing in more precise and realistic terms. A recent open space study in Islington, possibly the most deprived area for open space in Great Britain, has quantified playing pitch requirements showing the alternative methods by which their needs can be met using a combination of artificial and grass pitches (7.12). Such an approach might be built in to the revision of *Planning for Sport*, currently under preparation.

Artificial turf provides one answer to open space deficiencies, but further study is required to bring into use other alternative surfaces that may have environmental, playing or cost advantages. In London, two specially reinforced grass pitches have recently been installed. The performance of these two pitches, alleged to be capable of withstanding 30 hours of play per week, at a quarter of the capital cost of the synthetic turf equivalent, will be watched with interest. Further work on turf culture may indeed reveal other methods whereby improved drainage and irrigation can increase the capacity of conventional grass. Apart from the provision of the pitch, more needs to be known about the playing characteristics of those using the pitches. To provide a pitch capable of use throughout every day of the week is of limited value if players insist upon playing only on Sunday mornings. The introduction of these surfaces will certainly call into question the provision of separate school playing fields, currently justified on the basis of pitch vulnerability. A detailed study of playing fields, now being undertaken in London, may provide the answers to some of these problems.

The situation in urban areas is aggravated by the gradual erosion of privately owned open space for development. A number of private sports clubs, many owned by industry and no longer fully used, has been lost to development in recent years. Between 1970 and 1973, 140 acres of playing fields in London were lost to building. While in itself any one open space may appear insignificant, the cumulative effect of this in areas of open space deficiency could be critical. There are considerable difficulties in opposing this trend. In the first instance, the most vulnerable sites are often in the outer urban areas where local deficiencies are less acute. There is also the problem of purchase for public use. Authorities resisting development through planning controls may find themselves faced with a compulsory purchase notice to acquire the land at development prices. Outer urban authorities are understandably reluctant to pay inflated prices for open space which they may not themselves need, merely to satisfy the requirements of less fortunate inner areas.

There is a need for a positive and strategic approach to this problem. Such an approach might start by identifying those areas of open space that should be defended at all costs against development. More important, however, is the ability to guarantee the availability of finances to purchase threatened areas even at development prices. Joint financing by the local and strategic authorities is one approach, but there would seem to be a case for the introduction of central government support on the lines of that available for country park development. Close analogy can be made to grants from Central Government, available under the Countryside Act, to enable development of countryside facilities whose main use will be by those not themselves resident in the area. The availability of central grants at a high percentage – countryside grants are up to 75 per cent – could play a significant part in securing sufficient areas of open space in urban areas.

The most demanding single activity in terms of its open space requirements is golf; an 18-hole course can occupy 100-150 acres, During the past two decades there has been a most dramatic growth in the popularity of golf and all indications are that the demand will grow provided only that the development of facilities can keep pace. The conclusion that golf has one of the greatest growth potentials is confirmed by all the major surveys of demand.

A Sports Council assessment of the need for golf facilities, based upon the results of a comprehensive study of golf course provision has estimated a need for a further 485, 18-hole courses in England and Wales by 1981 (7.13). This target, based upon the projection of present trends in demand is, however, unlikely to be attained as land and financial availability must limit the potential.

Even at agricultural prices, land for an 18-hole golf course can amount to £200 000 and a comparable sum might be required for development of the course and its facilities. This order of investment is felt more likely to be attained by public authorities, although commercial interest in the game is at present higher than ever before.

The present growth in interest in the game has been reflected in a slight growth in facilities, but the rate of progress is too slow to meet the existing demand to say nothing of that anticipated. The national survey, *Planning for Leisure* found that 6 per cent of males and 1 per cent of females played golf regularly and that 9 per cent of males and 3 per cent of females would like to take it up. To meet such a demand, Britain's 1500 existing courses, most of which have their origins at the beginning of the 20th century, are far from adequate.

The problem is aggravated by an unequal geographical distribution of courses – 30 per cent of courses are in Scotland – and by an inadequate mix of private and public facilities. Ninety-two per cent of existing courses are in private clubs, most of which have full membership at high subscriptions, predominantly drawn from an upper social class structure and with long waiting lists for vacancies. The public courses freely available to all at reasonable fees, are extremely busy – queues at weekends form up in the early hours and annual figures for the number of rounds played frequently reach 70-80 000 – but are insufficient to meet the growing demand from beginners and from those unable to join established clubs. Again, Scotland with 50 public courses is in contrast to Wales and many parts of England where until recently no public courses existed. The Sports Council has set as its target not only to provide 30 per cent more courses but to improve the ratio of public to private from the present level of 8:92 to one of 30:70. While provision is falling well short of its overall target, it is significant that recent golf course developments are increasingly in the public sector.

The main deficiencies are in the urban areas where land shortages are most acute. In these situations new golf courses can only be expected on the perimeter, or in the case of conurbations in the designated Green Belt. The case for recreational development of the Green Belt for golf and for other countryside activities is strong. Many golf courses are already provided in association with common land, and with careful management it is possible to achieve a satisfactory co-existence with other casual users. The provision of golf courses in association with picnic areas, nature trails and other countryside facilities would be an effective means of conservation of Green Belt land and should be encouraged.

As with other facilities, golf can develop its own hierarchy from the championship course capable of staging major tournaments, through the club facility, to the public course, possibly designed for the beginner with wide open spaces and few hazards to hold up play. At this lower end, the par 3 and pitch and putt courses and golf driving range have a contribution to make to total provision, and can be provided on the small areas of land that might be available nearer to the centre of urban populations. The need for a positive approach to planning for golf is apparent. Few sports have such an evident growth potential but the extent of land required (used to a relatively low capacity) make it a great challenge to the recreational planner.

Specialist Facilities. In addition to the basic facilities for general community recreation, there is a second and related need for specialist facilities capable of providing the opportunity for training and competition to the highest possible levels of performance. Although specialist needs are of more than local significance, in many cases they can be developed from or alongside community facilities. Some activities will require entirely separate provision but by considering the needs of both community and specialist sportsmen together, it is possible to develop the hierarchical approach, thus gaining the opportunity to include specialist provision within long term planning and to secure the best utilisation of limited resources. The requirements of each sport are classified in the Sports Council's publication, *Provision for Sport*, 1973 (7.14). These requirements can in some cases be met within community provision by the inclusion or addition of certain items of equipment or additional buildings. In other activities, the need for specialist facilities such as skating rinks, rowing courses, diving pools, indoor athletic or cycling tracks, will require expensive developments. Because of the lower level of demand and high capital cost, many of these facilities can only be provided at a national and regional level, but the need for these facilities to encourage high level performance is an essential ingredient of the recreational plan. To encourage the development of these facilities, the Sports Council has powers to financially assist local authorities and other bodies providing specialist facilities.

Countryside and Water Recreation. This book is devoted to the problems of the urban community, and therefore, only minimal attention can be given to the important aspects of recreation in the countryside and on water. Leisure activity on, in and beside inland and coastal water, is growing rapidly. It is estimated that more than half of all countryside recreation is closely related to water. Within urban areas, the opportunities for water recreation may not be extensive, but nonetheless they do exist. The reclamation and development of disused canals and the opening up of reservoirs previously not available for recreational activity, has extended the recreational opportunities in many urban areas. The provision of a recreational environment as close to people's homes as possible is certainly a desirable objective and may assist in preventing conflicts that arise in the countryside. In this respect, the opportunities that exist for urban renewal as, for example, in the Lee Valley Regional Park, or the redevelopment of London's Dockland areas, may well make possible the provision of countryside and water areas fairly close to the heart of the population; this not only contributes to an improvement in the quality of life of those in urban areas, but also reduces the pressures on the countryside. Water is a strong focal point of any amenity provision and in planning for a recreational environment, the part it can play should be fully considered. One of the main obstacles to such development may be the lack of availability of direct financial assistance from central government. Grants are available for certain urban aid programmes and for the reclamation of derelict land, but countryside grants are not available in urban areas, although there are often opportunities within urban areas to provide countryside facilities within easy access of the town dwellers. A change of policy in this direction to provide greater flexibility in the award of grant could assist considerably in creating a satisfactory recreational environment.

Housing the arts

It has become a common practice to talk of recreation as embracing on the one hand, sport and physical recreation, and on the other, the arts and cultural pursuits. The range of activities embraced under the umbrella of the arts, is as extensive as is found with sport. Artistic activities can be grouped under four headings — music, drama, visual arts and literature — and within each there is a great diversity of further activity. There is a considerable area of overlap between sport and the arts. Activities such as dancing can claim an affinity in either direction, and many sporting activities and competitions judged by style, have much that is akin to artistic disciplines. The similarity, for example, between floor exercises in gymnastics and ballet is such that both dancers and gymnasts can benefit from close involvement in each other's activity.

If a broad view is taken of this cultural field, the activity could take in a spectrum from opera to bingo, from Covent Garden to Butlins and from a South Kensington museum to a Wembley pop festival. Given this wide field, a significant sign in recent years has been a shift in emphasis from passive interest as audience to active involvement as participant. The move is away from the elitism and exclusiveness that has surrounded the arts in the early part of the century, and especially the immediate post war years, and towards the participant arts. The street theatre, the wide interest in folk groups, the revival of music, dance and even drama in the pubs, the discotheque and the open air art gallery, are all part of this scene and involve far greater numbers in a creative sense than ever before.

This tendency is also reflected in the administration of the arts. The Arts Council has been receiving increasingly large amounts of government funds to dispense in grants. During its early years, it was predominantly involved with quality and standards of performance and was preoccupied with support to the major performing companies and national institutions. Even today, one third of the Arts Council grant goes to four major professional companies, but the emphasis is changing and great effort is made to spread this influence throughout the country and to every level.

The encouragement of Regional Arts Associations with grants both from central sources and from local authorities, is having a significant effect upon participation at the grass roots. But as in sport, the main responsibility for the encouragement of the arts is more and more that of the local authority. Local authority involvement in cultural activities has been, and still is, uneven but from April 1974, new local authorities have amended powers for the encouragement of the arts.

The only service that has essentially been provided by local government in the past is the library service, but many authorities have over the years taken an interest in providing other facilities, such as concert halls, theatres, museums and art galleries. Many library services in local authorities have seen their role as extending beyond that of the arts. Examples of extension activities frequently promoted through library services, are lectures, film shows, gramophone recitals, play and poetry readings, art exhibitions, concerts and drama, and library authorities have encouraged festivals and competitions of artistic work of many kinds. A Library Association study (7.15) in 1968 reported that approximately half of the library authorities were extending their work in one or other of these directions, treating the library building as a social and cultural focus for the community, rather than as a repository of books. The library is an important component of the local authorities' total recreation resources. In some areas it may become the focal point for the arts; in others the hub of activity may be an arts centre, one of the components of which might well be a library outlet.

The development of the arts centre in the local authority has been slow moving but there are several good examples. There is, however, great variety in the type and scale of provision. In many authorities, attention has been given to housing the performing arts and the emphasis placed upon providing a comfortable auditorium in which to stage a variety of professional productions. Elsewhere a more balanced approach has been adopted with attention given to the needs of the participant in the form of rehearsal rooms, workshops and studios. A good example is at the Midlands Arts Centre in Birmingham. This Centre sets out to provide 'a new kind of place'. On a site leased from the City of Birmingham and carefully landscaped into a public park, the Centre has tried to show that, in all its forms, the arts can be practised and enjoyed by far more people than has traditionally been accepted. It aims particularly at young children and to expand their knowledge and experience right through adolescent to adult years and is especially concerned to attract the family. In attempting this, it provides a warmly attractive and exciting centre of activity, adequately equipped with both practical facilities and professional expertise. Among the facilities planned over a ten year building programme are a film theatre, exhibition hall, music and dance pavilion, visual arts gallery, restaurant, theatres, studios, an arts club, swimming pool and squash courts. The sports facilities complement those already existing in the park for outdoor games. The success of this Centre in providing new horizons for many young children, adults and families in the area, has been an encouragement to many other authorities.

Elsewhere, even greater attention has been given to cultivating the link with sport. Billingham Forum, Wythenshawe Forum and the proposed centre at the Elephant and Castle in South London have combined arts and sports facilities. At Stevenage a special study of the needs of both sport and the arts was conducted which has resulted in a design for a centre combining these interests. Among the common amenities proposed are an entrance foyer, creche, administrative suite, publicity and box office, sales area, meeting rooms, lecture theatre, exhibition areas, cloakroom and toilet facilities, dining and bar facilities. To cater for the interests of the arts, is a main auditorium with fully equipped stage, fly tower and facilities for projection, dressing and make up rooms, rehearsal rooms, workshop, storage areas for properties and scenery, wardrobe facilities, band room and separate bars for quick interval refreshment services. An exhibition area, studios, craft rooms and music practice rooms, complete the arts facilities. Sports provision is to include a large sports hall, ancillary halls, equally capable of use for artistic or sporting activities and squash courts. The building is based on the concept of a centre embodying a multitude of activity and designed to provide the leisure heart of the town.

The hierarchical approach to the provision of facilities for the arts is equally as appropriate as it is for sports buildings. Very little detailed study of arts facilities has been undertaken to help establish standards of provision in the arts. The type of facility considered earlier would indeed be towards the upper levels of the hierarchy. If the concept of participation by the masses is to be encouraged, there would obviously be a need for substantial provision at the neighbourhood level. Some of this could be provided in schools and much already exists within the adult education system. Nor indeed are large scale and costly facilities the only solution. Many activities, for example, gramophone recitals, chess, rehearsals for music and drama, can take place in quite modest surroundings. Some facilities will be provided by voluntary societies perhaps acting in concert with each other or with the local authority through the medium of local arts councils. In other instances, existing premises, churches, halls, pubs, branch libraries, and a variety of other buildings can be adapted. There is, however, a case for permanent provision, particularly at this modest level. A number of arts centres have been established in large houses, perhaps run by the local authority or alternatively purchased by the local authority and handed over to local arts councils to manage. With local government reorganisation, many properties suitable for such conversion may emerge. The amalgam-ation of several local authorities has, for example, released from use a number of public buildings. It would require little effort to convert, say a town hall, to this purpose. The Council Chamber, the committee rooms and ancillary facilities, would relatively easily convert to meet the needs of a variety of cultural activities and amateur groups. A centre of this kind is currently being provided in the Battersea Town Hall. But the development of such activities is dependent also upon the provision of enthusiastic leadership; increasingly this is now being provided by officers of the local authority who are able to co-ordinate and make more effective the work of voluntary societies and promote events even in circumstances where purpose-built facilities are completely absent.

Community recreation facilities

A number of community facilities for recreation fall outside the specific requirements of sport and the arts. Recreational open space includes more than playing fields. The provision of general amenity areas in the form of public parks has been an established responsibility of local authorities. Parks are getting away from their Victorian image of grass and flower beds and are providing a wide variety of activity and entertainment of all kinds in the open air. Musical concerts, whether of the 'pop' or classical variety, children's zoos, exhibitions of sculpture and paintings, floral art, enhanced by floodlighting or by Son et Lumière, are examples of the type of amenity use of open space commonly found today in public parks.

In urban areas it may be necessary to provide small oases of open space, in the form of attractive local parks and gardens which people can enjoy within easy reach of their homes. Similarly, small areas are required for children's play space. Standards of provision for children's play space have been issued by the Department of the Environment (7.16) and several research studies related to various aspects of children's play and methods of provision have been completed (7.17, 7.18). The needs of children's play have been categorised as follows:

1. Orthodox playgrounds – fixed equipment, hard surfaced.
2. General playgrounds – variety of equipment, sand pits, and paddling pools.
3. Ball games areas – possibly with goalposts and floodlighting.
4. Natural playgrounds – land left in natural state, with hollows, and bushes.
5. Toddlers' playgrounds – small scale equipment for confidence building.
6. Adventure playground – providing creative play involving play leadership and facilities for indoor and outdoor play.
7. Comprehensive playgrounds – providing as many of the above groups as space will allow.

These needs suggest a range of sites from small local amenity spaces of less than two acres to intimate play spaces of ¼–1 acre, which have to be provided within and adjoining housing estates, within easy pedestrian access of children's homes.

Another area of public amenity open space to be considered is the allotment. Many local authorities have a statutory requirement to provide allotments, but the extent of demand is variable. In some areas, allotments are lying derelict and overgrown but some authorities are reporting a revival in the interest in allotment holding. With many modern houses in towns having increasingly small gardens, it is possible that an increasing demand for allotments will be experienced in the future. The proposed 'leisure garden', replacing the old image of the allotment, holds out interesting possibilities (7.19).

At this point, we can refer to the section on recreational open space earlier in this chapter (pages 198-202) and bring together the total range of provision. A hierarchical approach to the provision of open space has been suggested within the Greater London Development Plan (7.20) as follows:

Type	Main function	Minimum size	Distance from home	Characteristics
(a) Metropolitan park	Weekend and occasional visits by car or public transport	150 acres	2 miles, or more where the park is appreciably larger	Either 1, natural heathland, down-land commons, woodland, etc., or 2, formal parks providing for both active and recreation e.g. boating, entertainments, etc. May contain playing fields but at least 100 acres for other pursuits. Adequate car parking essential
(b) District park	Weekend and occasional visits on foot	50 acres	¾ mile	Containing playing fields, but at least 30 acres for other pursuits (as in local parks) and some car parking

Type	Main function	Minimum size	Distance from home	Characteristics
(c) Local park	For pedestrian visitors including nearby workers	5 acres	¼ mile	Providing for court games, children's play, sitting-out areas, landscaped environment; and playing fields if the parks are large enough
(d) Small local park	Pedestrian visits especially people, children, and workers at midday particularly valuable in high density areas	Under 5 acres	¼ mile or less	Gardens, sitting-out areas and/or children's playgrounds

Apart from open space requirements, the other main community facility to be considered is the multi-purpose hall. A community hall can serve a multitude of functions and will also be suitable for use for many sporting and artistic activities. Many public halls already exist within communities in both public and private ownership and serve a variety of uses.   In small communities a multi-purpose building may be a more justifiable form of provision than a specialist facility for either sport or the arts. The principles of provision referred to earlier apply equally to this type of facility and particular attention should be given to ensuring the full use of existing facilities. Multi-purpose halls in schools, public buildings, old people's homes, or churches, can provide for a considerable amount of recreational activity (7.21). With new housing developments many community halls are being provided and with careful attention to design, these could be capable of housing a variety of recreational activity. In large urban areas, there could be a case for a planned mix of community halls with facilities for the more specific needs of sports and arts. The flexible use of facilities will help ensure a full and effective use and this can be encouraged within a comprehensive local authority recreational service.

The recreation service

The main emphasis, to this point, has been upon providing the right environment for recreation. It is very evident that if effective and co-ordinated use of facilities is to be ensured and opportunity given over such a wide field of diverse activity, a recreation service with wide ranging responsibilities is necessary. Local authorities in this country have long recognised their role as providers of recreation, but traditionally the service they have given has developed in separate and often fragmented departments. Thus in many local authorities separate libraries, baths, parks and education committees may have existed for many years, each with its own chief officers and separate professional staff, and frequently duplicating both the service offered and the facilities provided.

In 1967 the Maud Committee reviewing the management of local government, criticised this absence of unity in the internal organisation of a local authority, and recommended that councils should be reduced in size and that the number of committees should be reduced, both to avoid overlap, to provide a better service and to allow members time free from committees to make contact with their electorate (7.22).

Prompted by this advice, a number of authorities, in some cases on the advice of independent management consultants, streamlined their committee structures. The pattern varied; some committees covered physical recreation, while in others a single committee which was responsible for all amenity aspects of local authority provision, was formed. Having created the committee structure, several authorities realised that for an effective service to be provided, it was essential also to provide the professional officers to co-ordinate and develop this work within a recreation department. Early thinking on this topic largely prompted from experience in Europe, had been to establish machinery for sport and recreation in isolation from other leisure requirements. Changes in thinking on leisure over the years and the experience of the pioneer departments in this country at, for example, Teesside and Greenwich, has confirmed that there are great advantages of carrying the service throughout the recreational spectrum. The effect of reorganisation of local government covering larger geographical areas, with both enlarged resources, and greater needs, has brought into focus the need for a comprehensive service staffed with officers of high standing and capable of making the case for recreation within the management team of the local authority.

Prompted by the strong support given to the recreation department in the House of Lords Select Committee Report on Sport and Leisure and in line with the concepts of corporate management outlined in the recommendations of the Bains Report on Local Authority Management Structures (7.23), a large number of new local authorities have elected to appoint chief officers within their management teams responsible for the whole field of leisure and amenity. Local government reorganisation has provided a substantial fillip to recreation planning, and there are now about 140 local authorities with recreation and leisure departments.

The House of Lords Select Committee's recommendation that "every authority on whom the recreation duty is placed, should have a Recreation Committee and should set up a Recreation Department under its own chief officer", would therefore appear to have already been taken seriously. A recreation department can achieve a much fuller use of existing resources – whether private, commercial or public – and the more effective siting and administration of new facilities. Working within the local authority in collaboration with other departments a positive plan for recreation can be developed; in its collective form it will be a major service commanding a budget only surpassed by housing, education and the social services. The challenge is to prepare and implement a total community recreation plan that can harness all the resources in the area. Given a balanced range of community provision catering for all interests, well publicised and imaginatively marketed, urban recreation planning can play an important part in enhancing an acceptable quality of life. It can do much to extend areas of personal choice in every day life, to release individual aspirations and preferences, to cater for family and group needs and to provide a new cohesive force in community affairs. This after all is what recreation planning is all about.

References

7.1 M. Dower, 'Fourth Wave: The Challenge of Leisure', *Architects Journal*, 20th January, 1965.
7.2 University of Keele/British Travel Association, *Pilot National Recreation Survey*, 1967.
7.3 K.K. Sillitoe, *Planning for Leisure*, HMSO, 1969.
7.4 The Sports Council, *Research Priorities for Sports Provision*, 1971.
7.5 North West Sports Council, *Leisure in the North West*, 1972.
7.6 House of Lords Select Committee Report on Sport and Leisure, 1973.
7.7 The Sports Council, *Planning for Sport*, 1968.
7.8 The Sports Council, *Provision for Sport*, 1971.
7.9 The Sports Council, *Indoor Sports Centres*, 1971.
7.10 The Sports Council, *Planning for Sport – Indoor Sports Halls*, forthcoming.
7.11 Department of the Environment, *Open Space in Urban Areas*, HMSO, 1973.
7.12 Islington Borough Council, *Recreational Open Space*, 1973.
7.13 The Sports Council, *Golf Course Provision in Great Britain*, forthcoming.
7.14 The Sports Council, *Provision for Sport*, Volume II – Specialist Facilities, 1973.
7.15 Library Association, *Public Library Extension Activities*, 1968.
7.16 Department of the Environment, Circular No. 79/72, 8th August, 1972.
7.17 A. Holme and P. Massie, *Children's Play: A Study of Needs and Opportunities*, Michael Joseph, 1970.
7.18 Lady Allen of Hurtwood, *Planning for Play*, Thames and Hudson, 1968.
7.19 *Report of Departmental Committee into Allotments*, HMSO, 1969.
7.20 Greater London Council, *Greater London Development Plan*, 1968.
7.21 Department of the Environment, Design Bulletin No. 28, *Multi-Purpose Halls*, 1973.
7.22 Ministry of Housing and Local Government, *Management of Local Government* (The Maud Report), HMSO, 1967.
7.23 Department of the Environment, *The New Local Authorities: Management and Structure* (The Bains Report), HMSO, 1972.

Further reading

British Travel Association/University of Keele, *Pilot National Recreation Survey*, Report No. 1, 1967, and No. 2, 1969.
T.L. Burton (ed.), *Recreation Research and Planning*, Allen and Unwin, 1970.
I. Cosgrove & R. Jackson, *Geography of Recreation and Leisure,* Hutchinson, 1971.
Department of Education and Science, *Provincial Museums and Art Galleries,* HMSO, 1973.
M. Dower, *The Challenge of Leisure*, Civic Trust, 1965.
House of Lords Select Committee, *Sport and Leisure*, HMSO, 1973.
B. Luckham, *The Library in Society*, The Library Association, 1971.
P.C. McIntosh, *Sport in Society*, Watts, 1963.
Northwest Sports Council, *Leisure in the North West,* 1972.
S.R. Parker, *The Future of Work and Leisure*, MacGibbon and Kee, 1971.
J.A. Patmore, *Land and Leisure*, David and Charles, 1970.
K.K. Sillitoe, *Planning for Leisure*, HMSO, 1969.
M.F. Tanner, *Water Resources and Recreation*, The Sports Council, 1973.
The Arts Council, *The First Twenty Five Years*, Annual Report, 1970-71.
The Sports Council, *Planning for Sport*, 1968.
The Sports Council, *Provision for Sport*, Volume 1, 1972.
The Sports Council, *Provision for Sport*, Volume 2, 1973.
P. Willmott & M. Young, *The Symmetrical Family*, Routledge, 1973.

8 Urban Government

As cities have grown in population, in area and in the variety and richness of their activities, one thing has remained constant. Their governing has been experienced as a problem. The shape of the problem has appeared to change from time to time. In the 19th century the city was seen mainly as a public health hazard. In the early decades of this century architects worried about congestion and lack of open space in which the green influence of nature could work on city children. By mid-century it was anxiety about size and sprawl as London's growth alarmed the town planners. In the 1960's urban transport and its destructive effect on the environment came to the fore as a problem. Often one generation's policies have been the next generation's problem.

Underlying all these perceived problems there lay another, continually confronted but seldom understood: the design of institutions of urban governance and their policymaking processes. The 1970's have brought this meta-problem into the open. Why this has happened is uncertain. Perhaps it is because complexity and the rate of change have increased to a degreee that causes us conscious institutional discomfort (8.1). It has now become a focus for study and action. When Friend and Jessop (8.2) reported in 1968 on their research in Coventry Corporation they were among the first to bill the management of uncertainty and change as a major task for urban planning. This and later studies of policymaking for instance by Dror (8.3), Rose and Boaden (8.4, 8.5) are evidence of a reconsideration of the purpose, nature and behaviour of the institutions that govern cities.

Housing and social welfare, environment or transport, the themes that have occupied earlier chapters, are problems on which urban government has powers to decide and resources to act, for continuity or for change and for good or ill. The theme of this chapter is urban government itself. It sees urban government as a problem: how to create an adequate system of governance.

In one sence the chapter is descriptive: what urban government is, what it does and how it is changing. But it is also a tentative explanation of some of the changes. I therefore focus on three issues in urban government that I believe are the cause of much worry at present and play a part in the change. The first is the question of how to achieve *coordination*, so that the actions of many different bodies in various policy fields make sense as a whole. The second question is how to get knowledge and information into decision making, how to maximise *intelligence*. The third is a question about *democracy*. While it far surpasses these two in significance it is furthest from being answered. Without a satisfactory answer to it, coordinated and intelligent decision making will bring us into worse trouble than we are in already. It is how to ensure that the responsibility for making decisions comes into the hands of ordinary people who are affected by them. The choice of these issues may be arbitrary, perhaps picked out at the cost of ignoring others. Yet they seem to me to make a useful framework for studying current trends.

Since I have used the words coordination, intelligence and democracy rather frequently it may be best to say at the outset what I mean by them. By coordination I mean recognising, taking account of and using creatively the relatedness that exists between urban phenomena; between agencies that make policy for intervention; between instruments of urban management such as the powers and responsibilities created by legislation; and perhaps most important, relatedness in policy and action. The idea behind coordination is that if people as individuals experience problems that are indivisible, so do communities. No community 'problem' can be 'solved' without either modifying or exacerbating another. Urban authorities with some claim to democratic representativeness, in so far as they seek to have an impact on conditions, should therefore share goals and objectives and negotiate mutually supporting policies.

The term intelligence I have used as short for a number of different things. It includes the most conscious and thorough use of empirical data and current theory in understanding cities and communities; the use of an analytical process to further the rational element in decision making; and the creation of an information cycle in the decision process that feeds back into decision facts about the state of the community, the impact of policy and the nature and behaviour of the decision making organisation itself to enable learning and adaptation.

As in all situations of change, the key words can be used in a retrogressive and progressive sense. In using the word democracy I am conscious that it has quite rightly fallen into disrepute because of the palpable shortcomings in what passes for democracy in Britain today. The electoral representational arrangements in urban decision making as we know them are called democracy but are far from satisfying the principles of democracy. I am using the term nonetheless to refer to a process that has yet to be created which would satisfy the ideals of equality of access to decision, full and open discussion as opposed to brute majority voting, the patient creation of consensus, immediate and responsive representation – and so on.

In the first section I look at the different institutions that make up urban government and the way they have developed over time. The several bodies serve one and the same public. Yet they often act as though each had its own client and its own objectives. As those who govern cities have come to recognise complexity and relatedness in society and the city, they have begun to look for relatedness in policy. Policies should serve compatible objectives and reinforce each other. This in turn has brought home the need for coordination. In the next sections I therefore describe some recent reforms whose main aim has been better coordination in urban government.

I then proceed to look briefly at the question of applying knowledge to urban policymaking. Some progress has been made in the last decade in improving coordination and intelligence, at least within local government. The result has been, however, to set decision making at yet more of a remove from the people and from most of their elected representatives, making it now more urgent than ever that we look for some radical solution to the third question, that of democratic usage. Reorganised local authorities may well give power to a few councillors chairing key committees at the expense of the majority; they may reinforce the dominance of the majority party. Special knowledge in the hands of professional officers of local government has made it difficult for the amateur, the councillor, fully to understand the reasoning behind policies he is called on to endorse. The long-term corporate planning process operated by a unified local government service is further removed from the intervention of the woman on the housing estate than were the *ad hoc* decisions of the old style single purpose departments.

People meanwhile have begun to have more, not fewer, expectations of urban government, and the tendency of the town hall to withdraw behind a smokescreen of good management practice and policy analysis has not gone unremarked. A wave of disaffection has spread through cities in the last few years. This ferment among small groups representing diverse interests has come to be called 'community action'. It is partly in reaction against the centralising and professionalising of decision making. It also seems to be a response to the failure of the big political parties to represent opinion of the deprived 10 per cent who are mainly found in the inner areas of large cities, or indeed to have anything relevant to say on urban affairs. These aspects are examined later in the chapter.

There has been anxiety within government, too, about the adverse implications for democracy of strong management systems. Small compensatory steps have been ventured in the other direction, devolving administration to smaller units. I mention some of these in a later section. Another response by urban authorities to community action has been a series of essays in the management of relations between themselves and the community in an attempt to bring the new dissent into a bureaucratic framework in place of the formal political context which it evades. I describe these towards the end of the chapter.

The series of related changes described here are adjustments along the axis that runs from a totalitarian order at one extreme to a kind of chaos at the other. They take place in two dimensions – the bureaucratic and the political, always interacting. The main development initiative in the late sixties and early seventies has been bureaucratic. The chapter ends in speculation about the future response of urban politics.

The scope of urban government

The three issues in urban government, but particularly the problem of coordination, can probably best be understood by looking at the scope of urban authorities and how they came into existence. The government of any one city region, say Merseyside or Greater London, today comprises many different types of body. They differ in the job they do, the way they are financed, the way they are controlled. At the core of the system are the county councils and district councils of local government itself. Local authorities are quite complex institutions. From the management point of view they are more challenging than most businesses because they not only cover many different fields of concern (ranging from education, say, to environmental health) but they play many different *kinds* of role. The authority is in turn a provider (for example, of schooling, of social care, of building work); a regulator (of cleanliness and of standards); a sponsor (paying grants to students); a purchaser of many different kinds of goods for the use of its own staff (e.g. stationery) and its clients (e.g. school milk). It is a propagandist, disseminating educational material about the danger of smoking, road safety and uses of family planning. It plays the part of censor (of films for local showing). It is a coordinator, attempting to negotiate shared objectives and complementary activities in a number of different departments within and a number of different institutions without. Finally, it is a cooperator, working along with other institutions involved in city governance.

In spite of deploying this extensive range of powers, the local authorities between them are by no means the whole of urban government. Health, water and transport authorities share the responsibility for urban policy and management. Statutory undertakings supply gas and electricity. Central government is active in the city too. In some of its aspects it is part of urban provision. Its departments run the post offices, the employment exchanges and the social security offices that spill their queues onto city pavements. It augments local authority rate revenues from the Exchequer. Its legislation creates the framework for local authority policies and its circulars to local authority committees chivvy or chide them into reflecting in their work the intentions of Acts passsed in Westminster and interpreted in Whitehall. Central government has long influenced the prospects of different localities of Britain through discriminatory regional development policies. More recently it has accepted first hand involvement in city government through the Urban Programme and other initiatives.

So urban government is shared by many bodies that between them have power to make policy relating to a wide range of matters. They generate an overall spatial policy to guide decisions on location of activities such as industry, shopping, housing and transport. They have a say in the use to which any plot of land or any building may be put. They supervise the shape and to some extent the pace of physical development. They manage or mismanage the environment, controlling or neglecting rivers, guarding against or ignoring pollution. They plant trees, kill rats and must provide each of us with a well-mown stretch of turf beneath which to rest our coffin. They protect the consumer to some extent against the cheating shopkeeper and the dirty restauranteur, the man in the street against assault and the man indoors from fire. They take responsibility for schooling children, they support individuals and families that cannot cope without help and they play a big part in housing the urban population.

In this sense, then, urban government does make itself felt by the governed. Ordinary people are affected both by the kind of policies the urban governors make and the efficiency with which their officers carry them through. But it has to be remembered that many of the things that may matter most, such as the buoyancy of the economy, the supply of jobs and the level of incomes relative to prices, are out of the hands of local urban government. Local government can do little to accelerate the overall rate of housebuilding and improvement, to influence the distribution of real incomes and of wealth, to maintain or wipe out barriers of class and race. These are partly accessible to national policy but they are hardly amenable to local control. Even the policy fields in which urban government does have power to act are influenced strongly by the centre, not only by legislative and financial control but by the right of central government departments, for example, to approve or reject forward plans of local authority departments or proposals for the appointment of senior officers.

The multiplicity of agencies involved in urban administration derives from the 19th century and before. The industrial revolution in Britain was a particularly formative time because the growth of industry and movement away from the land was transforming the settlement pattern beyond recognition. The population increased almost fourfold in the 19th century. By the end of that period one-third of the people had become city dwellers, living in places of 100 000 or more inhabitants. The countryside had lost many of its people to towns of smaller size too.

In those decades of stress the practical problems of housing, sanitation, health and education overwhelmed the new urban people, crowded into poorly served cities. The question of urban government became an urgent issue on the agenda of Parliament. Whether motivated by fear of crime, disorder and disease, or by sympathetic distress about ill health and poverty, many of the middle class, using as vehicles commissions of enquiry, official committees and voluntary pressure groups, urged on Parliament the reform of the machinery of urban government. The Municipal Corporations Act, 1835 was one of the more important pieces of legislation intended to strengthen local government. It liberalised the constitution of the Corporations and was a step in the cities towards the representative local authorities we have now across the country with paid fulltime officers and a range of practical responsibilities.

Central government intervened increasingly as the 19th century advanced, introducing Public Health Acts, town improvement and housing legislation. However, as each new set of powers was introduced and each new function created in the urban administration the tendency was to set up a new and separate authority to do the job. A proliferation of bodies was involved in the government of any one city: the Corporation, the Guardians, the School Board, Local Board of Health, a Highway Board, the Improvement Commissioners and others. This legacy of separate urban authorities has influenced local government behaviour even to this day and is one cause of the poor coordination that has motivated many of the reforms of the last five years.

The 20th century has brought two contrary trends in the assembly of urban powers. In the first thirty years or so local authorities gained many of the functions of formerly independent boards, becoming for instance (as they still are) education and highway authorities. Since the Second World War, however, the pendulum has swung the other way. The provision of many of the basic utilities has been hived off and local government has now lost the responsibility it used to have for personal health, water supply and, in some areas, for passenger transport.

The new urban institutions

In the last few years urban government has been subject to institutional change on a scale unprecedented in this century. Territorial boundaries have been shifted; functions redistributed; the nature of public control has been modified; internal organisation has been reshaped and the decision process changed. A big part in these changes is played by the three issues of urban governance I chose to look at earlier in this chapter. The reforms are explicitly intended to improve coordination; this is perhaps their main purpose. They seek better spatial coordination and better functional coordination. Less explicitly, I think, there is a feeling underlying the reforms that new institutions with new management structures will enable more rational management and planning, that it will allow decision making based on a study of facts and in pursuit of recognised objectives; in other words, that it is a move in the direction of intelligent government. The extent to which the reforms can or do achieve either of these objectives is discussed below. Meanwhile, however, it seems likely that they have exacerbated rather than do anything to heal the rift between governing and governed. The third problem seems further from solution.

What has happened? The Local Government Act, 1972, has introduced the most extensive reform of local government that it was politically feasible to push through. On April 1, 1974 the old system of county and county borough councils, urban and rural districts, inherited from the legislation of 1888 and 1894, gave way to a system of county and county district councils. Six of the counties are Metropolitan Counties and many of their Districts are large cities, formerly county boroughs. In these Metropolitan Areas the division of functions between the two tiers differs from that between the Shire Counties and their Districts. The net result is fewer, larger, more self-contained authorities in which cities are more closely related to their surrounding countryside and the big industrial conurbations are accepted for what they are.

The main impetus for this change has been population growth, commercial and industrial development, and the increase in the number of motor vehicles. The redrawing of boundaries has been a response to the nature of urban development. The Royal Commission on Local Government in England (8.6) and many others involved in local government wanted reorganisation as a means of rationalising the distribution of functions as well as coordinating spatial relationships, in such a way as to bring services together under a unitary management system in a unitary authority. This hope was disappointed by the Act. As it is, in the Metropolitan Counties town development, planning and transportation are separate from education, youth employment, housing and personal social services which lie with the Districts. The painfully accumulated powers of the old county boroughs, which were beginning to emerge as a powerful instrument for urban government, have been negligently dispersed. The Shire Counties show some gains in coordination, yet even there, though education and social services are at County level, the management and planning of housing services which tie in so closely with them are handled by the Districts. The detailed distribution of activities that emerges is still somewhat uncertain at the time of writing because the Act has made allowance for flexibility through agency arrangements and it remains to be seen how the new councils will use this power (8.7).

One aspect of local government not touched by the new legislation is finance. The Redcliffe-Maud report (8.8) had seen reform of local authority finance as one of the major purposes of reorganisation. The authors deplored the fact that local government was dependent for more than 50 per cent of its income on Exchequer funds and that this dependency was growing.

"The tendency is not a healthy one. It limits not only the freedom of local authorities in making decisions that should properly belong to them, but also their sense of responsibility, to the extent that they are spending money they do not raise and do not have to account for to their electors."

The Green Paper on local government finance (8.9) and a subsequent consultation document (8.10) have given little hope, however, of any fundamental improvement in local government's sources of revenue. The most that seems likely is an improvement in the rating system and the manner in which central government grants are made, but without additional sources of independent money for local government.

Alongside the new local authorities there are new regional water authorities and new health authorities. The water authorities have taken over the water conservation, water quality control, navigation and recreation functions of the present-day river authorities, and the water supply and sewage disposal work formerly handled by the local authorities. Local authorities keep only their local sewerage functions. The new bodies have the British Waterways Board's responsibility for canal and river navigation. They replace the existing joint water boards and joint sewerage boards. Only the statutory water companies continue to exist as agents of the Regional Water Authority. In the RWAs, spatial coordination of an internal kind, dictated by topography, has been gained at the cost of spatial coordination between local authorities and water authorities, whose boundaries are different.

The new National Health Service, brought into being at the same time as the new local and water authorities, comprises regional health authorities and area health authorities. They replace the former hospital boards and the personal health role of local government. The area bodies will have the same boundaries as the new district councils and this may go some way to help coordinated working.

Somewhat before these upheavals a related innovation had occurred in the management of urban transport. The Transport Act, 1968, gave the Minister powers to designate areas as 'passenger transport areas'. The authorities set up under the Act have a partially elected composition similar to that of water and health authorities and at executive level in each area a Passenger Transport Executive with a director general and from two to eight members. These authorities behave as self-supporting financial concerns, with power to carry passengers by road, rail or water, to pay agents to provide these services and to hire out vehicles for freight. The Act required them to prepare development plans for future passenger transport systems for approval by the local councils in their area and by the Minister (8.11).

Within their own institutional walls these new authorities have greater scope than the old for coordinated policy and action. They bring under one management system responsibilities that were formerly scattered among many. (An exception is the Metropolitan Districts that have fewer powers than the old county boroughs.) But the very act of bringing into existence powerful new bodies with clearly defined functions has increased the difficulty of coordination between them. Coherent government is going to depend heavily on the planning processes of the different institutions and the extent to which they enable them to share objectives and coordinate means.

Stewart (8.12) has called the new comprehensive and community-directed decision process that we need 'community planning'.

"Community planning is wider in scope than local authority policy planning. It does not take as its starting point those problems which are the concern of the local authority. Community planning is not restricted to problems which are the concern of any particular organisation. It is concerned with planning to meet the problems and needs of the community within a specified area, irrespective of the particular organisation that might be involved – or even whether any organisation would be involved."

Adapting the management structure of local government

The period of urban government reorganisation just ended has been seized by many authorities as a chance to rationalise their management structures in such a way as to take full advantage of those instances where they have assembled related responsibilities together and to mitigate the difficulties brought by sharing responsibilities with other organisations. The main aim, as it shows up in the various documents in which the changes were foreshadowed, has been efficiency. But significantly the concept of community purpose and responsibility has been re-emphasised. Urban government has begun to see its purpose and take its cue less from budgetary necessity than 'community needs'.

The development in management in local government was stimulated partly by the growth of interest in management in business, itself prompted by competition from the United States of America and Europe. There had been a rapid increase in the number of management courses for executives heading for careers in industry and commerce and changes in their content. The old O and M and Work Study schools of management were giving way to a more purposeful approach using 'management by objectives' and corporate planning. In the public sector, however, public and municipal administration and the educational courses that served them remained somewhat conventional, offering a broad understanding of the structure in which civil servants and local government officers worked but few concepts or techniques of planned policymaking or strategic choice. People were beginning to realise however that the management of Glasgow or Newcastle was no less demanding an activity than the management of ICI or Fords, indeed it was more difficult because of the many more legitimate interests government has to satisfy than does industry. Yet the senior officers of local government were not yet thought of as managers, nor was the management structure of the local authorities in, say, 1965 the product of any conscious design.

In 1967 a committee under the chairmanship of John Maud reported to the Minister on the management of local government (8.13). It argued strongly against the tradition of specialist administration in local government.

"Individual services, however disparate, are provided for the community as a whole. Planning for the development of the community, the allocation of priorities for finance or for space on the drawing board, the timing of the various schemes all demand a coordinated approach. The establishment of a managing body can provide this necessary coordination and focal point; it can provide both a unifying element drawing together the disparate parts of the whole and also the impetus for action."

The origin of urban government in many separate bodies with unique functions serving the same locality has influenced the behaviour within local government ever since. This is perhaps most marked in the case of a local education authority, which can serve as an example. Although technically only a committee of the Council, it has tended to behave very much as though it were a separate authority. The school buildings are treated as though they are not communal property, they belong to the educational authority: community use is the LEA's to dispense or withhold. Its links with central government were often tighter than its links with neighbouring committees and departments in local government. The marked division of local government into separate departments was exacerbated by the tradition of limiting the recruitment of senior officers to a single profession. It is unusual to find any officer being appointed or getting preferment to a second or third tier job in education without having been a teacher, in social services without a professional social work qualification, or in town planning unless a member of the Royal Town Planning Institute. Likewise Treasurers and their staff are members of the Institute of Municipal Treasurers and Accountants. All but a few Town Clerks (and the great majority of the Chief Executives in the new authorities) are lawyers. This use of professional qualification in staff selection has made hard work of communication across departmental boundaries and allowed a close group identification to develop around areas of specialist expertise. It has also prevented innovation reaching local government by means of the educational system, since the same professions that guard the right to jobs in local government are also in control of the content of professional education.

During the late 1960's many local authorities of their own accord followed Maud's advice and reviewed their internal structure, either by means of their own committees or by obtaining management consultants to advise them. In 1971 the Local Government Training Board (8.14) responded to the new interest in management by setting up a study group on management education for local government. A year later a further study group of the Department of the Environment (8.15) reported on suitable management structure for the new authorities, then about to be created under the Local Government Act, 1972. This was the Bains Report. Bains' advice to local government, like Maud's, was to look outward to the community it served.

"Local government is not limited to the provision of services. It is concerned with the overall economic cultural and physical wellbeing of the community . . . The traditional departmental attitude within much of local government must give way to a wider ranging corporate outlook . . . Management is not an end in itself. Changes in management structure must be justified in terms of the benefit to the community."

The Bains Report also invited officers and members to look sideways towards their colleagues in other programme areas. It discouraged professionalism and proposed horizontal movement of personnel between departments to foster the corporate approach.

Prompted by the shake-up of reorganisation in 1973-4 many local authorities have reshaped or are reshaping themselves internally, and in doing so most have followed broadly the advice of Maud and Bains. There has been a marked reduction in the number of committees carrying on council business, from as many as thirty or forty to as few as nine or ten. The number of departments too has been reduced, and logically related functions merged together under a single directorate. It is quite common for example to find responsibility for building, valuation, spatial planning and roads, once administered by three or four units, now managed as one under the general title of 'development'. Many authorities have set up a Policy Committee, some with resource subcommittees on finance, land and personnel and, as Bains proposed, a policy review subcommittee to provide a continual critical reappraisal of local authority policy. The role of town clerk or county clerk has given way to the 'chief executive'. As leader of the officers and principal adviser to the council he has no specialist responsibilities and is free for the first time to be a *general* manager. Often he is advised by a management team of chief officers, sometimes by a corporate planning unit of some kind.

The Local Authority Social Services Act, 1970, also influenced the internal structure of local government, grouping under one Directorate the social welfare functions of a number of departments. It had much the same motives as the broader reforms: service to the community and coordinated decision-making. It is worth perhaps listing the arguments made for reorganisation of social services in the Seebohm report which preceded the Act, because they throw some light on the motives for change in local government as a whole (8.16). It was hoped the reorganised services would: meet needs on the basis of the overall requirements of the individual or family rather than on the basis of a limited set of symptoms; provide a clear and comprehensive pattern of responsibility and accountability over the whole field; attract more resources; use those resources more effectively; generate adequate recruitment and training of the staff skills which are, or may become, necessary; meet needs which are at present being neglected; adapt to changing conditions; provide a better organisation for collecting and disseminating information relevant to the development of the social services; and be more accessible and comprehensible to those who need to use them. The intention of coping with the three problems of coordination, intelligence and democracy are quite explicit there.

The management reforms then have been rational and long overdue. They have aimed for greater inward connectedness in policy making, so that whichever problems local government concerns itself to tackle it may bring to bear on them coordinated and mutually supporting actions.

Therein may lie better hope for the individual and his indivisible problem, who in the past has had to thread his way through a forest of departmental barriers. There is a real danger, however, that the individual has lost as much as he has gained with the elevation of decision to an even higher plane more remote from her or from him and perhaps remoter too from the elected representative.

The proof of the new structures has yet to be made. It will depend to a large extent on the nature of the planning process that enlivens them. So far it has proved more difficult to change behaviour than to change institutional form.

Changes in the planning process

There is a sense in which all the structural developments described above were motivated by the wish to create a better decision making process. There was a new, more purposeful idea of the work of local government. Two of the qualities that the new planning was intended to ensure – connectivity and the analytical use of available knowledge – were bound to depend as much on process as on structure.

The result of separatist administration in local government had been a partial and spasmodic approach to planned decision making. It was not that no plans or programmes existed, Stewart (8.17) writes: "There are few departments in which they cannot be found. The issue is their adequacy first as an instrument of specialist management, but critically as instruments of general management". There were ten year health programmes, rolling roads programmes, four year housing programmes, a development plan and the treasurer's budget. But there was no mechanism for treating the budgeting procedure as an opportunity for formulating goals that could be shared by all departments, for strategic choice between alternative courses of action. Decisions tended to be incremental and the implicit goal was often no more than the smooth operation of the administrative machine.

If the local authority was to look outward to the community for its legitimation it had to recognise that all its activities were serving one and the same population and the choice as to how to allocate resources between committees should not be a matter of bargaining between vested interests of different sections of the bureaucracy as it had so often been in the past but for overall policy planning in pursuit of community objectives. The introduction of policy planning to local government has been furthered by the work of the Institute of Local Government Studies at the University of Birmingham and the Institute for Operational Research that, with other research bodies created the beginnings of a methodology for corporate planning and strategic choice in local government (8.18, 8.19, 8.20, 8.21). Nonetheless change in the nature and behaviour of policy making bodies has had the support of considerably less research than has urban policy itself.

Corporate planning in local government is only in its infancy and what it aims to be may as yet in many authorities be at some remove from what it is. Unlike the old development plan process this is not a linear sequence leading to an end-state plan. It aims to be cyclical and to produce many different kinds of plan, budget or programme, with differing periodicity, detail and topic. An initiating moment is the setting of general goals for the local authority as a whole and their refinement into more operational objectives, with a time scale for their achievement. Planners then analyse resources of money, men, land and buildings available for the pursuit of objectives; they consider uncertainty and change, and the probable influence on local authority work of those many aspects of city life unamenable to local government management.

A social, economic and environmental analysis is usually made to give policymakers a better understanding of the community they serve, the areas of choice open to them and the constraints that limit them. The next stage in the cycle is the drawing up of a programme structure relating objectives to activities. Position statements punctuate the cycle. There is a continual interaction between policy planning for the local authority as a whole and programme planning within the individual programme areas such as housing, social services or environmental management. Alternative plans are generated, analysed and evaluated by officers. Choices are made by the council. An overall policy statement for the local authority is prepared. Some authorities are now publishing a version of this as the 'community plan' for public information. Action plans are prepared for implementation by departments and hopefully one day by inter-departmental teams. Some attempt is made to establish measures of output and above all of impact, so that it may be possible to know how well the authority is doing in pursuing its aims. But this is proving one of the knottiest problems of planning. Action is monitored and what is learned is fed back into the planning cycle so that objectives and goals may be periodically reviewed.

The rather specific formulation of the planning process known as PPBS (planning programming budgeting system) first used in defense budgeting in the USA and later in private industry has been introduced in some local authorities as the main planning procedure. Others have criticised PPBS as being too formal, impracticable and slanted too heavily in the direction of finance. LAMSAC (8.22) give a neat summary of the process and Eversley and Wood (8.23) and Stewart (8.24) make points for and against its use.

Central government has never legislated for any policy planning process in local government, though in accepting the recommendations of the Maud and Bains reports it has supported its introduction. In particular policy fields however central government has laid planning requirements on local government. It remains a challenge for the authorities to integrate these individual mandatory plans into an authority-wide policy planning cycle. Directorates of Social Services are now required to submit ten year plans to the Department of Health and Social Security. The Ministry of Transport Roads Circular No. 1/68 introduced the expectation of highway authorities to produce traffic and transport plans for the approval of the Department of the Environment.

A particular challenge to corporate planning is the Town and Country Planning Acts, 1968 and 1971 which have radically altered the development planning system. The 1968 procedure involved 'structure plans'. These are statements on strategic issues for as far ahead as can reasonably be foreseen and are concerned with the social, economic and physical systems of an area in so far as these are subject to physical control or influence. Town planners by their training as well as by virtue of the legislation take a broad approach to their work, bringing under their review not only the physical environment but activities such as work, shopping, housing, public services, leisure, transport and recreation. To some extent therefore structure planning is coordinative. Yet there was no provision in the Acts for inclusion of policies for the client-based services of local government or for submission for approval to any department but that of the Environment. Indeed the procedure for submission and for examination in public would have been impossibly cumbersome had more than one ministry been involved. They were town planning Acts, intended for implementation by Town Planning Departments in local government, not by the authority as a whole. There is thus some confusion in local government today as to how to bring into one process this spasmodic but statutory long-range overview of the environment, subject as it is to public enquiry, and the annual internal corporate planning cycle that guides the work of the authority as a whole.

The need for coordination and the difficulty it presents are still more marked in action planning under the 1968 Act, of which few authorities have as yet had experience. If corporate planning is to bring tangible benefit to individuals it has to be more than high level, long term and abstract. Where physical change is imminent for a neighbourhood, with all the shock and loss (as well as the recognised gains) such change means for its people, all the services and controls at the disposal of the local authority clearly have to be brought into play in a coordinated and intelligent way. This may well be a bigger challenge for local authorities than corporate policy planning. It is one thing to paint policy with a broad brush. It is another to carry it through in such a way that the costs do not outweigh the advantages. Those authorities that are beginning to think about action planning are feeling the need for new kinds of inter-professional inter-departmental project teams. The reality of such teams may turn out to do more to break down the box compartments of local government than any amount of fiddling about with the diagrams of management structures.

Nearly all of these changes in institutional form, management structure and planning process can be explained as attempts to struggle, among other things, with the problem of coordination between the actions of the different bodies that make up urban government. Many different bodies were serving one and the same public, but the individual's need was not easily carved up and distributed between public bodies. Many government policies of the past solved one problem at the expense of another. Some of the worst problems we experience are created *by* urban government, by positive policies of road improvement, slum clearance and urban depopulation. Even some of those who stand to gain most from post-war urban policy, the car-using middle class, are appalled by the impact of these policies on the environment and on the lives of many urban people. One could instance the devastation wrought by slum clearance in Liverpool and the abuse of the city centre of Birmingham by acres of urban motorway. Yet these policies were well intended. Their failure lay in the fact that they were one-dimensional, they did not have regard to relatedness in the problem nor seek relatedness in policy. The recent changes in urban government have been moved by an intention to make the actions of urban government make sense as a whole.

The reforms have tried to achieve spatial coordination, creating larger authorities that bring the city and its hinterland under a single unit of government. They have looked for functional coordination through unified management structures and the device of grouping related functions into fewer departments of greater size controlled by a smaller number of committees than before. Corporate planning aims to integrate decision about the allocation of resources through a comprehensive framework of goals and objectives. Forward planning is an attempt to coordinate actions over time. The limited success of the changes in achieving this goal is evidence of the depth of the problem. Coordination in one dimension seems always to be at the cost of disjunction in another. Long term planning is hard to combine with a continuous sensitive response to changing needs and the expression of minority interests. People tend to respond to a coordinative problem in one field by limiting the scope and complexity of the problem they tackle in another. An example is the way that development has been focussed on small isolated territories (take for example the Home Office Community Development Projects and the Department of the

Environment's six city studies) when a comprehensive 'total approach' is intended.

Applying knowledge and information

One of the lessons that has been drawn from the experience of uncertainty and complexity is how little we really know about cities and communities, urban government and policy, and the effect our actions have on situations. There are differences of opinion as to the relative importance of understanding and of will; but one argument runs that those problems that are allowed to remain unsolved by urban government and those others that are the results of policy are not all evidence of intention. Some are the result of error. Decision-makers have too little knowledge to go on. Not all of the costs of urban policies are necessary or even foreseen. If local government had more intelligent, informed decision processes, the argument goes, if it could know more about the city it governs and the result of the way it spends its annual revenue, policies might just possibly emerge that would please almost everybody.

This is the feeling that has led to the considerable input of research into local government, the employment of non-professional staff from academic disciplines such as economics or mathematics, and a preoccupation with information systems in the last few years. The changes implied are less dramatic but probably more far reaching than the structural changes. They are an aspect of the new planning process, one of the principles of which is to extend the uses of analysis and rationality, to reduce reliance on judgment to a residual role.

In the universities and polytechnics many of the traditional disciplines and their related research work, particularly sociology, economics, political science, geography and others, have been deepening knowledge about people, activities and places. More recently still these disciplines have begun to give just a little more attention than before to policy knowledge: gaining an understanding of the effects of different interventions on the urban system. There is still great need for more research in policy and planning, and for this to filter down into postgraduate and undergraduate courses of education.

The application of this slowly growing body of theoretical and analytical knowledge to urban government remains a challenge. Many local authorities have set up information systems to manage data about their own areas. Many are employing research staff. Urban research has developed mathematical models to describe the working of cities, relating qualitative and quantitative facts about the city and its subsystems of residence, employment, mobility and space. Other models enable plans to be tested in simulation before they are carried out in reality. These models make the connection between data and theory. Their use has grown along with the capability of computers, since much of the quantitative analysis involved would have been impossible without them. It is becoming a conscious aim of the bigger and better organised local authorities to monitor and understand change in the community and to learn from action, adapting policy over time. A more important field in which we have less knowledge and in which less interest is shown as yet is the monitoring and adaptation of the organisation itself, the way it arrives at policies and carries them through. In system language the search is for the ideal learning system, that generates and uses information and is responsive both to the environment and to the results of its own actions.

McLoughlin (8.25) sees local government as working towards "pervasive networks of data and information exchange which are so interconnected as to constitute an intelligence system . . . The system will include at different times and in different ways a very large proportion of a local government's staff who must receive information at the interfaces with the client groups, central government, universities and other institutions and also those in intermediary roles – project managers and other 'line' executives part of whose responsibilities is the collation, editing, interpretation and transmission of information both 'upwards', 'downwards' and 'sideways' towards or away from top management centres."

Urgent questions may be begged, though, by simple acceptance of the need for more facts and more theory to be at the disposal of official social and physical planners. The first is the question of what knowledge; because much that is generated and taught by the traditional academic disciplines (economic theory, sociological theory) is illdesigned for use in urban policies and tends to reinforce existing patterns of authority and threadbare policies. Second, there is a tendency to believe and behave as though intelligence were value free. This is quickly refuted by pointing out that even the definition of 'urban systems of interest' for inclusion in the data bank is a matter of judgment and is political. For instance, do we include data on the private property market, companies and individuals who are landlords of private rented accommodation and their relationships and dealings, or do we not? More fundamentally there is a possibility that the use of central and pervasive intelligence systems in government may be for the purpose of enabling governing institutions "to survive and adapt in the face of the 'buffetings' of change" (8.26). This implies that the survival of the governing system is more important than the felt needs of the community, when what we may well need most in urban governance is change that penetrates the defences of the systems of authority. Third is the question of who holds the knowledge and who, with it, wields the power? The likelihood of better theory and more empirical data leading to better decisions depends wholly upon who is able to use the knowledge and who shares in the decisions. As things are, indeed as trends go, policy information is becoming more and more the property, not of the public, nor even of the councillor, but of the officer and the specialists within urban government. Intelligence within the bureaucracy calls for countervailing intelligence without and raises questions about the working of contemporary urban democracy.

Representing people

Urban democracy has always been less a reality than an ideal. The survey of councillors and electors carried out in 1964 for the Maud Committee and published as Volumes II and III of their report (8.27) showed that councillors are untypical of their electors in social class and education. The average person had little knowledge of council affairs and little conception of the part she or he could play in them. Local government was in such low repute that the turn-out at elections was derisory. The infrequency of elections contributes to their irrelevance, since events on the urban front have an independent pace. There has always been a discrepancy between the national political platforms of the major parties that contest local elections and the local issues that really count for people. Elected members have always been open to the suspicion of being in political life for the power game. Since the Poulson case another illusion has been stripped away and we see that the rewards of urban politics do not stop short at status, they run to money and favours.

Now the weaknesses of democracy are aggravated by the measures which have been intended to correct the other shortcomings of local government. Local government reorganisation has brought some democratic gains. The abolition of the alderman is a plus. But there have been minuses too and they may prove more substantial. Take for example the health authorities. The personal health responsibilities of the local authority were subject to decision by a committee of members. On the new Area Health Boards council nominees share decision with Minister's nominees. The same applies to the Regional Water Authorities. In both cases consumer councils are to be a complementary means of representing the public interest but this may prove to be a pale kind of democracy. The emphasis that is placed in the official recommendations on management of the new water authorities (8.28) on expert and efficient management as opposed to open political debate encourages pessimism about the democratic quality of the new bodies.

Unified management structures in local government also may, unless great care is taken, damage the representational capacity of councillors. As urban government has become stronger, more coordinated, more professional, it is likely that the elected member has lost much of his power to officials. He is called upon to endorse policies and decisions that are created by professionals with whose reasoning he is unfamiliar and whose sources of information he does not share. The new, stronger and larger authorities with fewer committees and powerful policy groups may offer more power to a small proportion of councillors. But they may well relegate the majority to a less significant role than before. Those that succeed in influencing the management system may be distanced by this involvement from their constituents. Those that remain close to the community may be far from the sources of power.

The Bains Report (8.29) is an example of the two-way pull in local government, with efficiency competing with the democratic principle. The committee recognised that the councillor's role needed strengthening even while they called for Chief Officers to have more clearcut powers, in recognition of their training and skill. The councillor is treated as an amateur in a professional world. She or he has few supporting secretarial services, no financial reward and in the past quite inadequate expense allowances. Often the councillor finds it difficult to get access to officers below Chief Officer grade or to obtain information from the departments for the advantage of the constituents.

Bains recognised the deprivation of the member. "If it is to the community that local government is accountable for the effectiveness of its operation, then it is unlikely that one can rule out the elected representatives of that community from any particular part of the management process". The report went on "it is basic to the democratic principle that members should have full information on matters affecting their electoral area and we recommend that authorities should ensure that a member is kept fully supplied with up to date information on all aspects of the Council's activities".

In their political context, as party candidates, the councillors have to carry what is often the burden of the party's national reputation and to cope with the irrelevance of the party programme to many of the issues in their ward. On the other hand, there are few local issues that can generate sufficient votes to return a special interest independent to the council in opposition to the party machines.

It seems likely that the form of electoral democracy exemplified by local government is felt by many to be inadequate in a fast changing world of multiple interests and high expectations. The councillor cannot today, possibly he never could, alone transmit people's needs into the power system. The people feel further from the bureaucracy too. The town hall has always seemed remote and slow moving. But there was something more human about yesterday's Town Clerk than the contemporary Chief Executive; and if the heights of the Policy Committee where the most important allocative decisions are made seem remote to the average councillor, they are out of sight to the average elector.

Frustration with the irrelevance of party politics, the unresponsiveness of electoral democracy and the inertia of the town hall has led in many cities to a more direct approach to influencing decisions. There has recently been a rapid growth in the number of interest groups in the urban community organising for action. They have different kinds of purpose. Some groups, such as squatters and free schools, simply intend to satisfy needs, whether for housing or education, independently of local authority provision. Some of these are philosophically anarchist and wish to reduce the intervention of government in urban affairs. Others form around an issue such as playspace or rent rises and operate through pressure, lobbying councillors, using the local press, making demonstration.

Yet others use direct action. The occasion in 1973 on which councillors of the London Borough of Kensington and Chelsea spent the night locked into a church hall by their home-hungry constituents and forced to listen to their case, probably marked a new era in the relationship between elector and elected. *Community Action*, a national journal appearing for the first time in February 1972, illustrates the wide range of issue and type of action used to augment or bypass local electoral democracy. "We are the writing on your wall" was a graffitus painted by the Piccadilly squatters for their council. The walls of the city have become a kind of correspondence column to be read by the local authority. "Thank you tree" is perhaps encouragement to the Parks Committee. But the sign that has survived for several years spray-painted on a wall near London's Euston Station is a finger pointed at the whole urban establishment: "The tigers of wrath are wiser than the horses of instruction".

A compensatory move to decentralise the administration

Community action is varied, uncoordinated response in the political sphere to the feeling that centralisation and specialisation in the bureaucratic sphere have gone too far. There are signs that central and local government too are aware that not all the advantages lie with centralisation. They seem to be acting on this awareness in two ways. First, they are trying to decentralise a few of their own functions and encourage into existence responsible semi-statutory bodies such as tenant groups in housing management who may take on some of the less controversial services. Second, and this has had by far the most committed effort, they are experimenting with new ways of managing relations between the local authority and the community.

There is a sense in which the very strengthening of local government that has been undertaken in the last few years is itself the product devolution of power — from central government. Redcliffe-Maud (8.30) wrote:
"In a period of great change, when huge unrepresentative organisations seem to control the lives of individuals and restrict personal freedom, people might be tempted to give up as a bad job the effort to master these impersonal forces. If they yielded, the loss would be irreparable. In this situation, local self-government should be a crucial influence. It should represent the citizen and be the means whereby he brings his views to bear on those public problems that touch most nearly his personal and domestic life. If local self-government withers, the roots of democracy grow dry. If it is genuinely alive, it nourishes the reality of democratic freedom".

Command Paper 4584 (8.31) demonstrates the decline in fervour that has come to be expected as time drags great ideas from Royal Commission, to White Paper, to Act, to the banality of implementation. Nonetheless it says: "The

Government are determined to return power to those people who should exercise decisions locally . . .".

Another illustration of some intention to decentralise administration was the adoption of the area team principle in the Social Services, recommended by Seebohm (8.32) and embodied in the Local Authority Social Services Act, 1970. A more far-reaching innovation would be the decentralisation, being discussed by a number of local authorities, of several town hall functions to shared area offices. Speaking of the 'micro-politics of the city' Donnison (8.33) called for experiment with "decentralised local service centres, combining the functions of a citizens' advice bureau and the local offices of housing, social services, education and other departments — doing as much work as can be devolved to this smaller scale of administration from town and county hall". The parent departments of the local authority should delegate officers to these service centres under the leadership of an area officer who would be, as he put it, "a company commander generally responsible for this bit of the front". The unit should have financial resources to deploy, should serve an area of about 25 000 people, and committees of elected members and perhaps a local MP and others, would act as the management committee for this local service centre. The joint committee of councillors responsible for the new Metropolitan District of Stockport recently announced plans for this kind of structure, using area coordinators and area committees.

The neighbourhood council movement is in a sense complementary to this mini-town hall concept. The Association of Neighbourhood Councils pressed unsuccessfully during local government reorganisation for a grassroots level in the structure of electoral democracy in the shape of a system of statutory urban neighbourhood councils throughout urban areas, comparable to parish councils which continue to exist in rural areas. The ANC wanted to see councils, properly elected, with funds of their own and some executive power to provide local amenities, that could hope to be more enduring and more likely to get a hearing from the local authority than voluntary bodies alone can do. Michael Young, who helped to organise neighbourhood council movement, wanted councils that have "boundaries which correspond . . . to the mental maps inside people's minds" (8.34). The main duty of a neighbourhood council, as he saw it, was to "represent local public opinion on anything that local people care about, whether it has to do with the impact on their community of national or local government, of public services like railways or privately owned services like shops. They should be far more effective in this representative role than most present councils". In reorganisation Scotland and Wales obtained provision for such councils, but in spite of ANC campaigning, they have not featured in reorganisation in England. Though neighbourhood councils have come spontaneously into being in some areas, for practical reasons they seem more likely to swell the ranks of community action than to play the role of urban parish councils.

Managing relations between authority and community

Central government has intervened in several different ways in the last five or six years to encourage local government to modify the style of its relationship with the community. Local authorities have cooperated in these exercises and in some cases have innovated on their own initiative. These steps seem to be an adjustment to the interface between governing and governed, or between the formal and informal systems that make up the urban community.

'Participation' has been a key word. Committees, commissions and government departments are now clearly sensitised to the consumer rights problem. A number of policy measures in the last five years have included a requirement of 'participation' by the public. The recommendations of the Skeffington committee (8.35) on participation in development planning were perhaps the clearest statement. "We understand participation to be the act of sharing in the formulation of policies and proposals". The Skeffington proposals were given modified expression in the Town and Country Planning Acts, 1968 and 1971 and the Secretary of State can now reject a city's structure plan if there is evidence that the people were not effectively consulted in its preparation. But structure planners are now facing the genuine difficulty of carrying them through. The Local Authority Social Services Act too mentioned participation by the client. Seebohm had said "the whole community 'consumes' the social services, directly or indirectly, as well as paying for them through taxation, and consumers have an important contribution to make to the development of an effective family service" (8.36).

As the public gains experience of the new procedures, the conviction is growing that participation cannot be more than nominal. There is a relentless tendency in the administrative machine to consult and then to go its own way, partly out of professional arrogance but partly also for reasons that have to do with differences of pace and style between the administration and the people. Efficiency is interpreted by the official (and indeed the councillor, whose time is short) to mean speed and clarity of decision. It may well mean to the ordinary person the full playing out of the democratic process. Wordy and deliberative as this has to be, it is clear to every officer that it will make his job more difficult. There may also be some reluctance on the part of councillors to allow their electors to confer, singly and in groups, directly with the officers rather than through their mediation.

An approach to the race problem was the first of a series of community initiatives by government. A problem faced by local authorities in the mid-sixties was the protection of immigrant groups from the racial hostility of host populations, particularly groups coming from the West Indies and the Indian sub-continent to settle in industrial cities. In many areas of heavy immigration voluntary or local authority-supported committees had formed spontaneously to help race relations and promote the social welfare of newcomers, but in 1965 it was proposed to make grants available to local committees so that they might employ fulltime officers. Local authorities were to help the committees with office accommodation and secretarial services. The Commonwealth Relations Committee created under the Race Relations Act, 1968 continues to give financial help to local community relations committees. It is normal for committees to have help in kind if not in cash from local authorities and to have a number of councillors among their members. These committees vary in the emphasis they give to political work, to expressing minority needs, aiming to bring about cooperation between racial interest groups, and to integrative services such as mixed housing schemes, playgroups and English-language tuition.

In the summer of 1968, the year the Race Relations Act was passed, the government announced something new, an 'Urban Programme', also to be administrered by the Home Office and, like the community relations movement, also involving the cooperation of local authorities. As the community relations measures had responded to the more particular urban problem of racial disharmony, the Urban Programme was a policy response to the general problem of localised urban poverty, then being urged on policy makers by pressure groups such as Shelter. Under the Urban Programme small grants of money are made available to local groups and local authorities for specific activities, especially in deprived inner areas of large cities. In the main these urban aid funds have gone to support social provision but since many bodies engaged in provision are also pressure groups for better service by local and central government, these funds have also had a small influence on community politics by fuelling protest.

A more direct experiment in governance has been the Home Office Community Development Programme also funded out of Urban Aid. CDP was described by the Home Office in initial press releases as a "modest attempt at action research into the better understanding and more comprehensive tackling of social needs, especially in local communities within the older urban areas, through closer coordination of central and local official and unofficial effort, informed and stimulated by citizen initiative and involvement". CDP was to be a five year programme. Local authorities were to find a quarter of the cost and the Urban Programme was to provide the remainder. Twelve local authorities are participating in the project and each has selected an appropriate locality within its area in consultation with the Home Office. In each locality a small project team has been set up, usually within the Social Services Department or under the aegis of the Town Clerk. Normally the project is managed by a special committee of the council and is supported by a research team mounted by a neighbouring university or polytechnic. It is clear from internal papers of the Project that the exercise is an element that has been consciously interposed between the bureaucracy and the community to test out new forms of relationship.

Three other initiatives are worthy of mention. One is the Educational Priority Programme of the Department of Education and Science, which stimulated experiment in the uses of schools in community development in deprived areas. A second is the Department of the Environment's 'six cities studies' begun in 1972. In this programme central government funds are being used to pay management and planning consultants to carry out studies in Oldham, Rotherham, Sunderland, Birmingham, Lambeth and Liverpool to reveal what would be the management implications of a 'total approach' to the environment. Some of the recommendations of these projects involve change in the shape or behaviour of local government.

Finally, the use by some local authorities of official community workers is turning out in practice to be more of an experiment in government and less an extension of social work than was perhaps originally foreseen. The Gulbenkian Foundation report (8.37) which provided much of the theory underlying community work had in fact defined the community worker in political terms. "Community work is only one aspect of the far broader issue of how to meet people's needs and give them an effective say in what these are and how they want them met. It is part of a protest against apathy and complacency and against distant and anonymous authority. It is also part of the whole dilemma of how to reconcile the 'revolution of human dissent' with the large-scale organisation and economic and social planning which seem to be inseparably interwoven with the parallel revolution of rising expectations. This boils down to the problem of how to give meaning to democracy."

Since that report was published a growing number of local authorities has appointed community workers to the area teams of their reformed social services departments. An evaluation of their impact remains to be made but it is clear from current practice that community workers, once they become involved with the community, go beyond community care and become highly political commodities because they are vehicles for information between the authority and its people and their existence alters the pattern of play between conflicting interests in an area. They are a lively illustration of the difficulties which arise when the bureaucratic and political spheres of urban government mesh in one role. It seems that community workers in the field are not sustained by theory and find themselves under pressure to abandon the attempt to be an interface, choosing quite early whether to serve the interests of the administration that employs them or to serve community politics and risk the withdrawal of backing by the authority.

Politics of street and housing estate

These official measures are efforts to open up, while still controlling, relations between the urban authorities and the community. It seems unlikely that they can mend the real weaknesses of urban democracy. The purposes of elected representatives and officials, those in the seat of government, are bound to be mixed and possibly conflicting. They will include the hope of defusing potentially critical or violent opinion; the desire to create a reciprocal structure in the community so as to ease the task of the administration in reaching the public with its services; a means for experimental exploration of new policies without heavy expenditure of money or political will. Community development and community work are thus partly social welfare measures and partly an attempt to minimise conflict. It may be through conflict alone however, that the deprived have a hope, in present circumstances, of making their needs painfully felt by those who are better off or who are in control. The dual source of legitimacy of community development policies, deriving as they do from both governors and governed, may render them at best ineffective and at worst buffer institutions to shield authorities from the full impact of criticism by the people and their representative groups. The anomalies and failures of the community relations movement have been detailed by Hill and Issacharoff (8.38). They illustrate the way in which "the community relations movement was a means by which government sought to divert the activities of immigrants and their supporters into non-political directions to prevent the development of an effective protest movement". In a similar way mini-town halls, unless their political committees are strong, may merely interpose between the people and the real source of money and place of decision a shopping counter where smallscale transactions may take place that give people a feeling of contact with the authority but have little effect on the real problem they are experiencing.

Something that these government actions may do, intentionally or inadvertently, is open up possibilities of confrontation and negotiation that may turn out to be of use to the community. They may provide new channels of information and that of itself is good. There is always a case for sensitising the local officials to consumer rights and needs, and helping people to be more aware of the possibilities of "community-defence against bureaucratic aggression" (8.39). It may be however that the quality of urban government depends more on initiative coming from the political sphere than from the administration. It seems to depend mainly on many informed people being prepared to press for real, not token, power over a wider range of issues. It requires people to be alive to any erosion of their rights and inventive in adapting democracy to make it more effective as changes in society and technology reveal flaws in it. We should therefore expect more, not less, political activity at local level.

The issues of coordination, intelligence and the 'who and how' of decision and control, on which this chapter has concentrated, are all closely related. It is enough to illustrate this to say: coordination and intelligence confer power. They who deploy them tend to be in control; and coordinated intelligent management is itself a method, a 'how' in decision making. Likewise bureaucracy and the political sphere are less clearly distinct than I have portrayed them. In the first place political organisation has its own bureaucracy, its own internal decisionmaking method. The major political parties are as conventional in their decision processes as the bureaucracy and it is not to them that people are looking for new ideas about democracy. Secondly, the bureaucracy has its own politics. There are competing and contrasting values and goals within the bureaucracy and they show up not least in the struggle over different forms of management organisation.

Coordination and intelligence in administration, in the bureaucratic sphere, make for centralisation, specialism and mystification. They can be mitigated in the administration by efforts to decentralise, to disseminate information, to demystify. But they still remain a threat to political life. Indeed, even bureaucratic decentralisation may result intentionally or otherwise in defusing political protest or at least preventing the upsurge of discontent from achieving its own coordination and intelligence and getting a more serious impact at the higher level of the town hall where relatively more power lies. At present the coordinated element in politics comprises the conventional political parties, who are indeed growing in strength in the urban scene as the majority party in any one urban situation responds to the new power that lies in stronger, larger authorities, more resources and unified management structures. The Liberal party is showing signs of embracing community interests. Towns are becoming more politically volatile even in the party political sense, as recent elections show. But the traditional political organisations as we have seen no longer satisfy many elements on the left, either in their policies or in the way they arrive at them. The new wave of urban activism however is as yet uncoordinated. Indeed much of it is still apolitical. Much community action is working class, concerned with the nature of the distribution of real income and services, and as such is potentially part of a wider left-wing political movement. It should be recognised, however, that much of the action is middle class and is a protest less at the system in which we live than at local government behaviour.

Some interesting questions seem to hang over the future of urban government. Beyond working class community action in the dispersed, individualistic style we now experience it, will a more powerful and coordinated political movement emerge? If it does, will it avoid the dilution of democracy as it too becomes coordinated and systematic? Will it tame and manage the modern administration? Does urban government control sufficient resources and possess sufficiently powerful instruments for people to see it as a worthwhile field for political innovation? The aim of much urban protest and action is to improve the condition of those who have always till now been dealt a losing hand in urban life. The means seem likely to include changing the nature of the game and the person of the dealer, rather than merely reshuffling parties and policies. At national level there are signs that some pressure groups, the non-parliamentary socialist parties and the rank-and-file movement of some unions, may share this aim. It will be interesting to see whether the current vitality evidenced by community action means that urban government is going to be an arena for a new political movement that brings the politics of the urban street and housing estate into partnership with the politics of the work place.

References

8.1   D.A. Schon, *Beyond the Stable State*, Temple Smith, 1971.

8.2   J.K. Friend and W.N. Jessop, *Local Government and Strategic Choice*, Tavistock Publications, 1969.

8.3   Y. Dror, *Public Policy Making Reexamined*, Leonard Hill Books, 1972.

8.4   R. Rose (ed.), *Policy Making in Britain*: A Reader in Government, Macmillan, 1969.

8.5   N. Boaden, *Urban Policy Making: Influences on County Boroughs in England and Wales*, Cambridge University Press, 1971.

8.6   *Royal Commission on Local Government in England*, (The Redcliffe Maud Report), HMSO, 1969.

8.7   Department of the Environment, Circular 121/72.

8.8   *Royal Commission on Local Government in England, op.cit.*

8.9   *The Future Shape of Local Government Finance*, Cmd. 4741, HMSO, 1971.

8.10   Department of the Environment, *Local Government Finance in England and Wales: Consultation Paper*, HMSO, 1973.

8.11   Ministry of Transport, *Traffic and Transport Plans*, Roads Circular 1/68.

8.12   J.D. Stewart, *Management in Local Government: A viewpoint*, Charles Knight, 1971.

8.13   Ministry of Housing and Local Government, *Management of Local Government*, (The Maud Report), HMSO, 1967.

8.14   Local Government Training Board, *Management Development*, Training Recommendation 7, 1971.

8.15   Department of the Environment, *The New Local Authorities: Management and Structure*, (The Bains Report), HMSO, 1972.

8.16   Home Office, *Report of the Committee on Local Authority and Allied Personal Social Services*, (The Seebohm Report), HMSO, 1968.

8.17   J.D. Stewart, 'New Approaches to Management in Local Government', *Local Government Chronicle*, articles from 4th January, 1969.

8.18   J.K.Friend and W.N. Jessop, *op.cit.*

8.19   F. Wedgwood Oppenheim, 'Planning Under Uncertainty', *Local Government Studies*, No.2, April, 1972.

8.20   Tony Eddison, *Local Government Management and Corporate Planning*, Leonard Hill Books, 1973.

8.21   J.K. Friend, J.M. Power and C.J.L. Yewlett, *Public Planning: The Inter-Corporate Dimension*, Tavistock Publications, 1974.

8.22   L.A.M.S.A.C., *A Review of the Theory of Planned Programme Budgeting. A System of Management for Local Authorities*, Report of the O and M and Work Study Panel of the Local Authorities Management Services and Computer Committee, 1972.

8.23 D. Eversley and E. Wood, 'Strategic Planning and Programme Budgeting', *Local Government Finance*, April 1971.

8.24 J.D. Stewart, 'Corporate Planning and Structure Planning', *Local Government Finance*, May, 1971.

8.25 J.B. McLoughlin, *Control and Urban Planning*, Faber, 1973.

8.26 J.B. McLoughlin, *op.cit.*

8.27 *Management of Local Government, op.cit.*

8.28 Department of the Environment, *The New Water Industry Management and Structure*, HMSO, 1973.

8.29 *The New Local Authorities: Management and Structure, op.cit.*

8.30 *Royal Commission on Local Government in England, op.cit.*

8.31 *Local Government in England: Government Proposals for Reorganisation*, Cmnd. 4584, HMSO, 1971.

8.32 Department of Health and Social Security, *National Health Service Reorganisation*, 1971.

8.33 D.V. Donnison, 'Micro Politics of the City' in *London: Urban Patterns, Problems and Policies*, (ed.) D.V. Donnison and D.E.C. Eversley, Heinemann, 1973.

8.34 M. Young, 'Parish Councils for Cities?' *New Society*, 29th January, 1970.

8.35 Ministry of Housing and Local Government, *People and Planning*, (The Skeffington Report), HMSO, 1969.

8.36 *National Health Service Reorganisation, op.cit.*

8.37 Gulbenkian Foundation, *Community Work and Social Change: A Report on Training*, Longmans, 1968.

8.38 M.J. Hill and R. Issacharoff, *Community Action and Race Relations: A Study of Community Relations Committees in Britain*, Oxford University Press, 1971.

8.39 A. Jay, *Householder's Guide to Community Defense Against Bureaucratic Aggression*, Jonathan Cape, 1972.

Further reading

On the public planning and policy-making process in general:
R.L. Ackoff, *A Concept of Corporate Planning*, John Wiley, 1970.
Y. Dror, *Public Policy-Making Re-Examined*, Leonard Hill Books, 1973.
D. Schon, *Beyond the Stable State*, Temple Smith, 1971.

On the management structure and planning process of British local government:
J.K. Friend & W.N. Jessop, *Local Government and Strategic Choice: An Operational Research Approach to the Process of Public Planning*, Tavistock Publications, 1969.
Ministry of Housing and Local Government, *Management of Local Government* (The Maud Report), HMSO, 1967.
J.D. Stewart, *Management in Local Government: A Viewpoint*, Charles Knight, 1971.

On the political dimension of British urban government:
J. Dearlove, *The Politics of Policy in Local Government*, Cambridge University Press, 1973.
W. Hampton, *Democracy and Community,* Oxford University Press, 1960.
G.W. Jones, *Borough Politics*, Macmillan, 1969.

On community development and community action:
C. Cockburn & P. Marris (eds.), *Community Action*, David and Charles, (forthcoming).
P. Marris & M. Rein, *Dilemmas of Social Reform*, Routledge and Kegan Paul, 1967. Second edition – Pelican Books, 1974.

9   Conclusions and Reflections

Town planning is a form of urban (and regional) management. Its skills relate particularly to two basic aspects of the urban system: the spatial form of the city, and the social processes that go on within it, and it is always necessary to harmonise strategies in respect of both. On the one hand, there have to be policies which concern the location of such matters as houses, places of employment, shops, public and community buildings, sites for recreation, and lines of communication routes. So far, these locational issues have been considered the more important features of town planning. In professional practice the planner's work has focussed on land and development, and the statutory planning process, through Schemes and Plans, has emphasised the rational assembly of land according to some long term ideal. At the micro scale, the planner's association with the design of buildings and spaces between them has given town planning the reputation of a distinctive art form. On the other hand, there are also policies which are designed to affect the social structure of the city. These concern groupings of people, they affect formal and informal organisation, they give employment opportunities and access to housing, they relate to activities which also have land use implications, and they have consequences for choices in life style and behaviour patterns. These aspects of town planning have been of much less direct concern to practitioners, at least until recent years, but the two relate and have a distinct bearing on each other.

The matter is further complicated because spatial form and social process have the immediate context of an economic system. To date, urban land use theory has not taken us very far in our understanding of the dynamics of the urban system. Concentric zones, multiple nuclei and zones of transition were terms popular thirty years ago, but they suggested a mechanistic and rather stereotyped form of city structure, and in reality the situation is very different. Spatial patterns of distribution within the city are now more usefully seen as the consequences of a capitalistic market economy. It is from the land economist that we derive new insights into the workings of an urban system: for example, how monopoly rents arise, how artificial scarcities come about, and how urban areas grow and change as a result of these.

Town planning also exists in a political context. The political system whereby decisions are made and implemented by myriad private and public bodies has its own complexity; operational research is showing the complicated network of policy making which exists in any governmental organisation. All planning is a matter of decision making under uncertainty, and choices are made between alternative courses of action with a very inadequate understanding of their future implications. Planning is a question of response by the governmental system to a situation that is seen to arise within the community; the outcome is some intervention in the community system which is believed to be appropriate. In this situation, professionals, elected members and interest groups of all kinds combine and interact with their own prejudices, outlooks and requirements.

Town planning assumes its multi-dimensional flavour because it relates to cities and regions which are themselves complex, dynamic systems. The previous chapters in this book have given ample evidence of this. Michael Croft has pointed to the many factors involved in the spatial aspects of urban form. Edgar Rose has looked at issues involved in the design of the urban environment. Peter Hills has related to the question of travel and movement within the city. These contributors were concerned particularly with built form. Margaret Willis and Cynthia Cockburn, on the other hand, have examined the social dimension, particularly social structures and political processes within the community. Bridging these two sets of chapters, three contributors – Chris Watson, Barbara Smith and John Birch – have looked at matters where the relationship between urban form and social requirements is particularly close. The location of employment and residence is intimately bound up with the physical structure of the city as well as social well-being; the distribution of houses of different age, size, condition and setting adds to the physical description of a city as well as reflecting differential social opportunity; and land and buildings reserved for recreation constitute important land uses while at the same meeting community needs.

The city therefore has a spatial form which contains social processes in a continuous interrelationship. We should not be surprised at this, for historical evidence throughout the world suggests a clear connection between the two. The built form of a merchant city in the Middle Ages reflected the social order of the day: a fortification (say a castle from a former period), a group of religious buildings (church or cathedral), and a market place were central and in close proximity. The skyline was dominated by tower or spire. In the larger cities, particularly at a time when commerce was dominant, an internal structure evolved which segregated activities and residential areas into patterns and was the image of relative positions of social prestige. The built form of the present city is quite different and mirrors the changed social order of the new industrialism. First, in terms of visual townscape, the 19th century mill chimney has long been replaced by clusters of tall office blocks, the skyline reflecting changing economic function as well as technical innovations in building design and construction. Second, from the point of view of internal distributions, our exploding cities show clear patterns of residential segregation which fully express the inequitable social structure in the capitalist city, with its differential rewards to various social groups.

The urban management processes which we have evolved so far have not yet given us any real harmony in policy terms whereby we might achieve some coherent social objective. Town planning has produced strategies to deal with built form. On the macro scale it has favoured decentralisation and dispersal, though in a contained, non-sprawling way; while within existing areas it has sought to achieve a rational order in spatial allocations and a sense of convenience to all urban users. It has only been marginally successful in this, largely because of a failure to comprehend and grapple with the complexities of the urban system which it is seeking to control, and because of failure in powers of implementation. But above all, there has been little harmony with the package of policies designed to deal with social processes in the city. The control of development and planned relocation within the urban system, on lines laid down by land-oriented town planning policies, all too often has served to improve options for one group of urban dweller and limit the possibilities of another. By and large the affluent suburban dweller has come off best and the low income family in the inner city has come off worst. The 1947 planning system based on urban containment and satellite growth has given benefits to some and denied them to others, which could not have been the original intention.

We have learned the hard way that town planning as a form of urban management is an incredibly hard undertaking. If we approach it in any other way than as part of a much wider context then the operation is relatively futile. Town planning is of course only one of the elements of urban management. It would be nonsensical to pretend that all urban management (built form and social processes) could be subsumed under town planning, but what we understand as town planning (and let us for the sake of argument say that its focus is on land and the development process) must conform with the related package of social policies, and together they must seek to achieve some set of coherent objectives. This is not a strikingly new point (the sociological implications of slum clearance for example have been the subject of studies for many years) but it seems that it must be stressed repeatedly.

This task is not easy: indeed it is possibly the most demanding exercise in any sophisticated programme of self-direction of affairs in any western developed country. But the theme of this book is that we are helped at least some way along the road of understanding just what is involved by recognizing the nature of the various problems with which we are dealing. Much more, of course, needs to be done, and certainly the implications for planning education are profound. Sixth form education needs to do far more in an early exposure of the nature of urban problems while within graduate and postgraduate education the challenge of incorporating a multi-disciplinary approach to the extent that is required is a daunting prospect. Quite apart from training town planners, we also need to explore the possibilities of training urban managers.

In this summary chapter we might identify and expand upon four main themes which have emerged. First, the historical dimension of the problem. Not only would it be quite wrong to consider contemporary efforts at urban management as unique in time just because we have fashioned new words for what we do, but it would be erroneous to think that from the past we could not learn important lessons. Second, the question of interconnectivity within the urban system. The importance of thinking in systems terms has been usefully emphasised in recent years, and the implications are fundamental for any form of comprehensive management. Third, the recognition of territorial disadvantage in the urban system. This has highlighted the needs of the multi-problem areas, largely (but not necessarily) in the inner city, where difficulties are compounded in their severity and where the operation of the town planning machine has frequently ridden roughshod over local concerns of great sensitivity. Fourth, a definition of the urban problem with which we are faced. Urban research has tended to deal with problems *in* the city, rather than *of* the city: the city has thrown up a range of urban phenomena and we have investigated these as separate issues, but what are the key characteristics of the city as a dynamic system? What are their implications for town planning? Are we in fact on the threshold of experiencing an urban crisis of unparalleled dimensions? These four issues of course only cover some of the problems with which town planning and comprehensive urban management are concerned; the rest must be for another volume.

The historical dimension

One theme in the previous chapters is that our present approach to urban management is the product of perhaps a century and a half of community response to urban problems. Some of the pressing questions of the 19th century have now been largely overcome (health and sanitation for example), but others remain depressingly familiar. Engels' description of British cities in 1844 is not entirely removed from contemporary reality:

"Every great city has one or more slums, where the working class is crowded together. True, poverty often dwells in hidden alleys close to the palaces of the rich; but, in general, a separate territory has been assigned to it, where, removed from the sight of the happier classes it may struggle along as it can. These slums are pretty equally arranged in all the great towns of England, the worst houses in the worst quarters of the towns; usually one or two-storied cottages in long rows, perhaps with cellars used as dwellings. These houses of three or four rooms and a kitchen form, throughout England, some part of London excepted, the general dwellings of the working class. The streets are generally unpaved, rough, dirty, filled with vegetable and animal refuse, without sewers or gutters, but supplied with foul, stagnant pools instead. Moreover ventilation is impeded by the bad, confused method of building of the whole quarter, and since many human beings here live crowded into a small space, the atmosphere that prevails in these working-men's quarters may readily be imagined."

(The Condition of the Working Class in England)

Housing standards have obviously risen greatly since early Victorian Britain (though like poverty, housing standards are only meaningful in relative terms). Good drainage and sanitation are now accepted norms of urban life: one of the great contributions of Victorian urban managers was in fact to be found underground in the miles of pipes and sewers which ultimately served to give freedom from water-borne disease. Residential densities have declined markedly and through public health and welfare measures infant mortality has been cut and wastage of human life greatly reduced. But the underlying nature of the capitalist city remains, whereby through a stratified society rewards are inequitably distributed, resulting not just in the existence of underprivileged groups throughout the urban area, but also in a territorial pattern of relatively advantaged and disadvantaged communities.

Many of the problems with which we deal are therefore of long standing and fundamentally relate to the same issues. The differential standards of housing accommodation amongst the community have been a repeated point of concern. Chadwick's *Report on the Sanitary Condition of the Labouring Population* was published in 1842, and the Royal Commission on the State of Large Towns and Populous Districts reported in 1844. Henry Mayhew contributed his letters to the *Morning Chronicle* between 1849 and 1850 dealing with communities of deprivation. George Godwin's *London Shadows: A Glance at the Homes of the Thousands* appeared in 1854 and his *Town Swamps and Social Bridges* in 1859. The tradition of both detached observation and inflamed protest literature was set and has continued since. Towards the turn of the century Charles Booth's *Life and Labour of the People in London* (from 1889) followed the *Report of the Royal Commission on the Housing of the Working Classes*, 1885. They were accompanied by a Congregational clergyman's denunciation in *The Bitter Cry of Outcast London*, 1883, and by General William Booth's description of the Britain of his day in *In Darkest England and the Way Out*, 1890. Cautious legislation gave some increased powers to local authorities to deal with their housing problems, but the *Report of the Royal Commission on the Housing of the Industrial Population of Scotland*, 1917, was eloquent testimony to the abject standards that had obtained so far and the particular needs that existed north of the Border. The Tudor Walters Report of 1918 set the seal on new standards of accommodation in the public sector in a flush of post-1918 determination at reconstruction. But failure to improve existing dwellings (as opposed to building new ones) led to renewed protest literature in the 1930's. War time Britain's new resolve to set things right led to the Dudley Report, 1944, and a substantial programme of public sector building. The updating of standards with the Parker Morris Report and investment on an unprecedented scale in slum clearance, rebuilding and improvement has transformed the housing situation but left us with a housing problem seemingly as intractable as ever. Homelessness is increasing and the thwarted aspirations of millions are still unfulfilled. Absolute improvements in living conditions for the vast majority do not necessarily make relative disparity in accommodation standards any easier to accept.

Housing is just one example. Without going into further detail there is evidence in plenty that the subject matter of urban management exhibits repetitive themes. For instance, there has been and still is poverty; its incidence is a relative phenomenon and does not depend on absolute criteria. The problem of the destitute in 19th century Britain may have been alleviated but the challenge of today's Child Poverty Action Group is no less demanding. As another example, a recent concern has related to the pressure of urban populations swollen by immigrant communities, particularly those of coloured and/or commonwealth origins. The 19th century saw far more severe Irish migrations, as well as new waves of Jews and others from central Europe in the last decades. The problems of employment and job opportunity are also of long standing. In the last century it was more a question of irregularity and uncertainty of employment; in this century regional unemployment has become the problem. In very recent years a new phenomenon has been appearing, that of the disappearance of jobs in the inner districts of large cities: formerly the extravagant user and importer of labour, the inner city may now be losing employment to suburban locations. Urban recreation demands are not new either: the Victorians relied heavily on the public park provided by both the public sector and philanthropic institutions as an encouragement to moral regeneration as well as the banishment of health hazards. The search for fresh air, open space and sunlight has supported long term trends in the reduction of residential densities.

The problems of government also show similar features. Towards the end of the last century local government reform set up the London County Council and provided a system of county boroughs, counties and district councils that lasted up to 1966 and 1974 respectively. Throughout this period the process of urban management has been a partnership between central and local government. The centre has provided finance and broad directions of policy; local authorities have implemented policy in the light of their own needs and circumstances. There has never been much lack of comment from the general public on the inadequacy of government or of excessive bureaucracy. The search for government with a human face is not a contemporary phenomenon. Protest is no new thing, although modern sophistication of dissent may raise new complications. The enforced preservation of some of London's common lands in the 19th century, the Jarrow marchers, and the defenders of the environment against motorway noise belong to the same tradition. The relationship between the planner and the planned has been a central theme in urban management for decades. We might be accustomed now to the idea of alienation of many individuals and groups in society from government, and of experiments of new forms of participatory democracy. But there has never been much shortage of alienation from government, with crime and violence in Victorian London for example being almost a by-word. The new interest shown in micro politics has its roots in political deprivation in certain communities for generations.

The significance of all this is at least threefold. One is that the problems which we recognise today, and have sketched in this book, are of long standing: they are repetitive and they crop up in various guises from one period to another. In large measure problems do not disappear; they merely change. Management is not necessarily a question of solving problems; it might simply be a matter of amelioration of unhappy consequences of a particular train of events. There are implications for town planning, which by tradition has looked towards idealist long term strategies as its contribution. It may be however that it should regard short term gradualism as an alternative, and perhaps more realistic, way to build the future.

Another significance relates to the way we tackle problems. Recognising the complexity and sheer intractability of recurrent problems, approaches towards new policy have stressed the importance of two things: sensitivity of management and greater allocation of resources. Throughout the last 100 years or more, as we have groped our way painfully towards comprehensive social welfare policies, the twin factors of the human face of management and more liberal financial backing have been seen as the most likely avenues whereby more effective work might be carried out. From Octavia Hill and her own personal system of housing management to contemporary voluntary service this is true. Personal sensitivity leads on to bureaucratic sensitivity in the sense of the obligation to know and truly understand the nature of the social problem which is being tackled. Urban administrators are now asked to see the social consequences of a particular strategy. Norms of collective welfare are not enough; any situation must be analysed in terms of individual needs and preferences and individual benefits.

With regard to resources, a repeated plea has been for more money to launch or adequately equip a particular service: in due time education, health, pensions, social service and the urban aid programme have become bottomless pits of expenditure. With economic growth, increasing financial commitments are possible; with zero growth the only recourse is cross budgetary allocations from one sector to another (for example education to health) or within particular sectors. This calls for priority options which are very difficult to determine, while the departmental structure of government usually ensures that only minimal budgetary exchanges are permissible anyway from one year to another.

The third significance is the fact that although there is a basic similarity of the nature of many of the urban problems over the last century, nonetheless since the 1880's and 1890's at least, we have tackled the problems with our present day institutions. The remarkable fact of the partnership of local and central government is that it has proved flexible and resilient enough to deal with the issues it faced. Once the vestries, the Boards and the Commissioners of early 19th century Britain had been swept away and power vested in municipal corporations, an effective local government framework was possible. For many years there could still be considerable differences in performance between local authorities, but from early this century a set of national standards of provision has obtained. This has given a contemporary standardisation of government throughout British cities, not achieved previously. (Admittedly one can always find serious evidence of differences in performance, whether it be grammar school admission rates or length of waiting time for hospital beds, but the point is basically a true one.) Its importance is that our framework of local/central government has been sufficiently flexible and adaptive to take on board and administer ever expanding social policies dealing with such issues as health, education, employment and old age, as well as a set of interventionist policies dealing with the built environment. A diminution of the powers of local government in recent years has taken away responsibility for health, water and statutory undertakers, and *ad hoc* boards have come to occupy and operate in a very uncertain area between local and central government. If adaptivity and flexibility are the keynotes, perhaps we should not have any fixed view about ideal forms of local administration. This point is relevant to recent suggestions which have found favour with, for example, the idea of Special Development Units for Inner City Redevelopment almost on the lines of New Town Development Corporations, charged with a development job to do, and standing largely outside the local government pattern. This further diminution of local government powers will no doubt be considered unthinkable, but increasingly we have to ask whether we can continue to rely on the existing roles of local and central government and *ad hoc* bodies. Or do we say that our institutions have failed us because of a lack of response to recognising new needs and an inability to attend to them? Certainly the sheer scale of public intervention and the pace of change pose a completely new situation for government, and, moreover, community attitudes are different. There are different attitudes about power, consensus, and the nature of authority and, because of a long exposure to affluence and a raising of expectations through a popular belief in sustained economic growth, there are strident demands for evidence of reallocations in the distribution of rewards. It is a moot point whether our inherited political system of representation at local authority level will respond to this. Community councils or urban parish councils seem to offer hope of retaining the flexibility inherent in local authorities by creating a new channel for communicating needs, aspirations and wishes from an economically and politically deprived community to a bureaucracy.

Interconnectivity

Every chapter in this book points to some key features in the nature of the urban system with which we are concerned. The main ones are interrelationships and interconnectivity, and dynamism. There is a total system of interlocking parts, in continued interconnection one with the other. Sub-systems may be defined within the one system, and it is possible to talk in terms of a housing system, an employment system, and so on. In each of these a sub-division might be identified: in housing, for example, there are systems for the private sector or the public sector. And then, as we have described earlier, within the urban system the built form interacts with that of social processes.

The systems approach to planning was one of the fundamental discoveries of the sixties as far as urban management was concerned because of its profound implications for planning practice: both for the way urban problems were recognised and for the way solutions might be prescribed. The design bias of planning, supported by the intellectual traditions of architecture and engineering, has given way to a view which sees planning as process: management of a system, ongoing and with no fixed end product, rather than (as previously) a matter of preparing unitary plans for a fixed time scale. The difference in style is fundamental.

In considering urban form we can think of the obvious connections between density, location of workplace and residence, and methods of transport. The crucial differences between the 20th and the 19th century city are that one form was supported by personal mobility, the other by public transport. Urban form therefore is dependent on transport opportunities: the private car permitted post-war suburbia and public transport was associated with bye law, high density housing. The simple recognition that all land use decisions are transport decisions and that all land use activities have implications for movement supported the many Land Use Transportation Plans, commissioned during the last 10 to 15 years. We have now got used to the idea that there are functional linkages between land uses and that these contribute to the dynamics of changing urban patterns of distribution.

But there are just not interrelationships in a physical sense. The transport element of the built form interacts with social factors in many ways. For example, transport opportunities affect fundamental abilities to choose: personal horizons are widened or constructed through availability of transport, public and private. At the local level road schemes can have social and psychological consequences. Road proposals in the inner city can be frighteningly severe in their implications: an elevated motorway adjoining houses is an obvious example, but the result of a re-routing system by some traffic management decisions can affect property values and environmental quality and set in train population shifts which can have repercussions a long way from the actual scene of the original activity. One can think too of the social values attached to certain transportation phenomena. 'Congestion' and lengthy journeys to work were targets in the Barlow Report of 1940: decentralisation as a favoured option was strongly supported because popular opinion had it that these constituted unnecessary evils in urban life. We do not necessarily put such a heavy premium on journey to work today. Think too of the micro effects of transportation policy on housing areas: the possible extension of tube lines into south London, which many have thought desirable, is a case in point. Who would benefit from such an extension? Who would lose? Would such an extension encourage gentrification of older housing areas in a part of London where so far this process has been slow? We might also mention the problems posed by complexities of time scale: with roads for example what is planned now may never be ideally suited to the needs of the day when the road is actually built and opened. Perhaps eight years might elapse from the drawing of an urban motorway line on a plan to its construction: in the meantime, not only will different people be affected but the general situation will have changed. In west London a motorway is now closed at night in order that local residents might be spared the affliction of noise. What is a technical achievement one year becomes an environmental hazard the next.

There is no need to labour the point about interrelationships. We now recognise their force in planning, and perhaps their first effect has been to add doubt if not despair to those engaged in the planning process. The assumptions and methods of planning as management of process are so different from those of prescriptive, end-state planning. Given even the slightest evidence of dynamic systems of interconnected parts we realise only too quickly that we know too little about them. We lose confidence in advocating measures to deal with particular problems. We simply do not know very often where to concentrate effort in breaking into a particular cycle. In urban renewal, for example, do we focus on housing, employment opportunity, income, environment, or what? But if a particular situation demands that we do break in and follow a certain policy package, what institutional arrangements do we need? How far can one rely on the public sector? Just what is the role of voluntary associations? And then granted that attacks on a multi-dimensional problem need many operational foci, coordination of effort is demanded. Although corporate planning in local authorities shows promise in this direction, there is as yet no corporate planning by government departments. Collaboration for joint activity is an attractive notion, but in practice there may be very considerable difficulties: the nature of departmental loyalties or professional traditions may make it difficult for one department to yield (seemingly) to another. Moreover it still leaves unresolved the question of identifying priorities amongst problems. Not only have we to recognise the existence of political weight behind priorities (old age has a high political priority; mental health has not) but there are technical criteria to bear in mind as well as the need to be responsible to locally determined issues in the community.

Multi-problem areas

Urban problems compound in severity, and throughout this book evidence has been presented which shows how the incidence of problems can be concentrated in particular parts of an urban area. The changing role and function of city centres presents a fascinating situation for planners. But districts of the inner city have received greater emphasis in this book, with many references to territorial disadvantage. We would be wrong to consider that all multi-problem areas were confined to the inner city, because given certain circumstances some local authority inter-war and post-war suburban estates can exhibit social management problems, but it is in the inner ring that the most complex areas have emerged. The cycle of deprivation extends over environmental issues, access to housing, housing quality, poor schools, diminished job opportunities, low income, racial tensions, all mirrored in a quality of life with fewer personal chances than elsewhere in the city.

The first approach to tackling the social aspects of urban management was on an individual basis. People were the recipients of aid. There are many reasons for continuing this approach, but it does carry with it the obligation to know a good deal about people who are intended to benefit. One still has the problem of identifying people in need, and above all, making sure that they get the aid which is intended. (Rent rebates are a recent example where aid might not reach the needy for reasons ranging from ignorance to pride.) The recognition of geographical territories within an urban area which might receive assistance through positive discrimination in favour of their needs, has been relatively recent. But in the last ten years or so there have been a number of steps in this direction: housing improvement areas, leading on to general improvement areas, education priority areas, community development programme areas and most recently recreation priority areas. A combination of the area and the individual approach to dealing with multi-problem areas reinforces the weight of attack.

The inner city problem is not new, as we have already remarked. The Victorian city had its 'social settlement tanks' where the flotsam of society settled in the most wretched of housing conditions, moving about the inner ring as circumstances dictated. It might be the case of gradually taking over the housing stock of a formerly, relatively favoured area which entered on a period of decay; alternatively, traumatic dislocations, such as caused by new building operations like the construction of a new railway terminal which swept houses and tenements away in great numbers, might have an adverse trigger effect on the fortunes of neighbouring areas. Compared with the last twenty years, however, the inner Victorian city was relatively stable. In the post war years a totally new factor has arisen, namely public intervention as part of urban renewal on an unprecedented scale, which had totally disturbed the previously 'natural' processes of invasion and succession and territorial displacement. Formerly, inner area problems could be conveniently sidetracked, receiving much less than their due prominence because of public attention being obscured. The beginnings of slum clearance in an organised way in the 1930's began the new period. It was then that inner area problems became articulated in a new way: the fact that they were translated as public housing problems meant that public money had to be spent.

The point has been apparent since the 1950's. Inner city problems do not come to public notice with quite the same force when they are simply the concern of social worker case loads or police work or educational truancy or unemployment; when they are housing problems they have an emotive urgency of their own and a political significance because of the high level of public spending. Over the last twenty years (since in fact the Housing Repairs and Rents Act, 1954, which really set in motion the post-war slum clearance programme) vast swathes have been cut into the Victorian fabric of the inner city setting in motion a rapid dynamism of social change which has cruelly exposed the plight of the underprivileged in relatively tightly defined ghetto areas. The rapidity of change can sometimes be startling especially with an incursion of coloured immigrants which can precipitate a 'white flight'. In London, though rarely elsewhere, a reverse movement has taken place through genetrification consequent upon improvement of older dwellings.

The inner city must not be thought of as in any way homogeneous. It is in fact strikingly heterogeneous with pockets of very different community characteristics separated from each other, sometimes by sharp social gradients. In the worst areas we find the key housing features. There is old and obsolete housing with deficiencies in water supply and flush toilet. There is reduced access to housing; people are denied entry to the local authority stock because of shortage of supply and the need to comply with residential qualifications; to private housing because of cost and the inability to enter into mortgage commitments; and to the private rented sector because as a tenure option its supply is being squeezed through redevelopment. Everywhere there is insecurity and a very real prospect of homelessness. The New Towns programme has proved largely illusory as an option because the employment demands there are for skilled labour, and the inner city resident is largely not skilled.

It is here perhaps in this question of housing that the twin aspects of urban form and social processes come most clearly together. Planners who rely on a contribution to the former without appreciating the interaction with the latter are simply deluding themselves. One does not have to criticise an Abercrombie approach of reducing densities in inner London in a grand master strategy by allocating units of accommodation in preferable locations, both peripheral and out-country, as put forward in 1944. The same blindness has occurred much more recently as local authorities have produced tidy, land use/environmental design plans for General Improvement Areas with little understanding of the housing and social system in which they were intervening.

There are many other critical aspects of the total environment of the inner city. These have been touched on in previous chapters, but perhaps we might emphasise the question of job opportunity. This is a relatively new phenomenon. While always the big city was a magnet for labour and skills, the inner districts were areas of high opportunity and high income. But the situation is being transformed. Middle income jobs have been decentralised and high earning, skill-based jobs are now to be found largely elsewhere. It is not so much that firms have actually moved, but that new jobs have been created elsewhere and some existing jobs extinguished. Added to this, in London at least, the development of tourist policies has created another sector of employment in hotels and catering with its own low paid jobs. Cities vary a good deal in their inner city employment characteristics; it would be wrong to generalise (for example in the opportunities for women) and in any case statistics are relatively sparse and hard to interpret. But a general belief at least is that high wage jobs are not open to the inner city dweller and this contributes to and compounds the discrimination experienced. Indeed, it might be claimed that just as the regional employment problem became *the* issue of the thirties in planning terms, so the inner city employment problem should be recognised as *the* issue of the seventies.

The implications for town planners is that they should adequately recognise the problem of deprivation in the inner city. The old-style Development Plans usually reviewed, and prescribed remedies for, urban problems under topic headings such as housing, industry and employment, shopping, roads and transport, open space and community facilities. There may have been a special chapter on central areas because that was where immediate problems were acute. One hopes that new-style Structure Plans will avoid this form of analysis, or at least move on to other recognitions; the big cities at least should recognise the needs of particular areas in a spatial context. A reorientation of analysis is needed. It is not as though a local authority does not at the present time devote enormous resources to the deprived inner city, but it should be conscious that this is so, in order that greater departmental collaboration can make its programme more effective. Even so, new developments are necessary: area based programmes of work, area based priorities, area based statistics, area based allocations of resources – few of these are attempted at the present time.

An urban crisis?

It remains for us to consider, on the basis of the previous chapters and on other evidence that might be brought to bear, whether the combined effect and magnitude of the contemporary problems presented in the urban scene amount to a scale and dimension not hitherto experienced. Are we, as some have suggested, experiencing an urban crisis which might indicate a critical phase through which our period of urbanisation is passing? Is this the real urban problem today, and if so, where does town planning stand in relation to it?

The critics of the big city have repeated a number of arguments for at least the years of this century. Urbanism as a phenomenon has been the subject of study certainly since, if only infrequently before, the masterly work of the American, Adna Ferrin Weber, *The Growth of Cities in the Nineteenth Century*, published in 1899 when he had just been appointed Deputy Commissioner of Labor Statistics by Theordore Roosevelt as Governor of New York. He considered the influence of city life on physical health, crime and morality and concluded that on the whole cities were benevolent rather than malevolent forces. Even from the point of view of social effects Weber felt that cities favoured liberal and progressive thought, and believed that it was "the fallacy of averages that obscures much of the best in city life". There had been voices before him which had not seen cities in such a favourable light: Jefferson had regarded cities as "ulcers on the body politic", and Rousseau had described them as "the final pit of the human spirit". In Britain, however, Victorians had generally been proud of their cities: Britain led the world through industrialisation, and big towns were part of that achievement. Cities represented progress.

But increasingly there were insistent voices raised against cities, and two favourite targets were linked: cities were environmentally undesirable for the great proportion of the people, and a combination of overcrowding, excessive densities and poor living conditions had social and moral consequences that were unacceptable. In large measure, at the turn of the century if Britain had an urban crisis then it was seen in those terms. The state of our towns demanded some halt to, or control over, unrestrained territorial growth (this applied particularly to London); reduction of densities through a new form of suburban architecture or dispersal to garden cities or colonies; and a marked rise in standards of environment, especially the dwelling house. We recall Ebenezer Howard's three magnets: town, country, and town-country. The town magnet contained many characteristics which were frankly unacceptable: "closing out of nature, social opportunity, isolation of crowds, places of amusement, distance from work, high money wages, high rents and prices, chances of employment, excessive loans, army of unemployed, fogs and droughts, costly drainage, foul air, murky sky, well lit streets, slums and gin palaces, palatial edifices" (*Garden Cities of Tomorrow*, 1902). From this popular conception of the late 19th century city sprang much of the force which supported a 20th century town planning movement.

This view of cities was to be reinforced by an economic argument which held that social costs rose as a function of urban size, and that consequently, cities were frankly inefficient. The Barlow Report of 1940 popularised this widely held view. There were social disadvantages of large urban concentrations: Barlow listed bad housing, lack of space for recreation, difficulties of transport, congestion, smoke and noise; also lengthy journeys to work, and unsatisfactory accommodation in flats. In addition, there were economic disadvantages: high land values, high transport costs through congestion and adverse effects on health and efficiency on people with long, uncomfortable journeys to work. Post-war Britain attempted to remedy many of these (largely unproven) disadvantages in a policy of decentralisation.

Up to recent years we have continued to review the urban problem from the point of view of these three criteria: adverse social consequences of an urban way of life particularly where high densities are concerned; environmental impoverishment of extensive urban areas without ready access to open country; and economic disadvantages of congestion and over-centralisation. This could well describe the 20th century 'state of our towns' and account for the town planning system we have devised: improvement of dwelling stock, environmental enhancement and a loose urban form.

Talk of a contemporary urban crisis has come from another aspect all together. This has stemmed from a heightened or a renewed sense of social concern and an evaluation of the effectiveness of our post-war spatial planning policies and statutory planning system. It began perhaps with a sense of despair at what was happening to the American city where inner area environmental decay was seen in close association with the plight of the underprivileged and racial minorities. In short, the urban problem can now be seen as a failure to harmonise public intervention in the built environment with social processes within it, in order that necessary social reallocations be achieved. The title of David Harvey's book *Social Justice and the City*, 1973, captures this concern.

The difficulty at this point, in our concern with urban problems, is to decide what are specifically city problems and what are problems of national society. It is not easy to distinguish between them, and issues such as breakdown in family life, general frustrations through a sense of powerlessness to direct change, anonymity, struggles with authority, delinquency, disintegration of a common purpose and a materialist surge through acquisitive values can have national, as well as specifically urban, cultural origins. But the fact is that we have begun recently to talk about cities in terms of reaching a breakdown point. Essential services only keep going with difficulty; in parts of the bigger cities transport, police and education are sectors where dislocations are touch and go. Standards seem to have fallen, particularly in street cleaning and refuse disposal. The management of cities is under stress. We cannot improve things fast enough, nor provide required facilities. Old solutions have been found wanting and there is uncertainty about the future. Above all there is a polarisation between the fortunes of the disadvantaged population in the deprived inner city and the relatively favoured suburbanite. There is a fear of social strife. The real essence of urban management is now seen as a question of reallocation of opportunity and rewards.

This interpretation is supported by the view that cities are now a focus of capitalism; urban land and property, largely in private ownership, is the subject of profitable speculation. Industrial capitalism of the 19th century has changed. The real problem is now a territorial one — it is the city where profit is made through dealings in land, as witness Centre Point and the question of rising land values. Moreover the city, as a function of modern capitalism, is considered to have an inherently inequitable structure. Hence, there can be no guarantee that our urban social system can achieve any real equilibrium; the system may indeed be explosive and conflict ridden. In this way, we might see the problems of the inner city in the context of a capitalist economic system, in which we seem to be moving towards a state of greater inequality and injustice.

There is real value in having this viewpoint as a background to our urban studies. But we should not accept uncritically the hypotheses presented. We should not necessarily take the American city as a parallel to the British scene. There are many reasons why the American city can be very different. Nor should we assume that London, with its inner city problems, is typical of other British conurbations; sheer size is one important difference. Moreover hard evidence is very lacking, particularly with regard to job opportunities which seem to be critical in spatial patterns of urban deprivation. In this situation therefore it would be necessary to exercise care and some caution in fashioning new tools of intervention in urban planning designed to tackle head on the capitalist market economy in order to deal with the underlying nature of urban problems. We do not know sufficient about the nature and function of modern capitalism to allow us to do that.

In the meantime, our urban planning will no doubt continue to be essentially incrementalist, gradualist and ameliorist. There can be no reliance, for example, on a single spatial strategy for redistribution of population and jobs; no slavish regard for one set of long term solutions to the exclusions of other options. Hence, there can be no 'final solutions' to the housing problem, transport, locations for commercial activity, land use and other standards of provision, or any other urban problem. In recent years, town planners have been roundly criticised for these characteristics from at least two sources: those who cry for fundamentalist policies based on a long term plan and those who deride gradualism as failing to achieve the reallocation of resources that is required. But if the British city is as inescapably inequitable as has been claimed, is not gradualism an acceptable policy to adopt? In any case, an incrementalist approach is perhaps more effective than we have realised hitherto: is it not a surer way of moving towards the future rather than determining an ideal future and forging our policies accordingly? It is of course a matter of balance and degree: the complete absence of long term goals would be undesirable; the complete subjugation of the short term to the long term is equally unrealistic. In any event, the implications for town planning practice, as well as other aspects of urban management, are profound.

We began this book with a lengthy extract from Louis Macneice's *Birmingham*. His description conjured up all the vitality and complexity of a modern city: ugliness and noise; beauty and stillness; industry and relaxation. Forty years on it remains so, just as it is still a place where "men as in a dream pursue the Platonic Forms . . . and endeavour to find God and score one over the neighbour". As we look at the city and unravel its problems, the challenge is to devise forms of public intervention that can create urban environments, beauty, convenience and order, that can serve as settings of justice, opportunity, satisfaction and stimulation. One thing we can be sure of: while the challenge may not change, our ways of meeting it certainly will, because town planning and all aspects of urban management are evolutionary in both concept and practice.